The idiom of the time

The Sign of the Four

The idiom of the time
The writings of Henry Green

ROD MENGHAM

Cambridge University Press

Cambridge
London   New York   New Rochelle
Melbourne   Sydney

Published by the Press Syndicate of the University of Cambridge
The Pitt Building, Trumpington Street, Cambridge CB2 1RP
32 East 57th Street, New York, NY 10022, USA
296 Beaconsfield Parade, Middle Park, Melbourne 3206, Australia

First published 1982

Printed in Great Britain by
New Western Printing Ltd, Bristol

Library of Congress catalogue card number: 82–9716

British Library Cataloguing in Publication Data
Mengham, Rod
The idiom of the time: the writings of Henry
Green.
1. Green, Henry, *1905*- —Criticism and
interpretation
I. Title
823'.912   PR6013.R416Z/
ISBN 0 521 24813 2

NWP

Contents

Preface   vii

Acknowledgements   x

1 *Blindness, Living:* the living idiom   1

2 *Party Going:* a border-line case   31

3 *Pack my Bag:* the poetics of menace   53

4 *Caught:* the idiom of the time   68

5 *Loving:* a fabulous apparatus   109

6 *Back:* the prosthetic art   157

7 *Concluding:* the sea-change   181

8 *Nothing, Doting:* something living which isn't   207

Notes   216

Bibliography   232

Index   243

Preface

The *public* at whom [the artist] aims is not given; it is
a public to be elicited by his work. The others of
whom he thinks are not empirical 'others' or even
humanity conceived as a species; it is others once they
have become such that he can live with them.

Maurice Merleau-Ponty, *The Prose of the World*
(London: Heinemann, 1974), p. 86.

'Henry Green' was the *nom de plume* of the industrialist Henry
Yorke: an industrialist who, according to his own son, wrote
during the lunch-hour; he was an obsessive man who preferred
not to be photographed, except from behind. With or without
this minimum of information, one tends to come from a first
reading of any of Green's works with the feeling that something
has been withheld, that the writing is an elaborately organized
ruse, that to a greater extent than is perhaps normal, it simply
does not mean what it says. The approach taken by this study
is that one should distrust such a feeling of distrust; that if anything is being concealed by Green it is not the essential meaning
of his text but the nature of a reader which only his text will
be able to elicit.

I mention the circumstances of Green's life only to make it
perfectly clear that this study is not biographically-based. If a
number of correspondences between the life and the work are
subsequently maintained, these are for the most part in view of
broad strategies like the use of the pseudonym. The continuities
in Green's work which I do want to bring out are not in respect
of biographical reference or of theme, but of what attracted me
to the writing in the first place: the peculiarly recreative quality
of the prose, whereby those passages which seem most irregular,
bizarre and superfluous in terms of story and characterization,
seem also to be the most important and irreducible units of the

text, because so much more intense, resourceful, and enlivening. I regard Green's work as bringing a kind of leaven to the comparative inertness of the novel with its cautious regard of figural invention.

However, this is not a structuralist study of specific texts in relation to the poetics of the novel, but a process of accounting for the recreative element of each text in terms of 'conditions of knowledge' (Empson's phrase). 'Conditions of knowledge' vary, of course, from text to text, and so each one is handled in chronological succession. The repeated emphasis is on finding a means, issuing from a broad view of the social and literary context, to account for the waywardness of a writing procedure. This account cannot be rule-governed, because the writing edges its way across a whole range of different, conflicting versions of contemporary history.

No attempt is made before chapter four to formulate the 'idiom of the time' (the phrase is Green's, and appeared in an essay in the autumn of 1941). There is a tendency in preceding chapters to regard the earlier work as in some sense pre-adapted to the 'idiom of the time'; but this should become obvious only in retrospect. To begin with the 'idiom of the time' is implicit rather than explicit so that, to begin with, there are certain discrepancies of critical approach. In the first chapter, for instance, psychoanalysis is used to a greater extent and advantage than elsewhere; the result is, properly speaking, a 'wild analysis', but this is because I have not been concerned to give a psychoanalytical reading of a text: rather to submit a few elucidating ideas to a particular textual constraint.

I have also introduced at decisive points ways of thinking more recent than those of the conditions of knowledge with which I am mainly concerned. This is not defensible simply from the point of view that Green was ahead of his time, that we are now ready to be the public elicited by his work; although in all sincerity this can be held to be part of the answer. The important point is that Green's work is not simply reflective of its time, and that its least reflective part, what for the moment I am calling a kind of leaven, is precisely what brings in question received ways of thinking, so that to juxtapose ways of thinking which do not synchronize with one another is to produce exactly the same kind of differential which gives this writing its edge.

Green's work deliberately sets out the limits of ruling perspectives; and in this connection, it is animated by a composite idea involving optics and representation. From the beginning, the obstruction of vision is explored as a means of interfering with a dominant point of view. The logical terminus of interference comes in *Concluding*, which contends for the absence of any dominant point of view anywhere in the universe. The writing has a strong sense of being within a field of vision, and the desirability of *not* being within it. And just as the man did not want to be photographed, so the author prefers to disappear from his work: '. . . if you are trying to write something which has a life of its own, which is alive, of course the author must keep completely out of the picture. I hate the portraits of donors in medieval triptychs' (Terry Southern, 'The Art of Fiction xxii. – Henry Green', *Paris Review*, 5 (Summer 1958)). This remark preserves the visual context of a dislike of being caught in position and scrutinized. Visibility is felt to correspond to, and indeed communicate with, the biographical accountability of so much fiction. In his own 'interim autobiography', *Pack my Bag*, Green tries to maintain an alternative self, one that can rival his own, which remains hidden.

This persistent removal of perspectives and lines of approach cuts short the possibilities of interpretation. Readers who have enjoyed a long acquaintance with Green's work, and who value this situation, may be dismayed by the exhaustiveness of my analysis. But I have tried to cover as much as possible, to take account of as much as possible in order to leave it free from explanation. The leavening quality remains finally inscrutable. Every critical method inevitably abstracts what it needs from its chosen object. And it is in the knowledge of this, and with the desire to do so as little as possible, that I have framed my work in the cause, not of interpretation, but of a description of strategies, devices, intensities, and proportions. In a sense I have wanted to write a continuation of Green: on a different level, and in a different accent, but in acknowledgement of the principles on which the writings of Henry Green have been based.

All page references are to the Hogarth Press edition of Henry Green's works.

Acknowledgements

This book started out as a doctoral thesis, the result of my postgraduate research at the University of Edinburgh, where I was extremely fortunate in having Dr Valerie Shaw as a postgraduate supervisor; her wise attention to my work has proved invaluable, and I owe her a great deal. I am also indebted to Professor W. W. Robson, who guided me through the early stages, and who was one of the examiners of the thesis.

My other examiner was Professor Frank Kermode, and I was lucky indeed to have the benefit of his advice and comments before recasting the thesis as a book. It is the more blame to me for any faults that the book retains. The rites of passage from thesis to book were made easier by the skill and tact of Dr Andrew Brown of the Cambridge University Press.

This study is the first, as far as I know, to make use of Green's manuscripts and typescripts in British Library Loan 67. Mr Sebastian Yorke has kindly given me his permission to quote from these papers, and I would like to express my thanks to him for doing so.

I am grateful to the Librarians and staff of the following libraries for their assistance: Edinburgh University Library, the National Library of Scotland, the British Library, the Bodleian Library, the Cambridge University Library, and Birmingham Reference Library. Thanks are also due to Elizabeth Yates, for typing a manuscript at such short notice.

My work was sustained by the interest of many friends, among whom I should particularly like to mention Geoffrey Ward, a devotee of Green, since the conversations I had with him really helped my understanding of particular texts. I am pleased to have the opportunity of thanking my parents for the generosity of their support during long years of research.

Finally, I simply do not know where to begin in thanking my wife, Dr Catherine Neale, both for the quality, and for the quantity, of her encouragement, inspiration, and practical help.

I   *Blindness, Living:*
the living idiom

ROSS: Could you define the compulsion behind your writing?
GREEN: Sex.
> Alan Ross, 'Green, with Envy', *The London Magazine*,
> vol. 6, no. 4 (April 1959), 23.

Henry Green's first novel, *Blindness*, is largely the work of a schoolboy. Not surprisingly, it lacks the peculiar savour of his later work; there is no manifold syntax, no leading motif, no refulgent texture, no cherished surplus of data. Where *Blindness* does join with the rest of the oeuvre is in being somehow unduly evasive, and shy of its own meanings. It combines reluctance with extravagance, wariness with magniloquence, in the manner besetting all the later work. This study will show how the later work is written almost to escape being understood; how it is totally committed to a method of the unexplained.

Blindness was drafted, and then typed, under the title of *Young and Old*; this was subsequently emended to *Progression*.[1] The novel includes, then, a developmental option, upheld through the tripartite division of the book into sections headed 'Caterpillar', 'Chrysalis', 'Butterfly'. But the writing itself tends, as will be seen, towards retardation; so that the scheme canvassed by the description of contents is a kind of ruse. Right from the start, *Blindness* is constructed on a cross-purpose.

The first part, 'Caterpillar', takes the form of a diary by schoolboy John Haye whose ambition is to become a writer. This section ends with a letter recording his blinding, but the final entry of the diary is a tribute to the epileptic author of *Crime and Punishment*. It is balanced at the end of the final section, 'Butterfly', by John's own epileptic seizure, which seems to bring him the power to write. The intermediate section, 'Chrysalis', is set in the kind of large Country House to which Green's fiction would often return. Here, John becomes selfishly attached to the poverty-stricken Joan, while growing impatient of life away from the town.

The diary part seeks to establish the immaturity of John, allowing the reader to anticipate maturation. But the writing is essentially disconcerted by obsessional previews of the blindness itself, and of the accident that will cause it, when a small boy throws a stone to smash the train window behind which John is seated: 'it is "the thing to do" now to throw stones at me as I sit at my window . . . Rather a funny thing happened while fielding this afternoon. I had thrown myself down to stop a ball and I saw waving specks in my eyes for two minutes afterwards' (p. 7); 'An awful thing happened. It was towards the end when I was so tired I could hardly see' (p. 12). The writing follows this plan even on the peripheries of meaning, on the level of casual phrase: 'Very interesting . . . in fact a great eye-opener' (p. 6); 'the athletic type, who sink their whole beings into the school and its affairs, and are blind and almost ignorant of any world outside their own' (p. 10). The diary section is really only there to foreshadow the blindness, and the kind of reading which enquires after blindness for its effect on the development of John's character is usurped by one which turns on the discursive figure of blindness itself, along with its adjuncts. Thus, a reference to 'the sound of disturbed water' although made to seem inadvertent is actually thoroughly attentive to the following chapter, where the now blinded John finds himself encompassed by the sounds of falling rain and running water. And the weight of this manner of reading is borne during moments which seem even more remote from its pressure:

29 January

But surely this is most beautiful:

The trills of a lark fall drop by drop down an unseen aery ladder, and the calls of the cranes, floating by in a long string, like the ringing notes of silver bugles, resound in the void of melodiously vibrating ether.

He is a poet: and his book is in very truth a poem. It is Gogol. (p. 25)

The context of this fragment of *Dead Souls* involves the return of a young landowner to his country estate, which he fails to become a part of – it provides an unexpected parallel to the situation of John Haye – but the nature of the description is even more to the point; in the Russian novel 'the entire country-side had been *transformed into sounds*'.[2] The excerpt from Gogol is a silent reference to what will be the most audible enigma of the book – the rustlings and murmurings of nature.

In *Blindness*, the loss of sight corresponds to a very specific kind of openness to noise, an oversensitiveness to the sounds of nature which are characteristically whispered and indistinct, only partially given: 'The air became full of messages' (pp. 132–3); 'the wind brought things from afar to hang for a moment in his ears and then take away again' (pp. 244–5). The inconclusiveness of these disclosures is less a product of reluctance, or indecision, than of furtive obscuration: 'The air round was stealthy. It was all so full of little hints; the air carried up little noises and then hurried them away again' (p. 151); 'For the trees crowd about us, and their branches roof us in slyly, with sly noises that one can just hear' (p. 184). The secrets of nature are clearly not to be shared but are meant to remain secret, they are confidences withdrawn as soon as given; the intimacy for which they show their desire is defined by a sense almost of shame. This retraction that is literally in the air is equalled by the evasiveness of John himself: ' "you are always like that, you know, John, always hiding things . . ." ' (p. 41). And his own 'secretiveness' is affected by the same correlation of desire and shame; its focal point, an obsession with the image of his own mother, holds the text in a claustrophobic embrace. Before he is anything else, before he is even the potential writer, John is a *son*; the first story he manages to write is actually called *Sonny*. His mother, who is in fact dead, is virtually the only mother in the book; she takes dramatic precedence over the stepmother, who resents the fact that 'there was always her between them' (p. 47). Joan's mother, also dead, serves nearly entirely as a type of John's. Several of the village mothers are periodically remembered but never featured in any important sense. In effect, the only other mother made conspicuous is in the authorial dedication of the book.

John's mother is supposed to have 'whistled most beautifully'

(p. 156), a trait which coincides with the typically sibilant communicativeness of nature. John imagines that 'she must have linked everything up with it' (p. 156), although the Nanny had regarded it as 'senseless' (p. 173); like nature, the whistling is endowed with vital meanings both proposed and rejected. But it lacks the 'slyness', the 'stealth', or any connotation of guilt, despite the fact that the mother's image is quite obviously the focus of an erotic desire: 'so tantalising, so feminine. Mummy would have been like that' (p. 50). As his mother had died giving birth to him, John has never actually seen her, and so his image of her is a total fiction; he pictures her as a woman of about his own age, eternally youthful and ideally beautiful.

Elsewhere in the text, erotic interest is gauged by a kind of light in the eyes: 'There would be something behind his honey-coloured eyes, a strong hard light' (p. 114); 'There had been a queer light at the back of Mother's eyes about then – how she understood that light now!' (p. 130). This light is what gives one away, betrays the nature of one's desire; it presupposes the scrutiny of some external agency – a threat of exposure that could come from anywhere. The mirror in John's bedroom, for example, although useless once he has been blinded, nevertheless remains on the look-out, 'mimicking the chalky white, and waiting for something else to mimic' (p. 40). In effect, John is blind to prevent the discovery of his desire. At the same time, blindness allows the guilt suffered over the fantasy of his mother to be converted onto a physiological basis – this is the punishment which he feels he deserves; the complete removal of both eyeballs is the symbolic equivalent of a retributive castration. And even after their removal, his eyes are still under the observation of the nurse: 'they were now in spirits on the mantelpiece of her room at home in the hospital. When she got back she was going to put them just where she could see them first thing every morning' (p. 58). This sense of being persecuted, continually and from every quarter, requires a further displacement of guilt, onto the correspondingly ubiquitous and inexhaustible whisperings and murmurings of nature; they are the constant reiterations of a compromise between the disclosure and concealment of desire.

At one and the same time blindness punishes and gratifies;

it privileges the sense of touch, which is the means of only
contact with the dead mother: 'And now that he was blind he
had come to treasure little personal things of her own, a prayer-
book of hers, though that, of course, was mistaken; a pair of
kid gloves, so soft to touch, and they had a faint suggestion of
her about them, so faint, that gently surrounded them and
made them still more soft' (p. 156). But the major compensation
comes from allowing the image of the dead mother to flood the
entire field of vision, obscuring the actual presence of living
surrogates; the reality in which an incestuous desire is forbidden
is simply eclipsed in its entirety: 'Then it was lucky perhaps
that he could not see any more, that the little boy had taken
his sight away. For she was nearer than she had ever been
before, now that he was blind' (pp. 161–2). By a curious para-
dox, John's sexual gratification shifts entirely into the realm of
seeing; blindness enables an exclusive investment in the image
of the mother while reducing the likelihood of a physical union
with anyone else. The stepmother dwells on the idea that 'he
would not meet any nice girls now, he could never marry' (p.
71). One of the diary-entries excised from the published version
provides a gloss on this situation:

April 20

In my tiny experience women are so very much nicer to look at
and to vaguely romanticise over than to get acquainted with.
Surely just as exquisite and certainly a more durable emotion could
be gained through the soul than through materialism. Corot had a
soul. (TS, p. 65)

The allusion to Corot is exemplary in its indirectness – giving
the main point of the *sententia* as an afterthought. Corot had
the reputation of great secretiveness and celibacy; his voyeur-
ism took the form of an exceptional possessiveness over his own
figure paintings, which were kept locked up in his studio until
after his death. There is no doubt that he abhorred his own
father, and his paintings are filled with images of truncation.
Gout kept him in the studio for long periods of time when, like
John Haye, he would invent the landscapes he could not see;
the work for which he *was* known during his lifetime shows a
predilection for remembered landscapes: 'Souvenir de Morte-
fontaine', 'Souvenir d'Italie: Castelgandolfo' and so on.[3] The

editing-out of this allusion, its absence from the final version, is further evidence of a strategy of compromise invading all levels of the text. The intimations of other literary work which would, so to speak, give the game away, are intermittently both acknowledged and denied. Another example of their denial is a quotation from *King Lear*, excluded from the final version, which is unavoidably explicit in connecting loss of sight with sexual passion:

> Why dost thou lash that whore? Strip thine own back;
> Thou hotly lusts to use her in that kind
> For which thou whipp'st her.

The lines quoted are preceded in *King Lear* by an advertence to the topic of obstructed vision, a figure to which the play is addicted:

What! art mad? A man may see how this world goes with no eyes. Look with thine ears: see how yond justice rails upon yond simple thief. Hark, in thine ear: change places, and, handy-dandy, which is the justice, which is the thief?[4]

Blindness is determinative of punishment, and this circumstance is the foreground of a quotation laying stress on a passion which is categorically unlawful (the apostrophe is addressed to any 'rascal beadle'). By obstruction of vision one set of criteria for lawfulness is replaced by another, cutting out reality as effectively as death; indeed, throughout *Blindness*, blindness *and* death emerge as equal means of emptying the sphere of the real in order to fill it with the imaginary. The fantasy can only be sustained if the mother is dead – this is grasped in one of the moments of acknowledgement, an allusion to Browning which is retained in the final version. John remembers the poem, 'Porphyria's Lover', in which the loved one is throttled because the lover can only completely possess her once she is dead.[5] Death marks the limit of change and allows the fantasy to stabilize around the chosen image; blindness answers the need to arrest the image and makes it extremely difficult to do much else but attend to it. John maintains the ambition of writing, but delays any performance that would mean a distraction from the central work of the fantasy. The developmental aspect of the text is subject to a progressive diminution. It is in desire's own interest to retard everything not itself, and the narrative dreams itself into an impasse from which it can only escape by means of an epileptic fit.

The ambition of writing is never allowed to recede; nor is the writing achievement of others, even though the published version omits the catalogue of forty-nine titles, 'A List of the Library of John Haye by the end of the Easter Term at Noat' (TS, p. 71). The constant premeditation and the bookish allusions both serve the work of the fantasy. The literary hyperaesthesia is part of the same strategy of evacuating the real; desire confounds the weakness of its unlawful position by making unlawfulness the means of its strongest support. It derives authority for its own transgression from other literature, sounding for precedents among a set of criteria which only apply in the world of the text. Within a community of writings, the fantasy can assume another kind of lawfulness. The special prominence of *Crime and Punishment* gives ground for the interaction of criminality and delay. But, in a more submerged aspect, the project centres on a mythography with even greater leverage, the Oedipal theorem, and it reaches back via Oedipus to the most inevitable of all laws, Fate; desire wants to arrive at the ultimate sanction for its unlawfulness, as if the constraints upon it were the business of an oracle.

All the mutilations of Oedipus are reproduced in John: the ruined eyes, the scarred visage and, in the form of hammertoes, the swollen foot implied by the Greek name. Both characters are fostered by aged couples, in John's case by his own grandparents. The Oedipal career, turning from exile to a marginal position at Colonus (he is both accepted and rejected in a place outside Athens but within its jurisdiction), is mirrored by John's retreat to the country before partial instatement in the city, where he is neither insider nor outsider in his temporary lodgings. The transfiguration at Colonus corresponds to the epileptic fit. The division of the book into three parts representing three developmental stages becomes more plausible as a reflection of the Sphinx's riddle concerning three ages of man. In John's evocation of the strangling of Porphyria, he changes the loosely wound string of 'all her hair' into a pigtail, reinforcing comparison with the 'plaited noose' that hangs the Sophoclean Jocasta.[6]

The specifically Oedipal relationship of mother and son
colonizes the entire text, and there is no significant divergence
from its pattern in any of the other relationships portrayed.
That between John and Joan contracts for as long as it lasts,
since Joan is basically a type of John; she is virtually his
doppelgänger. Her face is similarly scarred, the injury likewise
inflicted with broken glass, and in her case the father is direct
punitive agent; a marked dissatisfaction on her part is the
result of his refraining from punishment on other occasions:
'She feels cheated. He had been so mad underneath. Why
hadn't he battered at the door? What a shame. All that
trembling for nothing' (p. 134). The Oedipal lameness is
transformed into the birthmark on her leg, and, although she
is not afflicted with hammer-toes, she does remember one
occasion when she had dropped a real hammer on her toe. The
lesion of her thumb, a kind of transposed castration, is paralleled
by John skinning his knuckles and running a splinter into his
finger. Joan's memory of her own mother is only a reduplica-
tion of John's memory of his; both women had been sexually
promiscuous, and Joan's mother had taken as her lover the
postman named *John*. The fluidity of names – 'John' being as
close as possible to 'Joan' – is enhanced by his deliberately
mistaking her name as 'June'. The text operates by a constant
metastasis of the Oedipal disposition into one circumstance
after another; Entwhistle is the type of John as Oedipus at
Colonus, dependent on Antigone/Joan. He occupies a liminal
position, on the borders of the community from which he has
been expelled, earning himself the nickname of 'the Shame'.
Although his eyesight is intact, the windows of his house are
broken, or 'stare vacantly with emptiness behind their leaded
panes' (p. 98); the generally 'neuter' aspect of the house
suggests an eradication of desire on the strength of the usual
metaphor – Joan is no longer attacked by her father because
'the light in him had gone out' (p. 134). Like John, Entwhistle
is a 'poet' who adopts the same line of deferred action, failing
to write his own 'great book'. The purpose of writing for
Entwhistle is 'to link everything into a circle' (p. 111), a
desideratum supposedly shared by the whistling of Mrs Haye
– the two codings are themselves linked by a circularity whose
connecting medium here is the Ent*whistle* name.

Taken together, Entwhistle and John accommodate the symptoms ultimately diagnosed as epileptic. Both are prone to imagined levitations, interpreted as spiritual advance. Entwhistle is featured 'rising on a tide of knowledge' (p. 133) with the facility due to alcohol, while the rising sensation of epilepsy assures John that 'he would know all' (p. 253). The ascent to omniscience fortifies the text's oracular pretensions. (The ancient epistemology, unable to account for epilepsy, explained it as inexplicable, as 'the sacred disease'.) [7] The credentials of this knowledge are all variations of insight and vision; John's feeling of elevation in a religious setting is the implicit basis of ever being able to see: 'The church music went round and round the walls, and then rolled along the ceiling till the shifting notes built walls about you till you were yourself very high up, *so that you could see*' (p. 150, my emphasis). This is the frame of reference for his characterization of Dostoevsky, 'with his epileptic fits which were much the same as visions really' (p. 33). Epilepsy is a kind of superior vision whose reparation of blindness has a specifically religious overtone; vision partakes of the Creation, blindness loses it – blindness is atheistic. (This may seem a wayward hypothesis, but in 1749 the implications looked radical enough for Diderot to be imprisoned for linking godlessness with sightlessness in his essay *La Lettre sur les aveugles*.) [8] Blindness represents an estrangement from the world of the Father, and from a lawfulness that would underlie John's punishment by his own father; epilepsy is the metaphor of reunion – on the very last page of the novel, John treats it as a kind of return to the world of the father: ' "They tell me I have had some sort of a fit, but it has passed now. Apparently my father was liable to them, so that anyway I have one behind me after this . . . I have had a wonderful experience. I am going to settle down to writing now, I have a lot to tell . . ." ' (p. 254). Entwhistle is an unfrocked priest, which means another isolation from the world of the Father. These reproductions of the fall from God's grace authenticate the ambiguity of nature, as it constantly falters in the attempt to regenerate itself. But if nature cannot be reclaimed, it may be tranquillized, as the text implies in a rearguard action of allowing itself to be invaded by the word *green*.

Blindness often leaves itself no option but greenness, as if

greenness were the only occasion for writing; it appears overwhelmingly in trees and plants and leaves, but also in clothes
and the decorative arts, and in descriptions where it really has
no place at all: 'the blue that lay overhead was green' (p. 124).
It partly conveys a hope of salvation; Entwhistle had always
preached 'out of the green book on the second shelf in the old
study' (p. 134), while his inspired drinking is punctuated by
renditions of the hymn, 'There is a green land far away' (*sic*).
But this vague utopianism cannot restore the world of the
Father, and the only salvation whose success is feasible must be
like the amnesiac's fugue, in a setting which accounts for the
alteration of the hymn's 'green hill' to Entwhistle's 'green land':
'A long way away there might be a country of rest, made of
ice, green in the depths, an ice that was not cold, a country to
rest in. He would lie in the grotto where it was cool and where
his head would be cool and light, and where there was nothing
in the future, and nothing in the past' (p. 95). Greenness is thus
associated with a gap in normal consciousness, replacing the
agnostic with the anaesthetic – its elisions are identical to those
of blindness itself. In fact, the setting for the revelation of John's
blindness is almost totally green: 'Beyond, the door, green, as
were the thick embrasures of the two windows green, and the
carpet, and the curtains' (p. 39). The verbal superabundance
is made even more obtrusive in its control over several names;
there are Mrs Green, Greenham, Green the draper's, and
Lorna Greene. But the acme of interference is reached in the
exchange of the author's *nom de plume*; in the typescript of
Young and Old this had been Henry Browne – a name which
retains the final 'e' of the author's real surname, Yorke.[9] When
we consider the incidence of greenness in the writing, this
switch from Browne to Green argues for the reversion of the
work onto the life; later on in his career Green was to treat his
own life as a fiction to be read in conjunction with other
fictions. In *Blindness*, green stands for something like anaes-
thesia, but the film of obliviousness which it spreads over the
whole text is unable to swallow entire the burden of guilt; it
requires a final convulsion, with a profound gap in consciousness, to achieve that. According to Freud: 'The earliest
physicians described coition as a minor epilepsy, and thus
recognized in the sexual act a mitigation and adaptation of the

epileptic method of discharging stimulus.'[10] The epileptic attack in *Blindness* is preceded by the most intensely erotic episode of the book:

He leant forward further to where he felt her presence and the stand. Her breath burned in his face for a moment and bathing in her nearness he leant further forward still, in the hopes of finding her, but she dropped his hand and it fell on the slick edges of the pot in which the lily grew. Despair was coming over him again, it was too awkward, this pursuit of her under a lily, when all at once her arm mysteriously came up over his mouth, glowing and cool at the same time, and the scent was immediately stronger, tangible almost, so that he wanted to bite it. (pp. 241–2)

This passage brings to a head those libidinal tensions which now start to break out in secondary form: 'and then presences would glide past leaving a snatch of warm scent behind them to tantalise . . . and then mysteriously from below there floated up a chuckle; it was a woman and someone must have been making love to her, so low, so deep it was. He was on fire at once' (pp. 243–4). These erotic incentives, like the messages of nature, are always 'in the air', more or less unattached – the recurring adverb 'mysteriously' implies the lack of control over them. Their leakage undermines the method of sublimation and compromise, which is suddenly and violently overtaken by a method of discharge.

In the same way, the writing is all at once overlapped by the textuality of *Crime and Punishment*, whose effect on John is 'like dynamite' (p. 34). Although it has an idea of itself as a novel of continuous advance ('*Progression*'), *Blindness* comes to a halt with the shock of revealed truth. Green was later to refer suggestively to the Russian novelists as the 'novelists of persecution', a formulation whose premise of hysterical guilt makes it suitable for his own first book.[11] *Blindness* is a changeling fiction; its fantasy of parentage is matched by a fantasy of literary tradition – epilepsy is the perfect metaphor for its *seizure* of another lineage. The literary progenitor, Dostoevsky, identifies the source of the attack in his own interpretation of his own epilepsy:

The best account of the meaning and content of his attacks was given by Dostoevsky himself, when he told his friend Strakhov that

his irritability and depression after an epileptic attack were due to
the fact that he seemed to himself a criminal and could not get rid
of the feeling that he had a burden of unknown guilt upon him, that
he had committed some great misdeed, which oppressed him.[12]

Blindness ignores the lineaments of developmental time in
opening up a discursive space; it is least like a novel in the
blind paroxysm of its finale – it substitutes for analepsis *epilepsis*.
Its writing is deliberately 'blind', in the way of disinheriting
itself, giving up the enjoyments of a more seemingly legitimate
tradition of the novel in favour of going 'unseen' to combine
with its own illicit desires. The book is technically inferior to
the rest of Green's work, but its obsessional structure is the basis
of later refinements; it is already anticipative of the maturer
work in its sense of the inhibitions on a given literary form.

The mutation in Green's writing between *Blindness* and *Living*
is surely greater than between any other two of his subsequent
novels. This extremism of change is equal to the about face in
his way of life; after two years as an undergraduate at Oxford,
he moved to Birmingham to serve a three-year engineering
apprenticeship. The difference this makes to *Living* consists in a
fascination with working-class speech, and in the emulation of
this speech by the narration itself. The authorial voice is
submitted to the inflexions, the constructions, and the anecdotal
pace of inordinate talk: 'And Dale asked him why he went
round with Tupe then and Mr. Gates said me never and Dale
said he seen him and Joe Gates answered it might have been
once' (p. 29). Instead of correcting deviance and excess it
seeks to exploit it, rejecting the business of moderation, embracing the formalism of a waste of breath: 'Yes man in front
said turning back to him, yes all the evening but people in
front cried ssh: band was playing softly, softly' (p. 59). The
narration abuses punctuation and, to all intents and purposes,
authorial intent: ' "It's those that don't want a day's work I'm
for getting on." ' and ' "No but honest are you going?" ' (pp.
12–13). There is a measured emphasis on continuatives – 'and
. . . and . . . and . . . and' – which gives the impression of
lending equal weight to every clause, of a reduction in the
sense of controlling objectives, both locally within a sentence,
and generally. Attributions of speech, which are proof of

nothing if not an imposed control, are adapted into a similar pattern, made otiose, or sent out of control in a kind of exponential runaway: 'Once *she had said* to Mrs. Eames *she had said* it made you ridiculous *she had said* walking with him, yes *she had said* that to Mrs. Eames' (pp. 41–2, my emphasis).

The commonest mechanism of the text is co-ordination; and this occurs frequently in a precipitate form that is unusual for a novel, but which is typical of chronicles. Only three years before the publication of *Living* there had been a striking example of the chronicle in fictional form, in Anita Loos's *Gentlemen Prefer Blondes* (London: Brentano's, 1926). Loos's favoured continuative had been 'so':

So Dr. Froyd asked me, what I seemed to dream about. So I told him that I never really dream about anything. I mean I use my brains so much in the day time that at night they do not seem to do anything else but rest . . . So then Dr. Froyd looked at me and looked at me and he said he did not really think it was possible. So then he called in his assistance and he pointed at me and talked to his assistance quite a lot in the Viennese landguage. So then his assistance looked at me and looked at me and it really seems as if I was quite a famous case. So then Dr. Froyd said that all I needed was to cultivate a few inhibitions and get some sleep. (pp. 155–8)

This sophisticated artlessness cleared a way for Green's experimentally uncouth style. *Living* has a trick, of continually forcing the writing back to the present tense of anecdote, which is according to the poetics of the chronicle with its successive instalments of the historic present: 'She says what, only that much? He says yes and if that isn't enough well she doesn't have any, and snatches it back again' (p. 191).

There is a sharp sense in *Living* of the relations of chronology between the narration and the narrated events. And it is this sense exactly which Gertrude Stein appeals for in her 'Composition as Explanation', a lecture delivered in 1926 in Oxford when Green was still an undergraduate there, and published in the same year by the Hogarth Press, which was subsequently to publish *Living*. Stein argues that the contemporaneity of a writer should be measured by the intensity of his address to the problem of a ratio between time *in* the composition and time *of* the composition: 'In the beginning there was the time in the composition that naturally was in the composition but time in

the composition comes now and this is what is now troubling
everyone the time in the composition is now a part of distribution and equilibration.'[13] Stein adduces her own *The Making
of Americans* as the prototype for a continuous present whose
distribution and equilibration is achieved through 'beginning
again and again'. Her method of repetition with slight variations is simply usurped on occasion in *Living*: 'But he was
sincere *in his thinking* the old place wanted a rouser and *in his
thinking* he was *always building, always building in his thinking*'
(p. 57). This is little more than the garbled imitation of a
routine, but on another level the sense of a continuous present is
subliminally extended through the reconstitution of other, sometimes quite distant, parts of the text:

So her sanity, what there was of it, *so* it ebbed and she was drifting
back again to the gentle *undulations* which *heaved* regularly with her
breathing *like the sea, and was as commonplace*. (p. 106, my emphasis)

So sometimes when you work, daze comes over you and your brain
lies *back*, it *rocks like the sea, and as commonplace*. (p. 149, my emphasis)

This method of writing is a method of putting things into
circulation; *Living*'s alertness to the reiterations of factory
speech may have a documentary inspiration, but its first concern is with writing on a systematic basis of reiteration; not
with representing reiteration.

The dust-jacket for the Hogarth Press edition of the book
cites *The Times Literary Supplement*'s assertion that '*Living* introduced a whole school of proletarian literature', and yet it
contrasts strongly with many of those novels of the Thirties
which followed realist and even naturalist procedures in their
evocations of working-class life. The Hogarth Press itself was
to publish the kind of writer for whom there was 'the time in
the composition that naturally was in the composition'; in John
Hampson's *Saturday Night at the Greyhound*, for example (a
relatively popular book, which went through at least three
impressions in its first month of publication in February 1931),
the time-sense of the narration itself is as far as possible eclipsed
by the chronology of the narrated events, or characters' trains
of thought. This is, broadly speaking, the time-sense of realism,
in which time *of* the composition corresponds as nearly as
possible to time *in* the composition. *Living* is persistent in its

attempt to bring in question the generality of a realist contract; in one of the episodes set in a cinema, confusions of reference make the activities of the audience seem continuous with those on screen, so that any idea of a formal presentation being continuous with 'life' itself is shown to be a kind of delirium:

Later they got in and found seats. Light rain had been falling, so when these two acting on screen walked by summer night down leafy lane, hair over her ears left wet on his cheek as she leant head, when they on screen stopped and looked at each other. Boys at school had been singing outside schoolroom on screen, had been singing at stars, and these two heard them and kissed in boskage deep low in this lane and band played softly, women in audience crooning. (pp. 14–15)

In another such episode, the house lights stay on all through the performance, thus defeating any possibility of illusion; the screen is visible *as* a screen. And a comparable effect is obtained by studding the text with Arabic numerals, so that writing becomes that much more physically distinct from living.

There is evidently a close observation of film form, countering the illusion of reality with a simulation of blatantly artificial effects such as rapid montage:

'Oh' she whispered, 'Oh' and he felt quite transported.

Just then Mr. Dupret died in sleep, died, in sleep.

"'Ow are ye Albert?'

'Middlin' Aaron. The sweat was dropping from off me again last night from the pain.' (p. 124)

There is also the studied emulation of cinematic lighting effects, particularly in the dramatic intensity with which industrial work is portrayed: 'Arc lamps above threw their shadows out sprawling along over floor and as they worked rhythmically their rods up and down so their shadows worked' (p. 34). The writing is constrained less by any given 'reality' than by the features of another discourse; Green had specialized in artificial lighting effects even at school – one of the Eton Society of Arts puppet shows had been 'a strange amalgam based on the story of *Hansel and Gretel*, put into verse by Alan Clutton-Brock, the scenery designed and created by myself, the actors created by Mark Ogilvie-Grant, the music by Tchaikovsky (the *Nutcracker Suite*) and electric lighting effects by Henry Yorke, I

cannot remember who declaimed the words'.[14] While at Oxford
Green was a devotee of film, reputedly spending every afternoon
in a cinema.[15] What is especially revealing about these cinema
visits is that they immediatcly preceded his daily attempts to
write: 'I felt extremely ill and every day went alone to a cinema
after which I tried to write' (*Pack my Bag*, p. 201). When
Living presents the novel in the light of the film, it allows the
possibility of a different version; a difference which means that
the intelligible world is never the object of a simple attention,
but material in the formal play with a set of conventions.

The interest in film is an interest in the elements of its
language, parallel to an interest in literary language; syntax is
openly manipulated, and grammatical rules are regarded as
conventions to be modified: 'She met Mrs. Eames *who stood to
watch* potatoes on trestle table there' (p. 17, my emphasis). The
treatment of the verb 'to stand' as an auxiliary is a typical
irregularity. The word order is habitually irregular, but saved
from quaintness by a tireless impetus: 'With all senses fixed on
it yet in a sense he played with the job' (p. 195). Punctuation
seems virtually arbitrary, as if needed merely to dampen energy:
' "We shan't be up to much work not when you've been a man
for long so you'll look to our comfort when we'll have worked to
see you come to strength" ' (p. 24). The syntax is not held by one
or another constant design but shifts to meet new demands.
The sentence has a contorted logic which forms under the
impression of a complex agency: 'Mr. Craigan's face was
striped with black dust which had stuck to his face and which
the sweat, in running down his face, had made in stripes' (p.
34). This construction turns smartly through 180 degrees of
agency; the predilection for internal bracing tends to make the
hierarchy of subject and object a shadowy presence: 'Sparrows
flew *by* belts that ran *from* lathes *on* floor *up to* shafting *above by*
skylights' (p. 3, my emphasis). The deliberate variety of prep-
ositions necessitates a fluctuating stress which distributes the
attention. The sentence forces the exploration of a space,
enacting perception instead of registering something perceived.

Perhaps thc most celebrated excess of *Living* is the frequent
absconding of the article – a deprivation apparent at the same
time in poems written by Auden, in connection with whose
work it came to be known as 'telegraphese'.[16] Green has

provided his own explanation of this device: 'I wanted to make that book as taut and spare as possible to fit the proletarian life I was then leading. So I hit on leaving out the article.'[17] But the affected tautness and spareness is just as earnestly maintained in passages dealing with the ruling class as in those concerned with anything 'proletarian'. And its abstemiousness is even more emphatically the hallmark of writing which simulates the absence of any organizing intelligence: 'Evening. Was spring. Heavy blue clouds stayed over above. In small back garden of villa small tree was with yellow buds. On table in back room daffodils, faded, were between ferns in a vase' (p. 11). In fact the writing is the more severe and meagre in proportion to its assigned detachment from anything living: 'Water dripped from tap on wall into basin and into water there. Sun. Water drops made rings in clear coloured water. Sun in there shook on the walls and ceiling. As rings went out round trembling over the water shadows of light from sun in these trembled on walls. On the ceiling '(p. 40). Vacancies left by the departure of 'the' are often filled with alternations of 'this' and 'that'; and the resultant tension is a constant reminder that any *definitive* version of reality is spurious. The efficacy of the procedure is less as a reflection of a given way of life, as Green would suggest, than as a reaction against a particular convention governing reading and writing; the defaced language clearly operates as a type of antidote.

What the inflexions of 'spareness' or 'tautness' share is an unmistakably Anglo-Saxon character; there is a partiality for short clauses, co-ordinated rather than subordinated, for parataxis, even for an Anglo-Saxon word order:[18] 'Each life dully lived and the life next it, pitched together, *walls between built*, dully these lives went out onto streets promenaded dullness there' (p. 228, my emphasis). It is worth pointing out, in connection with this Anglo-Saxon interest, and in view of the chronicle approach, that fragments of the *Anglo-Saxon Chronicle* in Sweet's *An Anglo-Saxon Reader* (1876) would have been required reading for every Oxford undergraduate reading English, as Green did.[19]

The type of discourse which 'spareness' counteracts is present in a series of elaborate, overblown conceits: the ungainly stock-in-trade of a 'classical' style that will even attempt epic

simile; on one occasion (pp. 195–6) a single simile uses up over
five hundred words of text. Elsewhere, a florid and laboriously
unfolded comparison between the ailing factory owner,
Dupret, and a sinking submarine is brazened out over half a
page. The analogues are juxtaposed as abruptly as the vying
Anglo-Saxon and 'classical' styles: 'Mr. Gibbon said after he
had done the Holy Roman Empire he felt great relief and then
sadness at old companion done with. Mr. Dale wanted to feel
relief but felt only as if part of him was not with him, and sadness of a vacuum' (p. 121). The allusion to Gibbon brings to
mind a 'classical' eighteenth-century historiography, with
periodic sentences, which is poles apart from the austerity of
an Anglo-Saxon chronicle.

The awkwardness surrounding the interventions of a
'classical' author sponsors mistrust in an agency of regulation
which can also reveal itself as either dogmatic or flippant: 'it
is not known for certain . . .' (p. 90); '– how shall I say –'
(p. 134); 'But stretch this simile . . .' (p. 168); 'I don't
know . . .' (p. 189); 'how do I know?' (p. 228). A sense of
authorial intrusiveness is encouraged by the frequent parenthe-
sizing of informational comment: 'Then, as if she wanted to
explain asking her into the front parlour, (formal entertaining
of so young a girl compared with Mrs. Johns) . . .' (p. 193).
The parenthetical remark has the passing status of an ethno-
graphical note, as if the authorial tone was balanced in the
interests of social research; and yet the most confidently
authoritative passages in the book are also the most prejudiced
– deeply scored with an acidulous misanthropy: 'Thousands of
lamps, hundreds of streets, each house had generally a mother
and complacent father, procreation, breeding, this was only
natural thing there in that miserable thing home, natural to
them because it was domesticated. Procreating was like having
a dog, in particular spaniels. Fido who I'm so grateful to.
Miserable people' (p. 228). The graceless satire devalues what
pretends to have a special faithfulness to authorial responsibility. And yet this most self-conscious display of imposed
control is in fact a pastiche of *The Waste Land* – its real authority
derives from the imperative of style:

> he wants a good time
> And if you don't give it him, there's others will, I said . . .

Goonight Bill. Goonight Lou. Goonight May. Goonight.
Good night, ladies, good night, sweet ladies, good night,
good night.[20]

By gad didn't know it was so late well better be getting along now
or the wife won't have it eh, think I'm up to some of the old games
what well old chap I'll say goodnight now oh I say no I say old man
did you see your wife give me a kiss well perhaps it was a good
thing you didn't what, Gracie you're the sweetest little woman,
with another of course oh, that well dash it all that ever was. Well
goodnight and God bless you all – (p. 229)

Giorgio Melchiori, in his essay on 'The Abstract Art of Henry
Green', indicates a further parallel between *Living* and a
separate part of Eliot's poem, 'The Fire Sermon'. Eliot's river
images provide a setting in which Elizabeth's pleasure barge
is echoed by a 'party from Maidenhead in launch up the river,
men and women, a silver launch' (p. 114), watched by the
young Richard Dupret (one of Eliot's 'loitering heirs of City
directors') : 'Still flowed river Thames and still the leaves were
disturbed, then were loosed, and came down on to water and
went by London where he was going, by there and out into the
sea' (p. 115).[21] The author, or as much of an author as *Living*
allows, is exposed as a wholly literary invention.

And the manifestation of the author is politicized – through
a closeness, in both its accents and its sentiments, to the attitudes of Richard Dupret, the young ruling-class male representative of the greater part of Henry Green's experience:

And what was in all this, he said as he was feeling now, or in any
walk of life – you were born, you went to school, you worked, you
married, you worked harder, you had children, you went on working, with a good deal of trouble your children grew up, then they
married. What had you before you died? Grandchildren? The
satisfaction of breeding the glorious Anglo Saxon breed? (p. 187)

Living itself sprang from Green's own commitment to a new
way of life ('to work in a factory with my wet, podgy hands');[22]
and the energy with which the living idiom is pursued is
generated out of a tension between loyalty to one class and the
conventions of thought derived from another. The theme of
class division draws attention to the way the text is constructed
on a basis of discursive oppositions obtained by discursive

means; in the transition from one passage concerned with the upper-class Hannah Glossop to another concerned with the working-class Lily Gates there is a moment when the feminine pronoun 'she' is unassigned to either of these women: 'Another night. She had cleared table after supper. She went off out' (p. 118). The grammar allows us to briefly read Hannah in Lily's place – we hear elsewhere of her dilettantish interest in domestic chores: 'she enjoyed washing up' (p. 121). Hannah's attitude can be matched by Richard, who is, as his mother describes him, 'appreciative' in the face of heavy industry. He attributes a 'wild incidental beauty' to the machinery in the factory, striking the attitude of a posturing connoisseur – in fact, he reacts no differently to any sort of claim on his attention: ' "When I am with her I echo as a landscape by Claude echoes" ' (p. 35). He does, however, experience the odd revulsion at his own class: 'For in their games they sublimated all passions, all beliefs' (p. 138). This sublimation is sufficiently profound for Hannah Glossop to suffer a nervous breakdown when her doctor's chauffeur, a complete stranger, is killed: 'nothing had ever been near her before' (p. 117). Hannah's general apathy and total lack of responsibility mean that any and every experience is capable of trivialization: 'she had enjoyed enormously General Strike' (p. 117).

The book resorts to obsessively focussing on the material decay of the human body, as a constant dissolvent of class divisions. The name Dupret, carried by successive generations who inherit the factory, offers an illusion of perpetuity; it is a point of absolute fixity in language. But as a gesture towards repudiating material change it is a hollow compensation when Dupret is reduced to the common state: 'Whenever he spoke it was about the needs of his body' (p. 91).

The title, *Living*, is in itself redolent of process and change, as opposed to the conceptual *life*. All the older male characters decline remarkably in the course of events. At the outset, a great amount of play is made out of Tupe's falling over. Dupret also falls ignominiously, 'after slipping on dog's mess' (p. 56), and dies after an ensuing, protracted illness. Craigan takes to his bed and approaches his dotage; the storekeeper Albert Milligan is in and out of hospital; and Hannah Glossop's father 'also had been sick' (p. 117). The most vivid compression of this collective emphasis is given in the introduction at an early point of the image of a man 'that had lengths cut out of his belly' (p. 5). This violent decomposition is all too visible, displaying the kind of equality normally hidden. Craigan's senility is the vehicle of an apt allusion to the dying body of Falstaff:

for after I saw him fumble with the sheets and play with flowers, and smile upon his fingers' end[23]

He fell to picking at his coat. Then he held up finger squinted at it. (p. 161)

Falstaff is perhaps the most expressive example in English literature of what might be termed the Rabelaisian body, which is primarily an organic complexion rather than a visible structure. Obviously indicative of its hidden organs, and openly appetitive, the Rabelaisian body is crucially involved in a mutual transaction with the processes of the world.[24] It is of course the contrary aspect, of the body as visible and separate from the world, which strikes Richard Dupret on his initial round of the factory floor –

Young man passed by Mr. Dupret and works manager.
'What a beautiful face.' (p. 3)

– an observation which is nonsense to the working-class manager Bridges: 'What? Eh? Well I don't know.'

Class divisions hold good only in the divergent approaches to illness; Dupret becomes severely taciturn, while Craigan grows more freely responsive, to an extent that 'So much talk from him frightened her' (p. 94). And, while Craigan increasingly feels the need for Lily's affection, the ailing Dupret is to be consoled with a prostitute.

With these incessant pronunciations of mortality, the conflict of old and young is inevitably superimposed on the polarity of working class and ruling class. The succession of generations is more or less acute but never less than a disturbance: ' "Why do we bring kids into the world, they leave you so soon as they're grown, eh?" ' (p. 24). One generation does not simply follow another, but actively replaces it: during the course of the book the older workers are made redundant *en masse*. And antagonism is enforced between generations – an obscure

resentment is clarified by dividing them sharply into two age
groups: ' "I don't know what 'e's told Tupey" said Mr.
Gates, "but there's only men of 'is age and young men in that
place, so trouble's bound to be between 'em, the younger lot
trying to push the older out of the light. There's none that
comes between 'em, speakin' of age" ' (p. 151). It is safe to
suppose that this gulf would have been a legacy of the First
World War. And the division between the age groups is
augmented by the fact that, while all the younger men have
been born and brought up in the city, Craigan, Gates, Tupe,
and Aaron Connolly, all older workers, came originally from
the country.

　　The destructive competitiveness is concentrated in the outright hostilities of father-and-son relationships; of Mr Dupret
'pater', who is fifty years his son's senior, and of Bridges and
Tarver: 'Later Mr. Tarver was saying "Yes sir" and Father
said "my boy" often then' (p. 47). Considerable prominence is
given to the way in which most of the male characters per-
petually wish one another dead; this unblinking mercilessness
is even more transparent when its object is a parent: 'Why
could not the old man die?' (p. 110). The insistence of the son
replacing the father is always right on the surface; Bridges'
remark, ' "Can you work with a man like that, and when he's
old enough to be your son" ' (p. 67), includes a revealing slip
of the tongue. In place of the expected 'when he's *young* enough
to be your son', the substitution betrays an underlying fear of
'when he's *old* enough to supersede you'.

　　This undeviating pressure creates widespread instability. All
the older males take fright at the prospect of an impending
helplessness that would justify their replacement: ' "Don't do
that my wench" Mr. Craigan said, "I can still do that for
myself" ' (p. 141). Whoever fills the role of 'father' is bound to
retreat from the competition he is meant to lose; Craigan
spends a disproportionate amount of his spare time in the
isolation of his wireless head-set, even when the broadcasts are
in a language he cannot understand: ' ". . . 'e'd listen to the
weather reports so long that 'e wouldn't tell what it was doin'
outside, rainin', snowing or sleet" ' (p. 120). Bridges prevents
recognition of any threat to his position by the simple expedient
of 'always rushing out when he's crossed' (p. 82). He suspects

almost continually that he is being persecuted (' "What? Eh? What d'you mean? How do you know anyway?" '), and his anxiety is directly linked to physical degeneration by recurring images of body-infraction:

'I don't know what's the matter with me but I feel like someone had given me a cut over the brow with a ⅝ spanner. Worry, I've 'ad enough of that washing about in my head to drown a dolphin . . . Ah, so it goes on, every day, and then one day it breaks, the blood comes running out of your nose as you might be a fish has got a knock on the snout . . .' (p. 17)

"ow can you do your work conscientiously and be 'eld up like this and a pistol put to your heart . . .' (p. 30)

The waiting till you got back, that was the rub of it, was like having your arteries cut and watching the life blood spouting out. (p. 135)

And Bridges' alarmism is cruelly manifested in a moment of actual physical weakness, when his poor hearing converts 'defeatist' into 'diabetes' (p. 185). But the reader's own narcissistic security is threatened when Bridges' ridiculous obsession with Siam, associated with his own ruin, is suddenly substantiated by the unexplained arrival from Siam of Tom Tyler, a usurper in another context.

The rejection of one generation by another is further differentiated in terms of gender; which tends to complicate the settled oppositions of class. The working-class Craigan is a repository of regressive conservatism: ' "If I 'ad a son I wouldn't educate him above the station 'e was born in" '; ' "None o' the women folk go to work from the house I inhabit" he said' (p. 13). Lily's internal resistance to these obsolescent values finds expression in physical energy (' "You got a appetite" he said'), and her rebelliousness has a constructive ambition, while Richard's innovations at the factory are callous. Lily's dynamism provides a direct contrast in respect of class with the debilitation of Mrs Dupret, who finds a sense of purpose only when her husband falls ill; once he starts to revive and to reassert his control she reverts to 'her old helpless self again' (p. 105). Her relations with the working class are limited to the distribution of tips, the regulation of which obsesses her. The same principle governs Hannah Glossop's distribution of kisses – even kisses are given an exchange value: 'She made little rules about this for herself, one was she must not kiss him too often but let him kiss her' (p. 155).

The multiple polarities in *Living* (of class, gender, and age) are strongly reminiscent of D. H. Lawrence's vague, but precisely classified, levels of the psyche; Green has admitted the impact of Lawrence on his early work, and the interlocking mutual attractions and repulsions of *Living* are not inconsistent with the categories of Lawrence's scheme of consciousness in a work like *Psychoanalysis and the Unconscious*, which was first published in 1923, six years before *Living*.[25]

Green's compulsion to demarcate, throughout his text, thinking 'in feeling' from thinking 'in mind' answers to the modes of 'primal subjectivity' and 'mental subjectivity' in Lawrence. And a general inclination to impose negativeness on male characters, and positiveness on female characters, is worked out along the lines of Lawrence's discrimination between a 'sympathetic mode of communion' and a 'voluntary separative mode of communion'; the first of these is a 'love which gives its all to the beloved', while the second 'has its root in the *idea*: the beloved is a mental objective, endlessly appreciated, criticized, scrutinized, exhausted'.[26] For Lawrence, these different modes are successive stages of the same activity of consciousness, but in *Living* they are separated out into exclusive agencies.

Richard is the medium for an undiluted narcissism; he is found time and again picking his nose, often in close juxtaposition to the scenes of courtship between Lily and Bert Jones. His infatuation with Hannah Glossop is really a pretext for further self-indulgence – a mesmerized repetition of stagnant phrases, 'over and over again darling, darling, darling, like that, so like those old men squatting on the mountains' (p. 84). The love between Lily and Bert is conversely identified with a renewed purposefulness: 'When she was with Bert it was like she had just stretched, then waked, then was full of purposes' (p. 77). Lily and Richard react in an absolutely contrary fashion to the same refrain, 'Your eyes are my eyes / My heart looks through'; he 'felt quite transported' (p. 124), while for her it means 'Horror' (p. 227). Richard is of course predisposed to static formulae; his recitation of 'darling, darling, darling' is succinctly offset by Lily's reiteration of the word 'yes' in conversation with her lover: ' "Yes, and don't they keep the roads beautiful . . . Yes it's a pleasure . . . Yes it is . . . Yes we all went . . . Yes because you can get right out into the country . . . Yes . . . Yes that's what he says . . . Yes sometimes I wish I could go outside . . ." ' (pp. 45–6). The same word is elevated in the closely similar context of Molly Bloom's soliloquy at the end of Joyce's *Ulysses*. On different occasions Joyce made varying calculations as to its effect. To Jacques Benoîst-Méchin he said, 'The book must end with yes. It must end with the most positive word in the human language';[27] while to Louis Gillet he averred, 'In *Ulysses*, to depict the babbling of a woman going to sleep, I had sought to end with the least forceful word I could possibly find. I had found the word "yes", which is barely pronounced, which denotes acquiescence, self-abandon, relaxation, the end of all resistance.'[28] The language of active affirmation is also the language of passive assent; this ambivalence cuts to the heart of *Living*'s implied politics of gender. The energy released in Lily is transformed into an acquiescent energy, and the disaffection which had seemed to potentiate her for so much is retrospectively allayed in the serenity of prospective motherhood.

The definitive polarization of male and female, which occurs when Richard and Lily pass one another unnoticed in the street, turns on the question of reproduction:

What will they grow up to he thought in mind – they'll work, they'll marry, they'll work harder, have children and go on working, they'll die. He shuddered. Then he forgot all about them and thought about himself.

But Lily coming through the gate saw children running and those mothers and she stood and watched them, feeling out of it. 'I must have babies,' she said then, looking at baby in mother's arms. (p. 188)

The basis of this reduction to order could also have been provided by Lawrence, who reserved his most rhapsodical cogency for propagandizing the relationship of mother and child. Love between adults is always liable to cerebration, while the union of mother and child is galvanized by a 'lovely polarized vitalism', a nervous form of electricity conducting an 'unconscious sapience'. In *Living*, the satisfaction of motherhood is forcefully located on a semi-conscious level: 'Baby

howled till mother there lifted him from bed to breast and
sighed most parts asleep in darkness . . . She was not quite
woke up and said you wouldn't believe, she was so happy now'
(pp. 13–14). And a particular limpidity is uppermost in the
writing which celebrates the harmony of natural with maternal
bounty: ' "When the blossom was out the missus and I came
along and sat under it of a Sunday with the baby" ' (p. 48).
The most extended lyrical passage in the book is concerned
with the birth of a son to Arthur Jones, whose elated singing
draws an universally positive response: 'Soon each one in this
factory heard that Arthur had begun and, if he had 2 moments,
came by iron foundry shop to listen . . . each one was glad
when he sang' (pp. 89–90).

There is nothing to suggest that the novel's third term – an
implicit urgency, implicitly female, to transform the world –
has not receded behind the comprehensive image of motherhood, unless there is a possibility of its having been transmuted
into another aspect of the text. There remains the suggestion
of immense pressures in areas *other* than the question of female
sexuality. At the end of the book, the almost mysterious
quietness of the crowd on its way to the football match is an
obvious reflection of the daily march to work which opens the
book. The crowd's restraint exacerbates the subsequent effect
of mass hysteria in the football stadium, a hysteria whose
undirectedness is pointed by the indifference of '11 men who
play the best football in the world. These took no notice of the
crowd, no notice' (p. 266).

On balance, the violence of the crowd reaction is the measure
of a negative satisfaction. The writing is positive each time it
transmutes itself with an imagery of birds:

He saw these and as the sun comes out from behind clouds then
birds whistle for the sun, so love came out in his eyes . . . (p. 163)

Then, as after rain so the sky shines and again birds rise up into the
sky and turn there with still movements so her sorrow folded wings,
so gently crying she sank deeper into the bed and was quieted.
(p. 239)

Both these examples are reminiscent of Milton's epic simile in
Paradise Lost, Book II:

As when from mountain tops the dusky clouds
Ascending, while the north wind sleeps, o'erspread
Heaven's cheerful face, the louring element
Scowls o'er the darkened landscape snow, or shower;
If chance the radiant sun with farewell sweet
Extend his evening beam, the fields revive,
The birds their notes renew, and bleating herds
Attest their joy, that hill and valley rings.[29]

This 'classical' bias is corrected elsewhere by an Anglo-Saxon bias, shortly to be discussed; the recurring figures of birds transmute every species of discourse.

Among so many figurations, there is one where a bird trapped between the upper and lower sashes of a window may be taken to represent Lily. Craigan, Gates and Dale are all helpless to set it and her free. It is up to Mrs Eames to release the bird and to supposedly liberate Lily by her example of purposeful motherhood. But this symbolic interlude is only a momentary diversion from the series of very fitfully connected images of birds which is otherwise scarcely concerned to justify its determined hold over the text. The aspirations of every sort of character are subsumed in a vision of overseas, of Australia, Canada, and 'the East'; the text is correspondingly invaded by sensational metaphors and similes connecting birds with ocean travel:

She walked in misery. She tried not to think of him. But as sometimes, coming across the sea from a cold country to the tropics and the sky is dull so the sea is like any other sea, so as you are coming tropical birds of exquisite colours settle to rest on the deck, unexpected, infinitely beautiful, so things she remembered of him came one by one back to her mind. And as the ship beat by beat draws nearer to that warmth the birds come from, so her feeling was being encompassed then by the memory of him and it was so warm she sat down on the wet ground and cried. (p. 156)

The imagery seems primed for the merest pretext on which to present a maximum inconvenience to narrative exposition; its virtual independence of reference is so intensified that it can afford to make gratuitous forays into the text ('How can you darn when as it might be a bird is in your hand'). The writing is constantly waylaid by this imagery following a circular path; the living idiom evolved in complicity with the

subject-matter of factory life starts to predicate material of its
own.

But although it is not anchored in the tendentious formations
of the text – and indeed it appears to sublimate them – this
versatility does obliquely touch upon the tendentious design.
The first bird image of the book is a slight glance at Bede's
comparison of the life of Man with the flight of a sparrow:

Sparrows flew by belts that ran from lathes on floor up to shafting
above by skylights. (p. 3)

when we compare the present life of man on earth with that time
of which we have no knowledge, it seems to me like the swift flight
of a single sparrow through the banqueting-hall where you are
sitting at dinner on a winter's day with your thanes and counsellors.
In the midst there is a comforting fire to warm the hall; outside,
the storms of winter rain or snow are raging. This sparrow flies
swiftly in through one door of the hall, and out through another.
While he is inside, he is safe from the winter storms; but after a few
moments of comfort, he vanishes from sight into the wintry world
from which he came. Even so, man appears on earth for a little
while; but of what went before this life or of what follows, we know
nothing.[30]

The epigraph to the novel is only a concise version of this
analogy in the perfected form of a double-barrelled question:

>   As these birds would go where
>   so where would this child go?

And the very title of *Living* is paraphrastic of the 'present life
of man on earth'. The same combination of bird and child,
with bad weather, is the melodramatic hinge of Lily's dream,
which covers a vista – literally a bird's eye view – of industrial
life: 'Yes, and blackbird fled across that town flying crying and
made noise like noise made by ratchet. Yes and in every house
was mother with her child and that was grey and that fluttered
hands and then that died, in every house died those children
to women. Was low wailing low in her ears' (p. 108). The
weird pungency of the whole passage seems to confer with the
Anglo-Saxon tradition of dream visions, and its formal minia-
turism is of the same order as Bede's little parable.

Giorgio Melchiori considers that Green's bird imagery
'reaches at times the intensity of a symbol, but lacks all pre-

cision of reference and consistency'.[31] This is true, but the flight of birds in *Living* should be approached in the spirit of augury, where consistency is otiose; it calls rather for a method of reading which is organized around the anomalous, and the inadjustable.

The only common factor in the repertoire is the bird in flight on the wing, rejecting solidity for weightlessness; there is consistency here, consistency with the example set once again by Lawrence, whose 'Preface to the American Edition of *New Poems*' (1920) has a wholesale devotion to the preoccupying imagery of *Living*:

The bird is on the wing in the winds, flexible to every breath, a living spark in the storm, its very flickering depending upon its supreme mutability and power of change. Whence such a bird came; whither it goes; from what solid earth it rose up, and upon what solid earth it will close its wings and settle, this is not the question. This is a question of before and after. Now, *now*, the bird is on the wing in the winds.[32]

Lawrence reproduces the tension of 'whence' and 'whither' used by Bede in order to defuse it. But the attraction to vast scales of time in itself gives a kind of infinite backing to the 'now'; Lawrence is concerned for an *eternal* now, and the time-sense in and of his text refers to a temporality which simply flows over the text, sweeping away all questions of distribution and equilibration. *Living*, on the other hand, is closer to Gertrude Stein's requirements for a continuous present; when its epigraph reappears in the body of the text, it is in immediate proximity to a Stein-like procedure: 'Is nothing wonderful in migrating birds but when we see them we become muddled in our feeling, we think it so romantic they should go so far, far. Is nothing wonderful in a woman carrying but Mrs. Eames was muddled in her feeling by it. As these birds would go where so where would this child go?' (p. 246). The method of 'beginning and beginning again' is precisely what takes the text out of eternity and into history. And the Lawrentian crusade makes extraneous use of a bird imagery which *Living* incorporates with such thoroughness that its recurrence is the medium for presenting the text with its own history; the historic present of itself.

The increasingly independent dilations of the text suddenly contract to the same space in the final scene: 'When he came back he put grain onto hood of the pram and one by one pigeon fluttered off the roof onto hood of this pram. As they did so they fluttered round heads of these people in the yard, who kept heads very still' (p. 269). Purely in terms of its own textuality, the book appears to finish on a contradiction; the textual inertia of motherhood is contraposed to the textual volatility of birds. The transubstantiation of a desire for change into an audacious metaphor is overtaken by the articulation of a more complacent sense, which can rely on a more conventional method of reading for its superior intelligibility. On balance, *Living* fails to provide a satisfactory solution of its problems; indeed, its epigraph asks an insoluble question. But Green has discovered in the process of writing a new textuality, less conventionally readable, which he was to struggle to develop over the seven or more years that went to the making of *Party Going*.

2 *Party Going:*
a border-line case

He has said that his third book, *Party Going*, required nine or ten beginnings and became the novel hardest to write.[1]

The difficulty involved in writing this book corresponds to a certain stubbornness of texture which is the striking feature of any reading. The opening pages which bear the final brunt of 'nine or ten beginnings' seem to overtax the resources of a novel; we read with a hypnotized exposure to details, to an irreversible definiteness, which at first sight seems to communicate little more than the strength of a cryptic determination:

For Miss Fellowes, as they soon saw, had drawn up her sleeves and on the now dirty water with a thin wreath or two of blood, feathers puffed up and its head sideways, drowned along one wing, lay her dead pigeon. Air just above it was dizzy with a little steam, for she was doing what she felt must be done with hot water, turning her fingers to the colour of its legs and blood. (p. 9)

The deliberate attentiveness of the writing ought to reward a deliberate attentiveness of reading with a corresponding degree of purposed meaning. But the accepted means to achieve semantic cohesion – to condense these vaporous meanings – are used with a complete inadvertence. The organized weight of interpretation is forced into a startling texture which changes its line of pursuit, diverts it from knowledge: 'She turned and she went back to where it had fallen and again looked up to where it must have died for it was still warm and, everything unexplained, she turned once more into the tunnel back to the station' (p. 7). The novel's obsession with motive is replaced by a fascination with narrative where everything is 'unexplained'. On the other hand, there is an intense preoccupation with *motif*, which is perverse, since it does not inform

any method of integrating effects but generates a rising incom-
prehension as the writing returns with an awkward persistence
to the imagery of this incident:

'If he was a bird,' he said, 'he would not last long.' (p. 64)

'Go on if you like and pick up some bird, alive or dead.' (p. 159)

That is what it is to be rich, he thought, if you are held up, if you
have to wait then you can do it after a bath in your dressing gown
and if you have to die then not as any bird tumbling dead from its
branch . . . (p. 195)

Lying in his arms, her long eyelashes down along her cheeks, her
hair tumbled and waved, her hands drifted to rest like white doves
drowned on peat water . . . (p. 226)

Each time, it looks as if the image of a dead bird has been
displaced from somewhere else; the bird is a kind of negative
counterpart to the albatross in 'The Rime of the Ancyent
Marinere'. Both of these birds appear suddenly out of a fog:

> At length did cross an Albatross,
> Thorough the Fog it came;[2]

Fog was so dense, bird that had been disturbed went flat into a
balustrade and slowly fell, dead, at her feet. (p. 7)

In the poem the Mariner shoots the albatross, and so precipitates a narrative of guilt depending on a final redemption. This
determined scheme, which culminates in the revelation of
'truth', is reversed by *Party Going*; with the pigeon already dead,
'it did seem only a pious thing to pick it up' (p. 25). Miss
Fellowes's impulse is equivalent to 'blessing it unaware' – the
spontaneous compassion which brings redemption to the Mariner.
But in *Party Going* the pigeon becomes a morbid threat from
this point onward, and a pattern of reference is developed to
reject the implied ambition of Christian narrative, to revoke its
solution and keep alive a mood of crisis and questioning. The
poem includes a competition between 'LIFE-IN-DEATH' and her
'Pheere'; the Mariner is followed by the spirit 'from the land
of mist and snow' and hears two voices. Miss Fellowes holds an
imaginary argument with the waitress who was indifferent to
her: 'It might have been an argument with death' (p. 125).
She has a 'familiar spirit' in the house detective who can

employ a bewildering range of accents and who also appears to have a special relationship with death: 'And as he talked of death his speech relapsed into some dialect of his own' (p. 205). The dead bird is robbed of its interpretational value and returns the narrative to an impasse ('As idle as a painted Ship / Upon a painted ocean.').[3] The 'party' is unable to 'go' because the train has been immobilized by fog. The pigeon is comparably inert; like the albatross around the neck of the Mariner, it is a dead weight, burdening the narrative so that its removal brings a similar sense of relief: 'She felt better at once . . . she thought how wonderful it's gone, I feel quite strong again' (p. 12). But unlike the albatross the pigeon is immediately retrieved, and the measure of guilt implicit in the literary reference is not confined to an individual but transferred into a general unease; Julia also suffers from a bad conscience, and 'Few people passed her and they did not look up, as if they also were guilty' (p. 16). Instead of destroying a bird, Miss Fellowes (as the embodiment of her name) has demonstrated a 'fellow feeling', and it is this characteristic which makes *her* a dead weight on the hands of the party. Their response to every such liability is exemplified by Julia when she chooses to ignore a screaming woman in the crowd: ' "After all," she said, "one must not hear too many cries for help in this world" ' (p. 100). The indefinite pronoun is chillingly impersonal. 'Fellow feeling' becomes an issue tied up with class division; the crowd can encourage a harmony and spontaneity: ' "No it's fellow feeling that's what I like about it. Without so much as a by your leave when she sees someone hankering after a bit of comfort, God bless 'er, she gives it him, not like some little bitches I could name," he darkly said, looking up and over to where their hotel room would be' (p. 162). Thomson, who has just received a spontaneous kiss from a complete stranger, contrasts this example of 'fellow feeling' with the behaviour of members of the party; for Julia and Angela, kissing is chiefly a means of *regulating* social relations: 'As for Julia she had kissed Max to keep him sweet so to speak, and so, in one way, had Miss Crevy kissed her young man' (p. 115). Among the members of the party there is no question even of class loyalty – far from being attentive to each other's needs they often simply do not listen to each other: 'She looked round and saw her husband was not listening . . . And then, more embarrassing still, she realized Amabel was not listening' (pp. 141–2). The extreme to which this indifference can lead is shown by mention of a past incident when Julia herself had fainted and Max had left her to her own devices. Alex rejects any sense of community: 'not that even if it did mean fellow feeling' (p. 195). Kissing is no longer a pleasure shared but the quintessential act of insecurity:

'Is it gold?' she said, putting her hands up to it.

'It is,' he said and coming to sit by her on the stool in front of that looking glass he lightly kissed the hair above her ear. As he did this he looked into the glass to see himself doing it because he was in that state when he thought it incredible that he should be so lucky to be kissing someone so marvellous. (p. 127)

This narcissistic apprehension is shadowed by a more general testing of the significations of the body; and the particular focus of this general mood is on the illness of Miss Fellowes, which persists for the whole length of the novel.

Illness, as a means of articulating social complexities, is pressed into service again and again in the writing of the Thirties; indeed, the intellectual history of the time can hardly be separated from the theoretical course of psychoanalysis and related studies. Kenneth Burke, writing on literary form in 1941, summarizes a decade of finding out the implications of symptomatology:

The accumulating lore on the nature of 'psychogenic illnesses' has revealed that something so 'practical' as a bodily ailment may be a 'symbolic' act on the part of the body which, in this materialization, *dances* a corresponding state of mind, reordering the glandular and neural behaviour of the organism in obedience to mind-body correspondences, quite as the formal dancer reorders his externally observable gesturing to match his attitudes. [4]

At the beginning of the decade, in *The Orators* (1932), Auden included a 'Letter to a Wound' to be read as the sign of political crisis. The founder of psychosomatic medicine, Georg Groddeck, had maintained in an essay published in 1925 that 'the meaning of illness is the warning "do not continue living as you intend to do" . . . the patient is out to test every one of the doctor's measures for its usefulness towards its object of remaining ill' [5]. The need for a change of regime, both physical and political, is what gives *The Orators* its consistently imperative mood.⁶ The sociality of illness had also been demonstrated in Kafka's *Metamorphosis* (published in translation in 1933). In Kafka's story, the family of the patient develop an increasingly callous self-reliance conditional on the death of the patient, but in *Party Going* the problem is unresolved; the argument would run that Miss Fellowes remains ill because she reveals her unconscious in being ill – she has an interest in remaining ill to warn of a danger: 'If it is true that the meaning of illness is among other things a warning of danger, then the question is what is this danger that is common to all mankind. Everybody will think of the inescapable danger, death.'⁷

In *Party Going*, death has a kind of regional presence; it is a substratum into which the writing periodically strays or intrudes. The fog is more than once a 'pall' or 'appalling' as it hangs over the luggage which is 'like an exaggerated grave yard' filled with 'mourners' or 'the dead resurrected in their clothes'. Alex and Julia feel compelled to imagine a state of death: 'he likened what he saw to being dead and thought of himself as a ghost driving through streets of the living' (p. 37); 'what they saw was like a view from the gibbet' (p. 87). The emphasis here is not on the absence of the grave but on a haunted awareness, the anxiety of purgatory – the fear of a threshold: 'She thought it was like an enormous doctor's waiting room and that it would be like that when they were all dead and waiting at the gates' (p. 59). What Julia feels is a sense of vulnerability before the impending verdict, a quite precise form of uncertainty which would seem to have been endemic throughout the Thirties. At the start of *The Orators* Auden gives a diagnosis of society which makes use of a comparison with Dante: 'In the second book of this poem, which describes Dante's visit to Purgatory, the sinners are divided into three main groups, those who have been guilty in their life of excessive love towards themselves or their neighbours, those guilty of defective love towards God and those guilty of perverted love.'⁸ Here again the broad issue is 'fellow feeling' and its violation, which in *Party Going* takes the form of sexual intrigue: 'You know that thing of making up to someone else so as to make the one you really care about more mad about you' (p. 94). Any sexual relationship is thought provisional;

it is an arrangement to be manipulated, invariably by the use
of a third party. Angela uses Alex to make Robin jealous, and
Amabel does the same with Alex and Max.[9]

The mythical Embassy Richard – another third party to Max
and Amabel – is nothing if not the embodiment of intrigue
based on secrecy and guilt:

> He did not shake, he pressed as though to make secrets he would
> never keep, as though to embrace each private thought you had and
> to let you know he shared it with you and would share it again
> with anyone he met. As against this, when he spoke it was never to
> less than three people. It may have been tact, or that he was cir-
> cumspect, but he paid no attention to Amabel. (p. 254)

The second of three pictures in one of the party's hotel rooms
is an image for the loose, shifting triangles of sexual involvement:
'Another was one of those reproductions of French eighteenth-
century paintings which showed a large bed with covers
turned back and half in, half out of it a fat girl with fat legs
sticking out of her nightdress and one man menacing and
another disappearing behind curtains' (p. 92). The use of a
partition is extensive; both Robin and Alex wait on the
outside of a closed door which obstructs knowledge: 'When
Alex came to an end she had not properly heard what he had
been saying so she said something almost under her breath,
or so low that he in his turn should not catch what she had
said, but so that it would be enough to tell him she was listening' (p. 172). The partition is there to revoke knowledge, to
restore the state of incompleteness or ignorance: ' "Oh, but
they'll come up here and be dirty and violent," and she hung
her handkerchief over her lips and spoke through it like she
was talking into the next room through a curtain. "They'll
probably try and kiss us or something" ' (p. 235). To ward off
the kiss of knowledge, Julia interposes a threshold beyond
which it is forbidden to pass, like the original veto on the
apple: 'He could not hold that kiss she had given him as it
might be an apple in his hand to turn over while he made up
his mind to bite' (p. 203). Sex is a 'fall' into knowledge and
mortality – 'He stood in front of her and she fixed him with
her eyes which drew him like the glint a hundred feet beneath
and called on him to throw himself over' (p. 215) – a fall

which is self-destructive, combining the desire for knowledge with a simultaneous need to suppress that knowledge in oblivion. This double meaning is at the heart of psychoanalytic and psychosomatic theory:

> If there really is a fear of death and it exists universally, then there must also be a longing for death universally; for fear is a wish, a repressed wish . . . The Greeks, who were better at understanding the It than we are, gave the God of Death the same features as the God of Love . . . In reality we die when we love; our personality is wiped out in these rare moments of life . . . man has a longing for death because he longs for love, and a longing for love because he craves death, the mother's womb . . . after the union the man is no longer male, but child; he buries himself in the woman's lap . . . And illness, the meaning of illness, is this death wish and love fear, love wish and death fear.[10]

Party Going maintains the punning sense of this 'burying in the woman's lap'; as well as giving access to what is dead, it incorporates a recession of cavities. The train is relinquished in favour of the enclosing vault with its entrance tunnels, a damp and sticky fog which surrounds the warm, comforting hotel. The journey with a destination is replaced by a wandering through corridors, up and down stairs, in and out of rooms and into tunnels. The only travelling is done by Miss Fellowes – 'She looked as if she had been travelling' (p. 244) – and this happens *inside her own body*. The crowd is 'like those illustrations you saw in weekly papers, of corpuscles in blood, for here and there a narrow stream of people shoved and moved in lines three deep and where they did this they were like veins' (p. 86). The station is an arterial labyrinth which appears to recede to an inner sanctum. Regressive movement, similar to that in *The Castle*, *The Trial*, and *The Burrow* of Kafka, is repeated everywhere in *Party Going*; a 'guardian' is needed for the underground lavatory, 'and those stairs had LADIES lit up over them' (p. 8), where Miss Fellowes fills a basin with hot water to rinse the blood from her pigeon. Deep in the hotel is the room where Miss Fellowes lies on her bed, attended by 'those nannies, like the chorus in Greek plays' (p. 72). (The bed is like an altar – the focus of the curving, hollow structure of the Greek theatre.) It seems unlikely that the book is not complicit with psychoanalytic theory:

She was in a long hall with hidden lighting and, for ornament, a
vast chandelier with thousands of glass drops and rather dirty. It
was full of people and those who had found seats, which were all
of them too low, lay with blank faces as if exhausted and, if there
was anything to hope for, as though they had lost hope. Most of
them were enormously fat. One man there had a cigar in his mouth,
and then she saw he had one glass eye, and in his hand he had a
box of matches which now and again he would bring up to his
cigar. Just as he was about to strike his match he looked round
each time and let his hands drop back to his lap, his match not
lighted. Those standing in groups talked low and were rather bent
and there was a huge illuminated clock they all kept looking at.
Almost every woman was having tea as if she owned the whole
tray of it. Almost every man had a dispatch case filled with daily
newspapers. She thought it was like an enormous doctor's waiting
room and that it would be like that when they were all dead and
waiting at the gates. (p. 59)

The long hall with 'hidden lighting' is like the darkness of the
womb. Psychoanalytic theory suggests that there is vision in
the womb, but no eyesight – the eyes are 'for ornament'; the
glass eye and the glass drops are redundant because vision is
not 'outside-inwards' but 'inside-outwards' like that of the
'seer', whose eyesight is repressed to cut out the inessential, in
order to analyse a predicament.[11] The hall *is* 'an enormous
doctor's waiting room', outside the inner sanctum where Miss
Fellowes lies sick; it combines the idea of suspension before
birth with the purgatorial aspect present in the exhaustion and
hopelessness of the passengers. The people standing are 'rather
bent' as if confined by the womb; as the embryo grows there is
an increasing awareness that 'the time will come' and hence
the 'huge illuminated clock'. Infantile theories of pregnancy –
'most of them were enormously fat' – are coupled with the
denial of sexuality; the man who fails to light his cigar is like a
screen memory which repeats the imagery of sexual arousal to
censor it guiltily ('he looked round each time').

Moving slightly beyond the quoted passage, this censorship
is projected in the sealing of the hotel entrance which, although
it has 'RECEPTION lit up over it' (p. 56), is converted to an
'impenetrable entrance' (p. 61). Both foetal and purgatorial
aspects are combined in the notion of 'waiting at the gates'.

In an essay published in *Some Versions of Pastoral* in 1935,

William Empson had analysed 'The Rime of the Ancyent Marinere' in the context of arguing the synthesis of 'unusually intellectual with unusually primitive ideas; thought about the conditions of knowledge with a magical idea that the adept controls the external world by thought'.[12] The crucial text for Empson is 'The Garden' by Marvell, and in an examination of Marvell's symbolization of the mind as an ocean, he had made emphatic use of psychoanalysis: 'On the Freudian view of an Ocean, *withdraws* would make this repose in Nature a return to the womb.'[13] Psychosomatic theory also conceives of the sea as 'the mother symbol of all human beings' (Groddeck). And in *Party Going*, the feeling which is 'common to all of them' is a longing to return to the sea: 'But when it was fine and you sat on the terrace for dinner looking over a sea of milk with a sky fainting into dusk with the most delicate blushes – Oh! she cried in her heart, if only we could be there now' (p. 72). The sea is inextricably connected with the mother's bounty of blood and milk, and the reversion to this memory is covert and guilty since it is a relapse from knowledge: 'If they did not mention it, it was why they were in this hotel room and there was not one of them, except of course for Miss Fellowes and the nannies who did not every now and again most secretly revert to it' (p. 72). Fluid security is found in a number of annexes, in several images of containment. Behind closed doors, Amabel makes a ritual of her hot bath, and this oblivious amniotic comfort is what Julia reverts to: 'her feeling was just what she had when in a hot bath so exactly right she could not bear to wonder even' (p. 151). For Max the ideal woman is the warm, fluid, encompassing female – 'When they had been together she had warmed him every side' (p. 176) – under the influence of which he 'had come back to them, *unseeing* . . . his thoughts *hatching* up out of sleep' (p. 176, my emphasis). Even the fog 'came out of the sea', to become 'dim whirling waters' inside the station. The subject of centripetal forces, Miss Fellowes withdraws into her own body which she imagines as a violent sea that sweeps her from head to foot:

As this tumulus advanced the sea below would rise, most menacing and capped with foam, and as it came nearer she could hear the shrieking wind in throbbing through her ears. She would try not to turn her eyes down to where rising waves broke over rocks as the

nearer that black mass advanced so fast the sea rose and ate up
what little was left between her and those wild waters. Each time
this scene was repeated she felt so frightened, and then it was
menacing and she throbbed unbearably, as it was all forced into her
head; it was so menacing she thought each time the pressure was
such her eyes would be forced out of her head to let her blood out.
(p. 76)

A tumulus is the perfect image of a chamber to indicate the
symbolic relationship of the sea-womb with death. A representative image of birth trauma is superimposed with the attempt
to undo that birth: to replace the outside-inwards sight with
the original inside-outwards vision.[14] (In the very last stage of
revising his text, Green had deleted the sentence, 'Alex
wondered could Miss Fellowes be having a baby, and then he
wondered if she would not be too old for that.')[15] The illness
comes in waves – 'She waged war with storms of darkness
which rolled up over her in a series, like tides summoned by a
moon' (p. 72) – which, according to the psychoanalytical point
of view, the infant observer would relate to the loud breathing
of desire. The notion of the soul as the inspiration of breath
(τὸ πνεῦμα) is conventional, and in the description of Amabel
– 'under softly beaten wings of her breathing' (p. 176), and
'breathing like seagulls settled on the water' (p. 226) – it
rejoins the Christian imagery of 'The Rime of the Ancyent
Marinere' where the albatross is 'an it were a Christian Soul',
and of 'The Garden' (although Marvell takes a Platonic route
to the Christian figure):

> My soul into the boughs does glide;
> There like a bird it sits and sings,
> Then whets, and combs its silver wings;
> And, till prepared for longer flight,
> Waves in its plumes the various light.

Empson in his commentary on this passage employs a selection
of terms which surface intact in *Party Going*:

The bird is the dove of the Holy Spirit and carries a suggestion of
the rainbow of the covenant.[16]

Then three seagulls flew through that span on which she stood and
that is what happened one of the first times she first met him, doves
had flown under a bridge where she had been standing when she

had stayed away last summer. She thought those gulls were for the sea they were to cross that evening. (p. 19)

Although the doves are here transformed as seagulls, Julia forgets this later on and 'thought they had been doves and so was comforted' (p. 161). The span of the bridge repeats the arc of the rainbow, which is 'arc-en-ciel' in French, and referred to later as 'that promise of the birds which had flown under the arch' (p. 151)[17] The ship which she expects to board in the evening recalls the Ark of the covenant.

This cluster of symbols is familiar enough, apart from its allocation here; but if we take into account the date of the essay (and the fact that the novel 'required nine or ten beginnings'), the close attention it pays to 'The Rime of the Ancyent Marinere' and a keen interest in Freudian theory, it may look like something more than an accident, when Empson roots his argument in a reading of the couplet,

> Annihilating all that's made
> To a *green* thought in a *green* shade,

because the essay goes on with an exhaustive account of twenty-four occurrences of greenness in the work of Marvell. If a dependence on the poem might seem over-determined, a relationship between the novel and the essay seems more than likely.[18] The most striking co-ordinates arise from Marvell's connection of greenness with oceans – which gives it a magical security – and with mirrors and the partial knowledge of the mind. It is as well to remember at this point that Green is a pseudonym, the writer's real name being Henry Vincent Yorke. In other words, Green has once more been able to motivate his own name. In the text of the novel, the word 'green' attracts the notions of containment, fluidity, and reflection: 'Electric lights had been lit by now, fog still came in by the open end of this station, below that vast green vault of glass roof with every third person smoking it might all have looked to Mr. Roberts, ensconced in his office away above, like November sun striking through mist rising off water' (p. 28). The most radical interaction is indicated by the phrase 'green thought' which might be a compressed example of Green's own practice; Empson brings out the palpability of this figure:

The sea if calm reflects everything near it: the mind as knower is a conscious mirror . . . the unconscious is unplumbed and pathless, and there is no instinct so strange among the beasts that it lacks its fantastic echo in the mind. In the first version thoughts are shadows, in the second (like the *green thought*) they are as solid as what they image; and yet they still correspond to something in the outer world, so that the poet's intuition is comparable to pure knowledge.[19]

By an element of surprise the similes of *Party Going* 'are as solid as what they image'; the simile is already a lateral investment in language, but in *Party Going* it takes on a desultory extravagance, a manifest deviance away from the context: 'So that to be with her was for Angela as much as it might be for a director of the Zoo to be taking his okapi for walks in leading strings for other zoologists to see or, as she herself would have put it, it was being grand with grand people' (p. 140). It becomes almost impossible to return to the context of this figure without exerting some degree of force; and so the writing goes on, seeming to define itself by the width of its gap between discursive relations and representational reference: 'Aromatic steam as well from her bath salts so that if her maid had been a negress then Amabel's eyes might have shone like two humming birds in the tropic airs she glistened in' (p. 154); 'These two screamed now like rats smelling food when they have been starved in empty milk churns' (p. 178). Empson interprets the couplet as combining 'the idea of the conscious mind, including everything because understanding it, and that of the unconscious animal nature, including everything because in harmony with it'.[20] In this double articulation is the history of difference. Representation is perspectival – based on the eyesight it confirms the distancing of the conscious mind from its environment, and it suppresses the memory of interaction with the environment, blots out that history which is continually present in the unconscious. The collapse of representational depth allows an entry to the dialectic of 'harmony' and 'understanding', and its collateral expression of nostalgia for unity with the assertion of difference.

As a foil to what Empson refers to as 'the Orpheus idea, that by delight in nature when terrible man gains strength to control it', *Party Going* includes the illustration of another musician who is futile in the face of nature when terrible: 'One of these was of Nero fiddling while Rome burned, on a marble terrace. He stood to his violin and eight fat women reclined on mattresses in front while behind was what was evidently a great conflagration' (p. 92). The picture of irresponsible privilege, and flirtation set against an apocalyptic background, invites comparison with Max. He is prone to merge his identity with Amabel's in the attempt to retrieve an original harmony, to reunite with the mother, 'as he made himself breathe with her breathing, as he always did when she was in his arms to try and be more with her' (p. 226). The decisive point of consciousness must be the actuality of division; and the unconscious will form a neurosis to protect itself and withdraw to a stage before division: 'Illness is the expression of the wish to be small, to be given help, to have a mother, to be blameless.'[21] The fascination with a threshold includes this manoeuvre within its scope; as a compulsive repetition of the awareness of division, its concentration on what is constituted as unseen *because* it is implicitly known is like a sophistication of the principle behind the child's game of see-saw, which could be an unconscious dramatization of the separation from the mother.

There are several marks of infantility among the characters of *Party Going*.[22] Miss Fellowes drinks the whisky because she remembers having it as a small child after hunting, and this is what motivates the bizarre image of her on an antelope between rows of giant cabbages, because 'she was having a perfectly serene dream that she was riding home, on an evening after hunting' (p. 104). The unconscious does not recognize any age differences: 'But the voice asked why she had washed it and she felt like when she was very small and had a dirty dress' (p. 126). Alex's voice goes to a higher pitch, like a child's, when he feels he is about to be penalized. After the early death of his mother, to whom he had been 'simply devoted', he grows timid before the opposite sex: 'she was probably extremely powerful and he always had thought women were more powerful than men' (p. 191). The importance of 'fellow feeling' to this complex is clear when at the end of the book Julia sinks into the memory of a childhood happiness provided *by Miss Fellowes*. Robert shares with Julia a childhood fantasy concerning a patch of bamboo ('asparagus really'): 'When small he had found patches of bamboo in his parents' garden and it was his romance at that time to force through them; they grew so thick you could not see what temple might lie in ruins just beyond' (p. 47).[23] His imagination of a buried treasure in the heart of a maze-like undergrowth conforms to the obsessional image of sepulture in a labyrinth, while Julia buries in the same spot a number of objects which have no meaning apart from their very secrecy. These are her 'charms' which are complementary symbols of the sexual organs – a wooden pistol and a hollow egg painted with red rings containing three little ivory elephants.[24] Their burial has a dual purpose: censorship (sex is a secret which everyone knows about, while the knowledge of it is a white elephant) in the form of re-entry to the womb. The charms are directly linked with her mother ('of course'): ' "I don't know how I first got them," she said, for she was not going to tell anyone ever that it was her mother, of course, who had given them to her and who had died when she was two years old' (p. 108). And she relies upon them completely: 'it would be hopeless to go without them' (p. 18). In a childhood incident when the wind, caught in the umbrella she was holding, had seemingly lifted her 'as far as from cliffs *into the sea*' (p. 110, my emphasis) the only thing saving her from this experience of flight (another common symbol for sex) had been the hollow egg. Without it she is too nervous to use the hotel lift.

The bamboo patch is the last moment before knowledge, and hence Julia's fixation with her charms; they represent knowledge at the same time as the pretence not to know, just as the text diagnoses the novel as a fetishistic process – faced with irrational drives it constructs a reasoned alibi, it replaces the dissipation of meaning with a system of compatibilities. The individual 'who *could not or would not* light his cigar' (my emphasis) demonstrates the ambivalent motive of the fetish. Robert's apparent precognition of Miss Fellowes, a subliminal recognition producing an involuntary reference, is like the compulsion to give experience a narrative form. Just as the rules of narrative are subliminal, so we involuntarily read every situation in terms of narrative. The artifices of narrative are made prominent; *Party Going* evinces a certain willingness to proceed when all its characters are assembled: 'So now at last all of this party is in one place, and, even if they have not yet all of them come

across each other, their baggage is collected in the Registration
Hall' (p. 39).

It is the novel itself which is in the Registration Hall, observing the rules of a narrative contract by which the text is the
only site of certain correlations; it establishes special relations
which exist only for the duration of the text. The first word in
the novel is 'Fog', which spreads through the entire book, providing an image of opacity which stands for a continuous
metaphoric expansion which the text contains. Fog has a
symbolic presence almost identical to that in *Bleak House*
through the obstruction of 'fellow feeling' and the 'deadlock'
of fully comprehensible narrative.[25] Both novels employ
different kinds of diffuse syntax: 'Where hundreds of thousands
she could not see were now going home, their day done, she
was only starting out and there was this difference that where
she had been nervous of her journey and of starting, so that she
said she would rather go on foot to the station to walk it off,
she was frightened now '(p. 16). We expect 'this difference' to
supply more information about the difference between 'hundreds of thousands . . . going home' and Julia who 'was only
starting out'; instead of which it refers to a change in her own
state: 'where she had been nervous . . . she was frightened
now'. The usual method of guided invention by which we make
sense of a narrative relies upon directness and coherence, but
here the syntax is involute and oblique, and our small constructions of knowledge are shaken apart by a constant obscurity of reference, which loses us: 'As a path she was following
turned this way and that round bushes and shrubs that hid
from her what she would find she felt she would next come
upon this fog dropped suddenly down to the ground, when she
would be lost' (p. 16). The misleading path is reminiscent of
the bamboo patch, which is difficult to penetrate (the diction
of that passage is appropriate: 'it was his *romance* at that time
to force through them'). The text is frequently punctuated with
numerous images of obscurity and inaccessibility, the dispersion of focus:

In her silence and in seeming unapproachable . . . it seemed to him
she was not unlike ground so high, so remote it had never been
broken . . . that last field of snow before any summit . . . (p. 144)[26]
Through those lidded windows . . . there faintly whispered through

to them in waves of sound as in summer when you are coming on a
waterfall through woods and it is still unseen . . . (p. 149)

Although those windows had been shut there was a continual dull
roar came through them from outside, and this noise sat upon
those within like clouds upon a mountain so they were obscured
and levelled and, as though they had been airmen, in danger of
running fatally into earth. (p. 175)

At the junctures of dialogue the characters incessantly 'lose
track' or 'change ground' or 'lose the thread'. Then there is the
imposition of a barrier in the context of sexual intrigue; the
text is overwhelmingly coerced by a principle of interruption
at the verge of knowledge. It joins the image-repertoire of the
Thirties, transferring attention from the destination of a journey
to its nature as an obstacle-course: 'All she wanted from him
was something reasonable like a password which would take
her along without humiliation past frontiers and into that
smiling country their journey together would open in their
hearts as she hoped, the promised land' (p. 224). The frontier
is negotiated, the fog dispelled, the object revealed, the destination reached, the sentence completed, the sense achieved, by a
'password'. By a 'reasonable' passage to the referent language
would open up a perspective, travel a distance into the heart
of meaning. The interposition of a frontier is a sublimation of
meaning, creating 'thought about the conditions of knowledge'
below the threshold of promised meaning. That the 'border'
was a Thirties myth is apparent from a glance at the titles,
On the Frontier (Auden and Isherwood), *Journey to the Border*
(Upward), *Across the Border* (unfinished novel by Graham
Greene); the phrases 'smiling country' and 'promised land' are
like the standard properties of a style based on what was most
imitable in the characteristic work of Auden and those associated
with him.

Besides availing itself of the myths already in circulation, the
text invents such additional figures as the Embassy Richard
incident, which is 'discussed at length everywhere' and sustained 'in correspondence columns in the Press' (p. 21). The
entire effort to establish the fact of the matter is itself the
mythologizing process. Amabel also has a mythical status; her
face is familiar to 'shop girls in Northern England' because she
'had been sanctified . . . by constant printed references as

though it was of general concern what she looked like' (p. 145).

Myth has been characterized as the transmutation of what is historical into what is thought to be natural: 'In it, history evaporates. It is a kind of ideal servant: it prepares all things, brings them, lays them out, the master arrives, it silently disappears; all that is left for one to do is to enjoy this beautiful object without wondering where it comes from.'[27] The representation of the relations between man and his world is given a normalized form: 'There were in London at this time more than one hundred rooms identical with these' (p. 133). Max's and Amabel's flats are identical, and such is the extent of mythologization that 'in Hyderabad the colony knew the colour of her walls' (p. 140). It is the re-presentation of these forms, by constant printed references, that makes them increasingly natural, until: 'if their turns of phrase are similar and if their rooms are done up by the same firm and, when they are women, if they go to the same shops, what is it makes them different, Evelyna asked herself' (p. 145). If 'they' try to appear normal to one another out of fear of seeming different, then Evelyna's train of thought is leading towards an ironic misappropriation of the idea of a 'taboo of personal isolation', discussed by Freud:

Crawley, in terms that are hardly distinguishable from those employed by psychoanalysis, sets forth how each individual is separated from the others by a 'taboo of personal isolation' and that it is precisely the little dissimilarities in persons who are otherwise alike that arouse feelings of strangeness and enmity between them. It would be tempting to follow up this idea and trace back to this 'narcissism of small differences' the antagonism which in all human relations we see successfully combating *feelings* of *fellowship* and the commandment of love towards all men.[28]

Freud is considering how such taboos may be taken as evidence of a force that opposes 'fellow feeling' by rejecting the opposite sex as strange and threatening. Alex, who is impotent with women of his own class but not necessarily with Amabel's maid, considers that 'there was a sort of bond between the sexes and with these people no more than that, only dull antagonism otherwise' (p. 195); 'these people' are the ones in the room – 'that is what it is to be rich, he thought'. Evelyna puts much the same construction on the situation in answering

her own question – what makes them different is 'money'; the
'narcissism of small differences' is schematized as the outcome
of social disparity, and in *Party Going* narcissism is absolutely
associated with capital, ownership, nominalization. The central narcissistic image is that of Amabel in her bath; the
walls are of looking-glass clouding over with steam, and through
this opacity she scores her name.[29] An incident in her past has
set the link between the name and ownership on a grotesque
footing: 'Even those who went to bed with her never were
allowed to see her with no clothes on, because someone quite
early in her life had carved his initials low on her back with
an electric-light wire' (p. 155). Sexuality is based on relations
of direct exchange; Amabel is transformed into property:
'looking down on her face which ever since he had first seen it
had been his library, his gallery, his palace, and his wooded
fields he began at last to feel content and almost that he owned
her' (p. 226). Angela's face in a mirror 'had its ticket and this
had marriage written on it' (p. 197). Amabel gazes at the
reflection of her face through the written initial letter of her
name – an emphasis which refers her narcissism back to its
representational origin: 'She bent down to look at her eyes in
the A her name began with, and as she gazed at them steam or
her breath dulled her reflection on the blue her eyes were went
out or faded' (p. 171). The single letter 'A' is starkly reminiscent
of Hester Prynne's 'token of infamy' in *The Scarlet Letter*, where
it stands primarily for adultery – a suitable connotation in
view of Amabel's fondness for sexual intrigue. The last sentence
of Hawthorne's novel, 'ON A FIELD, SABLE, THE LETTER A,
GULES', is in point of fact a modification of the last line of
Marvell's 'The Unfortunate Lover' – 'In a field sable a lover
gules'.[30] The poem actually includes an image of giving birth
in a stormy sea 'as at the funeral of the world'. The disappearing
'A', with its hint of successively veiled texts, is thus an emblem
of the importance of subliminal meanings. The 'steam or her
breath', which falls over the mirror as a screen, dissolves the
illusion of the nominative and replaces one kind of perception
(outside-inwards) with another (inside-outwards). Vision itself
is construed as a gambit to gain control of the sexual identity
of another. The ultimate power of the eye – ' "Oh d'you
remember," she went on, "that time we were out at

Svengalo's" ' (p. 182) – is hypnotism; like the sexual act itself it removes identity. Amabel's eyes intimidate Max; he shrinks from the kind of proletarian fellow feelings of Ed, ' "It's her eyes enfold me and uphold me" was his gallant answer' (p. 177), turning his gaze to Amabel's feet instead. What he sees there is 'remembered beauty'.

The foot can be the object of a fetish which crystallizes the moment when the inquisitive boy is on the point of glimpsing the woman's 'member' from below. 'When the fetish comes to life, so to speak, some process has been suddenly interrupted – it reminds one of the abrupt halt made by memory in traumatic amnesia.'[31] In *Party Going*, memories are summoned up to freeze or stabilize character, to unearth a buried identity.[32] In the case of Julia 'it was her part she had to play to evoke good times' (p. 198), and Max is reassured by the consistency of his own behaviour: ' "Can't have it" he said cheerfully, as people do when they are living up to their own characters' (p. 189). But a converse *practice* of memory as a means of displacement is surmised in two generic sentences:

Memory is a winding lane and as she went up it, waving them to follow, the first bend in it hid her from them and she was left to pick her flowers alone.

Memory is a winding lane with high banks on which flowers grow and here she wandered in a nostalgic summer evening in deep soundlessness.[33] (p. 198)

A generic sentence is one in which the speaker asserts the truth of the predicate in respect of all possible referents of the subject noun phrase; but here the subject is repeated with variations to effect a de-stabilization of memory. The technique – which calls to mind the inexact repetitions of Gertrude Stein – diffracts meaning; it finds its visual counterpart in the prism: 'He felt as though he was gazing into a prism, and he could see no end to it' (p. 127). Summary, which is the periodic reassertion of memory, is here made completely inept: 'Now both Julia and Angela had kissed their young men when these had been cross, when Mr. Adams had made off down in the station and when Max had stopped chasing Julia to sit in his chair' (p. 114). Any 'privileged' information is deliberately banal – 'People, in their relations with one another, are continually doing similar things but never for similar reasons'

(p. 114) – and its redundancy makes it phatic, with little meaning except the maintenance of the narrative contract.

The novel is consecutive without rationale; it simulates a
continuity which is in fact absent, observes the mere formalities
of narrative with a groundless precision: 'And this affected
them, for if they also had to engage in one of those tunnels to
get to where they were going it was not for them simply to pick
up dead birds and then wander through slowly' (p. 8). The
usages of narrative are very conspicuous, but the narrative
purpose has been subtracted and replaced by a circumstantial
purpose:

Miss Crevy had hat-boxes and bags and if her young man was only
there to see her off and hate her for going and if Miss Fellowes had
no more to do than kiss her niece and wave goodbye, Miss Angela
Crevy must find porters and connect with Evelyn Henderson, who
was also going and who had all the tickets. (p. 8)

This grammaticality is a deliberate imposture of grammar;
the emphatic conditionals are purely technical – for her young
man to see her off and for Miss Fellowes to kiss her niece are
not the ostensible reasons that Angela must find porters. The
subjunctive is weakly qualified: the ostensible reason that
Angela must connect with Evelyn Henderson – because she
had all the tickets – becomes only the casual inclusion in a
relative clause. Even the conjunction is made to play a decisive
role:

Already both had been made to regret they had left such and such
a dress behind *and* it was because he felt it impossible to leave things
as they were with Angela, it was too ludicrous that she should go
off on that note, that kiss on his nose, he must explain, that Robin
came back to apologize. (p. 29, my emphasis)

In a standard grammatical conformation, we would extricate
from this one sentence the submerged two which would
normally shrink from contact. The principle of construction is
not subordination but co-ordination where even the logic of
selecting the means of co-ordination (*and* or *but*?) recedes:' Of
course she did not know them well enough to say things of that
kind he thought, *and* he was wrong' (p. 44, my emphasis).
Peculiarities of syntax impede the allocation of contextual
meaning, instances of which are supplanted by a persistent

metonymic disorganization: 'Fog darkened with night began
to roll into this station striking cold through thin leather up
into their feet where in thousands they stood and waited'
(p. 199). This sentence with its mania for precision risks an
unnecessary description of shoes, demonstrates the timidity of a
conventional realism which aims to depict a world whose
relation to language is assumed to have a finished form. This
writing declares the work of language to be unfinished; it
forces itself to ignore the rationale of literary conventions,
preferring its own reality, which takes place with the rising
deposit of grammatical marks:[34] 'As pavements swelled out
under this dark flood so that if you had been ensconced in that
pall of fog looking down below at twenty foot deep of night
illuminated by street lamps, these crowded pavements would
have looked to you as if for all the world they might have been
conduits' (p. 14). If the ideal of representational writing is to
suspend disbelief in a three-dimensional picture of reality, this
sentence is a paraphrase of that reality, and establishes its
distance from such a delusion by pushing up a rival set of
dimensions; it aggravates the rules of its own economy, straining against the prescribed limits with a substantial inflexion, a
design whose stress falls variably on the generation of different
tenses and grammatical moods: the constant secretion of
figures of speech: 'an aeroplane high up drones alternately loud
then soft and *low* it is so *high*' (p. 149, my emphasis).

This kind of productivity had perhaps been more apparent
in *The Orators* than in any other English text of the Thirties; a
brief glance at the Auden text might help in defining the nature
of *Party Going*'s brinkmanship. *The Orators* is saturated with a
competition of meanings, a massive display of contradiction;
its prodigality is an evasion of everything that it is not – a
crushing simplicity. Critics who ask 'is it Fascist or not?' miss
the point, because the text is constructed on the very question
of whether or not to be Fascist. *The Orators* is literally tantalized
by Fascism. Its prolific surface shows a proclivity for subordi-
nate noun phrases – the repression of the agency function
founds a history of subjection. If the writing is in flight from a
central dominion of meaning, it does nevertheless present itself
as under such a threat – that of the universal submission to a
single agency. This universality, 'turning towards one meaning',

whether it be accepted or rejected, is precisely what is absent from *Party Going*, whose writing stays alive when it puts one off the scent of meaning:

Where ruins lie, masses of stone grown over with ivy unidentifiable with the mortar fallen away so that stone lies on stone loose and propped up or crumbling down in mass then as a wind starts up at dusk and stirs the ivy leaves and rain follows slanting down, so deserted no living thing seeks what little shelter there may be, it is all brought so low, then movements of impatience began to flow across all these people and as ivy leaves turn one way in the wind they themselves surged a little here and there in their blind search behind bowler hats and hats for trains. (pp. 201–2)

The intricacy and angularity of syntax conceal from each other the blurred subject and predicate; and as the syntax is neither prospective nor retrospective the experience of reading is not one of finding a position in relation to the other parts of the sentence. The sentence and by extension the text is really utopian in that it does not place the subject it includes. The subject floats, is subject *to* the flow of the text (there is an extensive use of the dative of agency). The writing which takes place is *superfluous* to the novel; its highly visible construction is what detaches it from the history of the novel, and is what gives the novel that history.

3 *Pack my Bag:*
the poetics of menace

I was born a mouthbreather with a silver spoon in 1905, three years after one war and nine before another, too late for both. But not too late for the war which seems to be coming upon us now and that is a reason to put down what comes to mind before one is killed, and surely it would be asking too much to pretend one had a chance to live. (p. 5)

From start to finish, *Pack my Bag* is taxed by the prospect of death. Mustard gas, bayonets, and sirens are among its paraphernalia; mementoes of a future to which the writing continually reverts. This premonitory quality gives the life under review a spurious completeness; within the absolute limits of birth and death a life can be made into a career, and so answerable to certain conventional methods of inquisition.

But why have completeness at this particular time? Why, at the age of thirty-four, make an autobiography out of what 'otherwise would be used in novels' (p. 5)?

In a sense, the general understanding of events in the Thirties seemed to read its haphazard experience in the terms of a looked-for proof of consistency for the time being postponed – it was unconsciously writing itself in the terms of biography. The Thirties as a decade was felt to be moving towards some sort of objective:

There is a sense in which patterns await events, and in the 1930s the pattern of war grew darker and clearer with every month. It awaited the actual event so that in the end war itself came almost as a relief. The reality was better than fear and anticipation. But in this thickening atmosphere, at the time of Munich, there was little chance for imaginative writing of any kind. [1]

In the months following 'the time of Munich', the President of the Publishers' Association, Geoffrey Faber, was particularly

well placed to observe the paralysis which more and more
writers were submitting to:

For the last year shrewd observers . . . have been noting a progressive decline in the quantity and quality of worthwhile manuscripts. The reason is easy to see. Ever since Munich the atmosphere
of Europe has grown more and more unfavourable to creative
literary work . . . 'How can I write with the world in this state?'
is a cry I have heard more than once in the past few months.[2]

There was a widespread anticipation of the impossibility of
imaginative writing after the crisis; and it was this sense
exactly which prompted the hurried composition of Green's
book.

But the resulting text is not so rigorously inductive as its
predeterminants would lead one to expect: 'As I write now a
war, or the threat of war, while still threatening seems more
remote; a change of wind and the boat is blown in, there is
nothing to do but tie up and call it a day' (p. 54). In biography,
time is spatialized but here it forms unmeasured distances
without intervals. The account is only roughly chronological;
each section has an obsessional structure rather than a serial
development. The whole book only *drifts* to the present; the
conventional idea of narrative method is to be disappointed by
the irregular condition of another constraint, another urgency,
which is 'the mystery of sex'.

The unusual inflexions of this self-presentation are inflexions
in the present tense of desire, authorized by the moment of writing; moments in a life are not supposed to be converging on a
terminal point but emerge like tributaries opening onto an
aimless, ramifying flow of diversified impulses which they
simply interrupt. The interpretation of an individual's history
is not attendant on the establishment of any facts, but is produced in the material work of writing – the supposition that
lessons are to be drawn from experience is unambiguously
repudiated:

Most people remember very little of when they were small and what
small part of this time there is that stays is coloured it is only fair
to say, coloured and readjusted until the picture which was there,
what does come back, has been over-painted and retouched enough
to make it an unreliable account of what used to be. (p. 8)

The text becomes a series of substitutions, in which the clarity of testimony recedes under the addition of colour – a colourist principle of superposition which is reflected in the syntax:

But while this presentation is inaccurate and so can no longer be called a movie, or a set of stills, it does gain by what it is not, or in other words, it does set out what seems to have gone on; that is it gives, as far as such things can and as far as such things can be interesting, what one thinks has gone to make one up. (p. 8)

The transmission of information begins to look neurotically provisional, strengthening the position of the text as its own place, apart from the self, not merely an extension of it:

If I say I remember, as it seems to me I do, one of the maids, that poor thing whose breath smelled, come in one morning to tell us the *Titanic* had gone down, it may be that much later they had told me I should have remembered at the age I was then and that their saying this had suggested I did remember. (p. 8)

The construction of an identity, as the objective of experience, fails and the absence of an authorizing self is replaced by the presence of the text as a rival self: no longer dependent on a single retrospective viewpoint, but made to work by its component intensities. The attempt to recapture the self for identity will be dispersed by the urgency and insistency of desire.

In fact, writing and reading are virtually co-opted into a main project of giving oneself over to, of losing oneself in, desire. Without the 'great stimulus' of sex, Green speculates, 'a boy could have gone through school and not have read a single book outside of his lessons' (p. 125). The simultaneous inception of his own writing and love-making is so formulated as to suggest an equation of the two: 'I began to write a novel. / I began to meet girls' (p. 172).

The writing becomes a kind of chemical solution, breaking up those homogeneities which, during the Thirties, had asserted themselves with such violence. Throughout the decade, it was Fascism which offered the most powerfully and influentially maintained conspectus based on rigid distinctions of sex and race; according to Hitler, 'There are two worlds in the life of the nation, the world of men and the world of women.'[3] The men identified themselves by martial tendencies, the women by their usefulness in healing the wounds of the men; a

demarcation which, if it sounds too generalizing, is appropriate
for that reason because, as Virginia Woolf insists, 'there are so
many versions and all are so much alike'.[4] It is a representation
of Fascism derived from German and Italian sources, 'but it
is curious', Mrs Woolf continues, 'to find how easy it is to cap
them from English sources'. Evidence of Fascist preoccupations
can be found in the early unpublished version of Green's first
novel, *Blindness*, where diarist John Haye questions himself as
to whether prayer can weaken the 'really strong man' (TS,
p. 60).

For Green's generation, their obsession with death – an
obsession very close to the surface in *Pack my Bag* – seemed to
reach back to a sense of guilt over the sacrifice which had
been made for them by the victims of the First World War. In
his autobiography of the period, Isherwood relates that 'we
young writers of the middle 'twenties were all suffering, more
or less subconsciously, from a feeling of shame that we hadn't
been old enough to take part in the European War'.[5] Brian
Howard, a contemporary of Green's and a fellow-member of
the Society of Arts at Eton, apostrophizes the victims of the
war in verses written and published while both he and Green
were still at school: 'Oh, we will fight for your ideals – we, who
were too young to be murdered with you.'[6] With Green
himself, this feeling of belatedness, of having come at the
wrong time, is transformed into a sense almost of being *ex
tempore*: 'I felt I had to make up for lost time which I had not
had time to lose' (p. 196). By some obscure means, a whole
generation has been 'falsified' by the turn of events; and the
knowledge of having fallen short – in every way – is further
complicated by a rejection of the authority which had demanded actual sacrifices. Green regarded his two older brothers
as hero-types, although both of them had been too young to
fight. When his brother Philip died, he developed a nervous
condition: 'I had a great sense of shock whenever Philip's name
was mentioned and for some months had difficulty in not
crying' (p. 82). This was the outlet for self-pity at the 'menace'
of corporate doctrines – the attitude of a society which was
felt to exact death as a necessary sacrifice, a tribute to its
values. The set-text for this youthful animus would have been
Wilfred Owen's 'The Parable of the Old Man and the Young',

in which Abraham is advised by an angel to substitute for Isaac the 'Ram of Pride'. Unlike his biblical precursor, the twentieth-century patriarch refuses: 'But the old man would not so, but slew his son, / And half the seed of Europe, one by one.'[7] Green's brothers represented to him a kind of war-generation, coming between himself and his parents; and, according to Anthony Powell, his attitude towards his parents was that they were both extremely selfish.[8] He retained the feeling, however submerged, that some form of initiation was expected of his generation:

We may have revolted against fear but it is more likely we thought for once the world was ours who were so young we did not have to mourn the dead, who did not guess the price we in our turn might have to pay for other boys to celebrate the victory by, that which our lives must buy today sooner than tomorrow, no doubt to turn the worms again. (p. 104)

Isherwood perpetuated for himself the myth of a 'Test' in which he had never been required to prove himself. This persistent apprehensiveness suggests that conditions of knowledge from the First World War had prolonged themselves *ex tempore*, and were still available to a generation about to engage in a Second World War. *Pack my Bag*, although written in anticipation of this Second War, certainly reads like a memoir of the First, because Green's family home had been used as a hospital for wounded officers, so that for some years he had grown up in that same 'atmosphere of death, and of the dying' (p. 77) which pervades his text of 1938–9: 'They had been so close to death they had a different view of life . . . They were people meant to die' (p. 65). Another contemporary of Green's, Arthur Gwynn-Browne, is quite demonstrative about this continuation of 'the last war in our feeling of it':

When it ended, that is when an armistice was made it did not end it just stopped the fighting just stopped the rest went on, I was thirteen and I have often been surprised my mother saying I did not remember it I was too young. I was not too young and none of my generation was too young and none of this young living generation is too young to remember what war is in their feeling of it . . .

My generation knew that in its feeling of the last world war that the struggle had begun. It almost seemed that afterwards it might perhaps be defined and they tried to define it but it could not be

defined. It is growing. It is not formed but it is growing it is not
articulate but there is a feeling for it that it is growing and that in
growing that it will evolve and come.[9]

This Second War memoir, written in imitation of Gertrude
Stein, is clearly in accord with Stein's own thesis in 'Composition as Explanation' that military thinking, as a model for
consciousness, is always one war behind itself.[10] But the
Gwynn-Browne of 1942 reinforces the Stein of 1926 by the
idea of 'the struggle', or 'Kampf', with its overdue 'Test', and
likely sacrifice. This was the danger of Fascism for a guilty
generation – the new focus it gave to self-sacrifice: the replacement of a 'falsity', with a 'reality', of guilt:

What almost everyone refuses to acknowledge is that the fascist
machine, in its Italian and German forms, became a threat to
capitalism and Stalinism because the masses invested a fantastic
collective death instinct in it. By reterritorializing their desire onto
a leader, a people and a race, the masses abolished, by means of a
phantasm of catastrophe, a reality which they detested and which
the revolutionaries were either unwilling or unable to encroach
upon. For the masses, virility, blood, vital space, and death took the
place of a socialism that had too much respect for the dominant
meanings.[11]

What the rise of Fascism allowed was the reality of a timely
death; 'Better a terrible end than an endless terror' was an
actual slogan of the emerging Nazi Party in Germany.[12] It
suggests a fulfilment of the same wish animating those soldiers
billeted with Green's family in 1914–18: 'He was no longer
human when he came to us . . . he had haunted eyes as though
death to which he was still so close and which walked arm in
arm with him through our meadows could be a horror worse
than what he was still suffering' (p. 66). This purgatorial
awareness – *Party Going*'s 'waiting at the gates' – had become
an indissoluble part of conditions of knowledge. The expectation of war which, as Hugh Sykes Davies says, 'awaited the
actual event', is like the 'aggressivity of the slave whose response
to the frustration of his labour is a desire for death'.[13] The
phantasm of a catastrophe was almost indispensable to a
generation whose pubescent experience of discipline had
revolved on the question of forbidden knowledge, of an absolute

uncertainty whose only adequate correspondent was the absolute certainty of death: 'Sex was a dread mystery. No story could be so dreadful, more full of agitated awe than sex. We felt there might almost be some connection between what the Germans were said to have done and this mysterious urgency we did not feel' (p. 47). The urgency of incipient desire becomes compounded through having no specific objective: 'Boys think of sexual gratification long before they know what it is all about' (p. 116). Left to its own devices, this searching ignorance will conceive of satisfactions more impressive than any future performance: 'This kiss which was not exchanged has lasted on where others given or received would have escaped the memory' (p. 91). Desire outgrows the capacity for its fulfilment, finds itself on a trajectory which it can never cease to follow, always at one remove from knowledge, while credulous of a contextualization that memory will eventually provide: 'Then it is almost impossible not to remember adolescence, the imminent feeling that soon everything will be made known' (p. 138). But the adolescent consciousness is already totally possessed by ignorance – an ignorant congestion which the introduction of a sexuality produced outside of its own obsessions will fail to clear. Green's own self is in a limbo of frustration: 'All through my life I have been plagued by enjoying first experiences too much' (p. 63). The only decompression magisterial enough to cover the extent of repression is the inviting catastrophe:

And was it then or some time later that, as our school was on the south coast, some formation of the hills round brought no louder than as seashells echo the blood pounding in one's ears noise of gunfire through our windows all the way from France so that we looked out and thought of death in the sound and this was sweeter to us than rollers tumbling on a beach. (p. 40)

Although it was Fascism that seemed to provide a catch-point for this instinct of self-destruction, it was also Fascism which banalized the catastrophe: 'Fascism was brought back to these same dominant meanings by a sort of intrinsic bad faith, by a false provocation to the absurd, and by a whole theatre of collective hysteria and debility.'[14] The youthful Green excised all Fascistic notions from his first novel when revising it for

publication, at a time when he must also have been reviewing
the educational system through which he had just passed; the
adult Green could reject Fascism together with the authority
it would overthrow because of their communication with one
another along the channels of repression: 'I believe the whole
system of government in Germany is founded on that evolved
through centuries at the greater British public schools' (p. 94).

As far as Green was concerned, school was an experience of
penal servitude: 'We were almost prisoners from ourselves . . .'
(p. 21); 'There are terms of imprisonment and terms even at
kindergartens' (p. 24); 'We had calendars and each boy
marked off every day which brought him closer to term's end,
as prisoners notch the walls' (p. 49). He goes as far as to claim
that the school engenders a type of paramount convict ('purer
types, more perfect examples of liars thieves and crooks'), as a
direct result of the opportunities for relentless scrutiny by
authority, greater than elsewhere: 'there were no thoughts or
feelings we ought to have and if there were things we could not
say then it was a crime' (p. 24).

Every transaction in this context is interpreted with reference
to a criminal code. It is a society that forces the self into an
enclosure of meaning containing the impulses which traverse it;
forcing it to dispose itself into precipitates of meaning, so that
any divergence or attempt to readmit those impulses and
emancipate them is criminal, the infringement of a rigid code.

The fear that imaginative writing will be impossible in such
highly conditioned circumstances is transformed into a demonstration that the only free conditions are those of artistic
production. Writing is not the sedimentation of personal
marks, but the gradual attrition of a hard surface formed by
corporate doctrines which have a binding power. It becomes a
process of restoring the self to a critical state, of *un*learning: 'In
my case it has been a long and in the end successful struggle to
drive out what they taught me there and afterwards' (p. 22);
of disassembling a 'corpus' of knowledge; 'Their corporate
doctrines teach one ugly sides and it is when one has forgotten
to be as they taught that the experience begins to be worthwhile'
(p. 22).

School represents the institutional magnification of biographical accountability – the history of the individual *must*

be explicable: 'Any secret, our old tyrant had warned us, must be guilty, the secrets we were not allowed to have for fear they might be sexual' (p. 46). The only recess in this constant inquisition is in sleep:

Home seemed a heaven and that we were cast out and seventy five little boys when there was no more light lifted those lids to hide their letters back amongst their clothes and turning over went to sleep at once in the arms of whoever it was they had who loved them wherever the place was they called home. (p. 29)

The scene prefigures that of the girls' academy in the totalitarian state of *Concluding*: 'throughout the dormitories upstairs, with a sound of bees in this distant Sanctum, buzzers called her girls to rise so that two hundred and eighty nine turned over to that sound, stretched and yawned' (p. 19). The image has been turned inside out and the girls, statistically reduced, are waking up, to resume their allotted places under the surveillance of Miss Edge.

The limit of this administration is reached in its attempt to regulate sexuality, where it is bound by the terms of its own hold over the boys' imaginations, forced to resort to 'a warning against unspecified vice so appalling that I was as one who has heard too huge a noise, too vast a something that has been disclosed; it was too much to take in and I was left, in no wise the worse for not knowing, in a void of unmentionables, or as they say all at sea' (p. 37). The partial revelation drowned by disappointment will reappear elsewhere, intact by its incompleteness, so long as it is fragile enough to withstand systemization. To go beyond the enclosure of meaning involves an act of transgression, almost any transgression; Green became an outrageous liar: 'I could not help myself in railway carriages, and it took a form so obviously extravagant and false that I could never hope I should be believed' (p. 126). And thieving was widespread in the schools he attended; only the chests in which were stored letters from home – 'those secrets of tenderness' – were 'sacred'. But the most extreme transgression of all was betrayal, as the inverse of sacrifice: 'I, who had been so full up to that time of the story of Judas, I believe it haunts all little boys, went in after them to stand up for my friend' (p. 85).

Towards the end of the book, the General Strike disposes

Green to leave Oxford in sympathy with its aims; but when an elderly neighbour rings up seeking volunteers for 'national' work, the circumstances of Country House life entail a reserve of guilt that is bound to forestall the youthful Green's betrayal of his class: 'I had been eating the strawberries when I was told this man was asking for me' (p. 235). Later in his career, Green renegues on the falseness of his position, rarely allowing himself to be photographed without turning his head, as much as to say, 'the true self is not there to be seen, but at least the false self will not be seen either'. And he has trimmed the explanation of his attitude at the time of the General Strike to a simple observation that 'for some time I had been unable to look a labourer in the eye' (p. 234). There is evidently a physiognomy of reluctance and capitulation – 'toadying alters the expression of the face in extreme cases' (p. 108) – which engenders the strategy of the back of the head, a form of self-sacrifice that is equal and opposite to the adaptative variety. Already, as a schoolboy, Green had cultivated a distaste for any living space that was not devoid of possessions, 'or anything to give any line on what I was like' (p. 179). And a further correlation is implied in the, obviously inveterate, pseudonymous impulse: the *nom de plume* Henry Green being preceded by Henry Browne, and before that by the unlikely Henry Michaelis (p. 163); an impulse whose bearing on the need for betrayal constitutes the outspokenness of anonymity:

We might interpret symbolic parricide as simply an extension of symbolic suicide, a more thorough-going way of obliterating the substance of one's old identity – while, as we have said before, this symbolic suicide itself would be but one step in a process which was not completed until the substance of the abandoned identity had been replaced by the new substance of a new identity. Hitler's voting himself a 'blood stream' distinct from that of the Hebrew patriarchs is a symbolic transubstantiation of this sort – while an attenuated social variant of reidentification is to be seen in the legal adoption of a new family name, or in pseudonyms, *noms de plume* etc.[15]

Green expects to die in the war; in the 'absolute bewilderment of 1939' he faces the prospect of the 'Test' he had taken pains to circumvent years before by resigning from the school cadet corps: 'There was no valid argument against me, no war was threatened, we lived then in the fool's paradise of a peace the old fools had dictated' (p. 162). In case his death should be falsely interpreted, he kills himself off beforehand – suiciding the 'falsified' self in a history of its formation. Autobiography is a form of internalized surveillance; Green kept a diary at school, preserving 'exactly that sensation of being watched' (p. 112). *Pack my Bag* is accordingly the autobiographical form unlearned; the presentation of the back of the head; a transubstantiation of self into writing, rather than a transcription of self, under pressure from the dialectic of sacrifice and betrayal.

Betrayal suggested, to the generation that had been haunted little boys, the purest means of exonerating desire, and Green's analytical unlearning can be matched by the more symbolic revocations of certain of his contemporaries. Burgess and Maclean, who were of a generation only slightly younger than Green's, and products of the same milieu, were both anti-Fascist and both (Burgess in particular) notoriously given to sexual nonconformity. Auden said that he had gone to America for the same reason that made Guy Burgess defect to Russia – it was the only way finally to repudiate England.

Green recounts that his earliest memory is of a complex 'disloyalty' to his mother; within his adult milieu, for those who were not already homosexual, a temporary homosexuality was almost obligatory as a representation of disloyalty: a means of betraying the parental generation. Femininity was explored as the only available means of expression adequate to the realities of desire: 'We were feminine not from perversion although it is true that we were preoccupied by sex, but from a lack of any other kind of self expression' (p. 113). Since the imposed sexuality was one of Fascist virility, the 'underground' society of the school was adversely feminine: 'the general feeling . . . as it cannot be in the larger world outside, was feminine' (p. 96). To escape from a body which has been confined to a certain meaning it is first necessary to restore a radical inquisitiveness whose research can extrapolate a different meaning: 'Bodies should be objects of curiosity and it is a comment on the way we were brought up that we should find them exciting because forbidden' (p. 124). The official misuse of the body depends on an armature of meaning, which is removed by *dematerializing* that body. There is a remarkable celebration of the female body given a latitude, rendered fluid to become itself a medium of expression:

It was their skin got me which I had never touched except on hands and which I thought to be softer than I afterwards found, that skin down from the neck coming out of flowering summer dresses which sent me back to my room to read Spenser. It was their eyes I never looked into I was too modest and too modest by far to fall in love, their arms which I thought were cold and which I could not think they ever used to help them kiss, their lightness I did not know the weight of, the different way they moved and literally then it seemed as though they were walking in water up over their heads along the glaring street, all this bemused me although I had been reading Herrick. (p. 119)

The writing ramifies, refusing to solidify in a body which it melts into several effects; it does not accept the body as the objective of a determined meaning, it *reads* the body with reference to reading; and it sees the body as if with a compound eye, its vision forming with the loss of perspective. The visual sense in *Pack my Bag* is of a loss of consistency, a loss of conclusiveness; the eye experiences the shifting of surfaces, planes, and depths – the eye behaves rather as an organ of touch. In a certain sense, the body that is sensible to its touch is unrecognizable to the male view, because a 'female language of phantasm . . . could not be represented or circumscribed within a framework dominated by sight' – according to the feminist psychoanalyst, Luce Irigaray, for whom the genesis of a female language is synonymous with the unlearning, the forgetting, of male language:

a feminine language would undo the unique meaning, the proper meaning of words, of nouns; which still regulates all discourse. In order for there to be a proper meaning, there must indeed be a unity somewhere. But if feminine language cannot be brought back to any unity, it cannot be simply described or defined: there is no feminine meta-language. The masculine can partly look at itself, speculate about itself, represent itself and describe itself for what it is, whilst the feminine can try to speak to itself through a new language, but cannot describe itself from outside or in formal terms, except by identifying itself with the masculine, thus by losing itself.[16]

The feminine can only find itself by dissolving the homogeneities of the male. The unitary power of the eye disappears;

and so does the unitary power of the nominative, from a text that is spreading out to give a latitude to its own subjectivity: 'Prose is not to be read aloud but to oneself alone at night, and it is not quick as poetry but rather a gathering web of insinuations which go further than names however shared can ever go' (p. 88). Leaving out the names 'makes a book look blind', a circumstance which Green considers 'no disadvantage' (p. 88). In the novel he had actually titled *Blindness*, the undoing of proper names had been interrelated with a total blankness in the male domain; the indistinctness of names, *John, Joan, June*, occurred in a context of bisexualism, of the mutual replication of male and female characters. This sustained disunity, this simultaneity of opposites, is what the writing of *Pack my Bag* accomplishes in the question of a supposed propriety or impropriety of its meanings. The improper meanings are those which resist integration in their discursive context; and among them the most beautiful, as well as the most refractory, are those with a littoral setting:

As I see things it is sex in little boys makes them shrill out at times like these. They are so feminine they go on like women on the sands even when they can see no man within miles, scream after scream echoing up cliffs to the deserted top over which, and over a boy watching behind his tuft of grass a blade of which gets up his nose, sea-gulls soar on their white wings diagonally set to the sun-blue sky. (pp. 34–5)

The court was out at the back by stables which were built round three yards, brick buildings over cobblestones the colour in sunlight of dried seaweed on white marble with the smell so like but not the same as when under a hot sun the small wind blows inland the bite of sea on a temple grown over and uncovered at low tide. (p. 173)

In this way the bells, so overdone they soon lost their charm, by never leaving one alone seemed, as the sea eats out a temple to cover it with weed, to have bitten into the black porticos and walls their sound was forever lapping. (p. 200)

The littoral scene, with its ruined temple being eaten away, half on the land and half on the sea, is precisely suggestive of an incomplete stage of unlearning with an equal vantage on solidness, associated with the male, and fluidness, associated

with the female. The sex-act itself is thought of as 'a marriage
with sympathetic swans' precisely because this takes place 'in
an element like the air I could not fly in and was *half a stranger
to*' (p. 120, my emphasis). The sexuality of the book is half-
familiar, half-strange; it is the autobiography of *half a stranger*
– one who does not even have a proper name. The writing is
withdrawn from an isomorphism with the masculine sex; it
is no longer the expected accumulation of traits, evidence of an
identity, that will constitute authority but the elaboration of a
text in which the author is discomposed. The account and the
author are fictions together being produced during the writing.
The conditions of bilateral meaning, so alien to the conventions
of autobiography and biography, are recognizable as those
which are adduced for the psychoanalysis of hysterical phantasies:

In psychoanalytic treatment it is very important to be prepared for
a symptom's having a bisexual meaning. We need not then be surprised or misled if a symptom seems to persist undiminished although
we have already resolved one of its sexual meanings; for it is still
being maintained by the – perhaps unsuspected – one belonging to
the opposite sex. In the treatment of such cases, moreover, one may
observe how the patient avails himself, during the analysis of the
one sexual meaning, of the convenient possibility of constantly
switching his associations, as though onto an adjoining track, into
the field of the contrary meaning.[17]

The 'contrary meaning' fielded by Green takes the form of
the anonym: the true confessions of a cover-up; the conditions of knowledge as of 1939 have the readability of a 'strip-
tease', with people 'saying good-bye to what they could use to
drape their hearts where everyone now wears his in the stress
of the times, on his sleeve, not naked as hearts will be when the
war comes, still covered but in a kind of strip-tease with
rapidly changing, always fewer and ever more diaphanous
clothes' (p. 186). Green reveals no more than the back of his
head, since he cannot reveal the face of a woman. *Pack my Bag*
is an effacement, and the process of a disclosure in which one
can hide. When he departs school for Oxford – 'It was like
getting out of prison' – surveillance, at least in its cruder form,
comes to an end, and yet the account becomes more opaque;

Green shows even less of himself, and resorts to the camouflage of a literary exemplum:

The experience for those who have not had it can best be described by the picture of a traveller who has come some of the way and now finds himself bewildered, suspicious and rather tired because he has not found the sort of country he has been seeking, part of his difficulty being that he is not quite sure what climate or kind of scenery is necessary to his peace of mind. He comes to a place where the winding track he follows through nettles breaks into two and there above a great number of broken bottles are a profusion of signposts obviously false, giving details of the amenities offered by following the direction indicated. The day is hot, the way has been long, flies and wasps have been troublesome, and all the time there has been a persistent knelling in the distance to work up a feeling of foreboding. Also the sense is strong that it will soon be too late. At the intersection of this track however he comes upon a tall gaunt figure dressed neatly as if for London but with something untidy about him, perhaps in the uneasy protuberance of his eyes. He appears to be resting without discomfort just off one of these paths with nettles about but it is plain that in his case they do not sting because he outstings them and there are no flies on him. He speaks first . . . (pp. 203-4)

And so on, for another three hundred words. There could be nothing less particular and individual than this little allegory, this miniature Pilgrim's Progress, the formal equivalent of the back of the head. And yet its reversal of expectation is no less than should be expected from a text which starts at the end – with the prospect of death – and ends with a beginning: 'now . . . there was love' (p. 246).

4 *Caught:*
the idiom of the time

With the final onset of war on the Home Front, with the Black-out, aerial bombardment, and a prolonged dislocation of routine, there seemed to be a simultaneous crisis in the attitude of both readers and writers towards the novel. One way or another it was being uncertainly rejected as a contemporary form:

The actual number of fiction titles published fell from 4,222 in 1939 to 1,246 in 1945, which, taking into account the total decline in book production, means a fall from about a third to a fifth of the total of all volumes published annually – but this says nothing about the contents or quality of the work that was accepted, or refused.

Whatever their eventual decision, publishers had fewer manuscripts to consider, good or bad.[1]

The biggest change was the sudden popularity of collections of short stories by one author, or, better still, anthologies. Before the war these had not been popular with publishers or public, but that quickly changed. This was not just the result of circumstances of production, for writing and reading habits changed during the war.[2]

The short story seemed an obvious resort for the reader in need of a current for his imagination when the illusion of continuity which had made the novel so persuasive, and which his sense of his own life had confirmed, suddenly desisted. Replacing it was the experience of the Black-out, which the editors of Mass-Observation described as 'this contradiction in our civilization, the unlit city': 'On dark nights it is really a matter of groping one's way with nerves as well as hands held out into the future of the next second.'[3] Among writers, it was almost as if the novel itself had suffered physically from the disruptions; as if its role in the equation 'text is continuous with world' could only ever be passive and secondary; as if the novel would survive only on its ability to efface every unexpected difficulty. Now that there was nothing in the 'world' to invest with the claims of longevity, the novel was thought to be correspondingly inoperative:

These years rebuff the imagination as much by being fragmentary as by being violent. It is by dislocations, by recurrent checks to his desire for meaning, that the writer is most thrown out. The imagination cannot simply endure events; for it the passive role is impossible. Where it cannot dominate, it is put out of action.[4]

In other words, the imagination can only demonstrate the impossibility of its taking a passive role, by instrumenting the passivity of certain forms. It was indeed the case that many novelists, including Elizabeth Bowen herself, did not publish a novel during the war. But among those that did appear, the more remarkable – like *Hangover Square* by Patrick Hamilton, and *The Ministry of Fear* by Graham Greene – invalidate altogether the terms of Bowen's distinction. In general, it was the short story – categorically the form of the part, as opposed to the whole – which tacitly accepted the passive role: to an extent, at least, that when one reads Henry Green's short stories of the period one is made aware of a scandalous measure of independence from the convenient form adopted elsewhere. On the whole, a story was being regarded as a kind of evidence which the reader might use in his struggle for meaning: 'The pre-war *New Writing* had set the style for a form of documentary story that simply required the author to choose a situation, and describe it. For preference the situation was social rather than emotional, to do with work or class.'[5] As such, the story was most complete in seeming incomplete – its real meaning was elsewhere. Provided one treated an experience with apparent accuracy, it could be broken up for the sake of a resolution that was deferred. An alternative was to hallucinate a meaning. Fragmentariness could be overcome, appropriately enough, by exploding a situation; that way one could engross a particular detail in order to exhaust it. A noted example of this was William Sansom's *The Wall*, which expands the moment in which the wall of a burning house collapsed. But even in this experiment the writing is likewise concerned to take the measure

of its own accuracy: 'Even the speed of the shutter which closed
the photograph on my mind was powerless to exclude this
notion from a deeper consciousness. The picture appeared
static to the limited surface senses, the eyes and the material
brain, but beyond that there was hidden movement.'[6]

These aversions to the systematic requirements of the novel
were a means of keeping its requirements unchanged – they
avoided the need for a special resourcefulness, for the novel to
be as fully adequate to the contemporary situation as it apparently had been before. With the promise of meaning *after* the
event, the novel was released from the necessity of developing
a different kind of social propriety, since after the event it
would come back into its own, as it was. And in poetry, there
was a leading example of this kind of literary endeavour, where
the writing refers to a recapitulation, in the *Four Quartets* by
T. S. Eliot. Its publication was met with a great deal of accord;
Edwin Muir pronounced it 'the most original contribution to
poetry that has been made in our time'.[7] The composition over
many years of the four poems which comprise the whole
sequence was a process of reserving its meaning for a final
resorbence:

Even 'Burnt Norton' might have remained by itself if it hadn't
been for the war . . . you remember how the conditions of our
lives changed, how much we were thrown in on ourselves in the
early days? 'East Coker' was the result – and it was only in writing
'East Coker' that I began to see the Quartets as a set of four.[8]

Eliot's appropriation of a past work for inclusion in a project
governed by the promise of ultimate meaning is the outstanding
illustration of a consensus regarding literature; the contemporary response was regulated on this axis:

Time will give our confusion a perceptible character of its own.
When to-day has become yesterday, it will have integrated, into
however grotesque a form. Until then, the desire for the whole
picture must be satisfied by the contemplation of such whole
pictures as already exist – in fact, of works of art that came into
being either when there was a present that *could* be got into focus
or when time had had time to act on what was already the past.[9]

The most popular novel of the war was, rather predictably, the
most totalizing of all novels, *War and Peace*. Trollope was very

widely read for some years. The appeal of these books was clearly that of 'the whole picture', of a comprehensive image of society, able to feed the bewildered mind with a cogency it missed. In direct opposition to such a mood – which sought to revert to conditions in the past which it looked to resume in the future – Green welcomed the immediate challenge to the novel: 'The truth is, these times are an absolute gift to the writer. Everything is breaking up. A seed can lodge or sprout in any crack or fissure.'[10] His own short stories 'A Rescue' and 'Mr Jonas' both deal with the rescue by firemen of trapped individuals: one down a man-hole, the other inside a burning house. Green was an auxiliary fireman himself, and his own experience of the Phoney War and the Blitz contributed directly to the settings of *Caught*,[11] and of the two stories, both of which are distracted from the documentary style in passages of convoluted description. Neither of them makes any concession to the idea of a deferred meaning, the ending in each case being painstakingly offhand:

The injured man was taken away in an ambulance. We have not heard anything of him. He may have died.[12]

When the other crew took over we had fought our way back to exactly the same spot above that hole out of which, unassisted once he had been released, out of unreality into something temporarily worse, apparently unhurt, but now in all probability suffering from shock, had risen, to live again whoever he might be, this Mr Jonas.[13]

One receives the impression of a definite recalcitrance, as if there was implicit the pressure to simplify the account and render it more soluble. In his essay 'The Natural Man and the Political Man'[14] which drew a great deal of attention from other writers, Edwin Muir maintained that a stage was reached in literature where a 'simplification of the idea of man' had been evolved. This state of affairs was not confined to literature, which 'has not initiated but merely reflected' a gross reduction of human life to compliance with a given environment – what Muir contends is a 'mythology'. It is a line of thinking which bears out the assessments of contemporary psychology. Between 1940 and 1942 there were many published attempts to ascertain the links between war and mental illness.[15] A number of these were alive to the fact that psychoses were at least partially induced by the social idea of reality: 'The form of the illness is to be conceived as a product of inner factors in the patient, and of factors imposed by the environment. As the theories entertained by the observer are an important part of the environment, it follows that changes in theory and form will be closely related.'[16] The psychotic illness appeared in some measure as the accelerated form of a process at work in society as a whole – the circulation of 'theories entertained by the observer', which were excessively contrived. Among the governing influences on the social idea of reality, the official sources of information were heavily censored, increasing the amount of uncertainty behind the disuse of all but the more submissive forms of literature: 'This state of bewilderment and uncertainty helped to make people over confident, to make them give vein to their wishful-thinking inclinations.'[17] According to Mass-Observation, an unprecedented state of mind developed for which their chosen term was in fact 'wishful thinking': 'By wishful thinking we mean interpreting events to suit an individual's wish. This may result in extreme optimism (the commonest form), sometimes, however, alarm-ism and a tendency to welcome catastrophe. The latter type of wishful thinking helps to satisfy more obscure emotional needs.'[18] The construction of reality that 'wishful thinking' was meant to elide had become drastically overshadowed by the threat of aerial bombardment. The prevalent fantasies of air-raids were so horrifying as to be practically inadmissible to the balance of the collective mind. The *official* expectation was of a 'knockout blow', with 600,000 killed and 1,200,000 wounded in the first six months: 'The estimate was thus an overestimate by fourteen-fold . . . Madness on a huge scale was expected . . . In 1939 the Mental Health Emergency Committee reported that psychiatric casualties might exceed the physical by three to one: that is to say, between three and four millions of people would suffer from hysteria and other neurotic conditions.'[19]

Caught is set largely in the Phoney War period, and dealing with the Fire Service it refers directly to the structure of feelings outlined above. Its main character, Richard Roe, is in the habit of retailing the myth of catastrophe in the hope of having it explained away. He is like many people in the place and time under consideration – 'in this book only 1940 in London is real' – who were *caught* in the version of their existence which was forced upon them. It needs a foreigner, the Swedish girl Ilse, to disabuse him of his 'wishful thinking':

As he told Ilse, while enjoying a return to this oft-told horror story, he was watchful, expecting the usual 'Oh, you will be all right, we shall all be.' So that he was daunted when she said, 'Yes, and it is my thought that your people in this country have not done enough, not nearly, no, you are such a long way to go even yet, you will not realize,' she said. 'I was so surprised,' she said, 'to see those death bodies, skeletons, up there, such a lot think bombs do not explode because they come from Czechoslovakia . . .' (pp. 70–1)

This concern for guarantee corresponds to the way in which literature was being contained. One of the few serious novels to appear at an early stage of the war, *Night Shift* (1941) by Inez Holden, is a skilful evocation in the documentary manner of a factory waiting for the inevitable bomb, which comes. Regressing to the simple determinism of the bomb was a means of finding a position which made grim sense; it sponsored the survival of meaning unaffected by change among the social conditions in which it is produced, and as such was equal to a desperate nostalgia taking place elsewhere. Henry Reed, in his survey of the novel between 1939 and 1949, remarked on how often the theme of childhood occurred.[20] And among psychologists, there was no shortage of explanations for that:

The civilian has no really powerful check to the desire for self-preservation; indeed, he is licensed to consider his own safety to an extent that no soldier can be. The flood-gates are therefore open to desires for self-preservation which can take a form that is primitive and not well adapted to a reality situation. There is a real danger that he will seek, not security, but infantile security.[21]

The search for infantile security seems to haunt the imaginative writing of the time. It pervades *Hangover Square* (1941) and *The Ministry of Fear* (1943). The narrator of Sansom's *Fireman Flower*, reverting to scenes of his past life, more or less repeats the programmatic statement of Elizabeth Bowen: 'One wishes to envisage the future; one cannot; one casts around for a substitute; one substitutes the picture of the past, sufficiently alien from the present, a vision – yet one that can be controlled.'²² The overall drive was formulated simply by Stephen Spender at the beginning of his 'September Journal': 'During these first days of the war I have tended to live in the past, partly because the present is so painful, partly because it is so fragmentary and undecided.'²³

In sum, the self in 1940 looked to be in a position of fundamental eccentricity, and the novel was too concerted a form for the time; surely it could not provide a guarantee of meaning? The memory of a time when the self *did* occupy a more concentric position in its world insisted on reproducing itself, either by way of refusing access to the novel-form or by arresting its development. This persevering memory provides *Caught* with its moment of intervention among the conditions of knowledge of '1940 in London' through writing in which the novel-form is given the disconcerting element it needs.

Each character in *Caught* is captivated by a memory which provides him with the image he fixes upon himself. The adapted image provides a basis for the flights of 'wishful thinking' that each character, imperilled by the disorder into which he is thrown, uses to imagine himself in control of a situation – to introduce order into it. For Roe, the central image is the scene in the rose garden; for Pye, it is the incestuous encounter with his sister, extremely adapted. These are the most effective images in the book, but there is a constant activity of 'picturing': 'She had so often imagined what she would do . . .' (p. 145); 'She pictured at the back of her eye the descent she was going to make . . .' (p. 83); 'As usual he pictured himself involved in argument' (p. 84); 'As he pictured her she was pale . . .' (p. 85). This urge to float over the present with an effective delusion is the result of failing to come to terms with it; the present gets submerged in the attempt to 'create memories to compare' (p. 63), which is the identical stimulus behind the increase in short stories – providing a record of memories with a future purpose: 'She meant to make the few days they were to have together as much a memory to the boy as they would be to the father' (p. 29). Roe is found giving his past memory the same treatment, providing it with a hard surface to make it unimpressionable in the face of present threats to the order he contrives: 'he crystallized in his imagination a false picture of what his home life had been' (p. 92).

This tendency to 'disremember' is purveyed as being characteristic: the term is used with unconscious irony by Mary Howells, fabricating another memory: 'she would never forget, ever, and never disremember the sight of Brid standing at the door' (p. 82).

Roe's obsession with the disremembered rose garden, associated with his wife, is given extra force by virtue of his wife being dead. This was not the case until a very late stage in the composition of the novel, when Dy, the wife, became Dy, the sister-in-law, with a minimum amount of correction. With his wife dead, Roe is unable to realize a situation in which he 'imagined, as has been described, a great deal going on all round between girls and men. What he might be missing haunted him' (p. 99). And he eclipses the possibility of realization with his carefully nurtured image. The scene in the rose garden is artificially prompted; this is reflected in the forced growth of its description:

The roses, when they came to the rose garden, were full out, climbing along brick walls, some, overpowered by their heavy flowers, in obeisance before brick paths, petals loose here and there on the earth but, on each bush and tree of roses, rose after rose after rose of every shade stared like oxen, and came forward to meet them with a sweet, heavy, luxuriant breath. (p. 64)

The roses are coerced, like the fruits and flowers of Marvell's 'The Garden';[24] they are forced to participate in the world created by his own need. Nature is made to seem 'enchanted by terror into immobility as the two of them halted, brought to a full stop at the corner round which this impermanence caught them fast' (p. 64). The impermanent event is the basis of a fixation which persists in the memory; it can attain a permanence because it has been brought to a full stop. This permanence interrupts every attempt to realize a situation, tinting it with the same hue. Prudence, disturbing his reverie, is described as '*infinitely* young' (my emphasis). In this way, the fascination with a threshold of meaning reasserts itself:

But this day a permanence of rain softened what was near, and half hid by catching the soft light all that was far, in the way a veil will obscure, yet enhance the beauty of a well-remembered face or, in a naked body so covered, sharpen the sight. In such a way this stretch of country he knew so well was made the nearer to him by rain. (pp. 8–9)

The inevitable reimposition of a veil, a screen on which to project what is already known because it is 'well-remembered', predisposes the apprehension of knowledge. A manuscript addition to the typescript pointedly substitutes 'permanence' for 'veil' (TS, p. 8); elsewhere, 'brilliant sapphire blue' is changed to the 'permanence of sapphire' in the following passage (TS, p. 17):

The walls of this store being covered with stained glass windows which depicted trading scenes, that is of merchandise being loaded onto galleons, the leaving port, of incidents on the voyage, and then the unloading, all brilliantly lit from without, it follows that the body of the shop was inundated with colour, brimming, and this colour, as the sea was a predominant part of each window, was a permanence of sapphire in shopping hours. (pp. 12–13)

This brimming colour is described as 'fatal' (p. 11) – 'odd' in the manuscript. The oceanic blue, colour of the amniotic sea of oblivion familiar from *Party Going*, fascinates the boy who has lost his mother.

The purposive veil takes effect as an always insidious, and sometimes treacherous, snare:

He wished it had all been less, as a man can search to find he knows not what behind a netted brilliant skin, the eyes of a veiled face, as he can also go with his young son parted from him by the years that are between, from her by the web of love and death, or from remembered country by the weather, in the sadness of not finding. (p. 9)

In this way the time for father and son passed quickly. Neither was much with the other, the one picking up the thread where the war had unravelled it, the other beginning to spin his own, to create his first tangled memories, to bind himself to life for the first time. (p. 34)

Christopher is strangely attracted by the 'trap' for rooks. In their walk through the grounds, father and son stop by a 'domed triangle of concrete' padlocked fast, which is supposed to contain ice kept intact 'against the summer', unaffected by

the real climate. Roe is trapped by his deafness, a kind of veil
enabling him to retreat from his real surroundings. The deafness has some link with a boyhood incident in Tewkesbury
Abbey where Roe, on a ledge forty feet above the ground,
had been mesmerized by the flood of colour from stained
glass, paralysed by 'that height calling on the pulses and he
did not know why to his ears' (p. 12). Remembrance holds the
terms of a fixation that paralyses the real present – a paralysis
reproduced in the design of future 'tangled memories'. Character is made the vehicle of a kind of infinite memory:

Now that he was back in this old life only for a few days, he could
not keep his hands off her in memory, now that he did not see her
every evening, rather mocking, aloof, as gentle as he had been curt
always, the touch of her white rose petal skin an unchanging part
of what his life had been before, her gladness when she had been
with him a promise of how they still had each other, and of the love
they would yet hold one another in, the greater by everything that
had gone before. (p. 33)

In response to this idea, the syntax loosens itself, in a suffusion
by which the different tenses appear to blend in an 'unchanging'
confluence.

The rose garden scene in *Caught* seems to be overlaying a
passage from the opening of Eliot's 'Burnt Norton'.[25] The
recurrent thesis of the first part of Eliot's poem is that
'What might have been and what has been / Point to one
end, which is always present'; the memory holds a record
of what might have been – it echoes with the sound of steps
that were never taken in the direction of a never-opened door
giving onto a rose garden. The presiding spirit of this garden
is a bird, specifically a thrush, which encourages the pursuit of
'other echoes', to be found 'Round the corner'. At the heart of
the garden is a dried-up pool, momentarily filled with water
'out of sunlight, / And the lotos rose, quietly, quietly, / The
surface glittered out of heart of light'. Mysterious 'guests'
appear to be reflected in the water, which vanishes with the
passing of a cloud. The garden is also haunted with the sound
of children's laughter. The bird intervenes with its urgent
message: 'Go, go, go, said the bird: human kind / Cannot bear
very much reality.'

There is what is virtually a compressed version of the 'Burnt Norton' passage in *The Family Reunion*:

> I only looked through the little door
> When the sun was shining on the rose-garden:
> And heard in the distance tiny voices
> And then a black raven flew over.[26]

'Round the corner' is the point where reality intrudes on the rose garden of 'Burnt Norton'. In *Caught*, Roe stages the rose garden scene by throwing over it a compliant immobility, even though he is on the very brink of undeceiving himself 'at the corner': '. . . at the corner round which this impermanence caught them fast. He turned to her and she seemed his in her white clothes, with a cry the blackbird had flown and in her eyes as, speechless, she turned, still a stranger, to look into him, he thought he saw . . .' (p. 64). The cry of the blackbird is almost a signal to refer to the cry of the thrush in 'Burnt Norton', or to the raven in *The Family Reunion*. As in *Party Going*, the twisting and turning of a path represents a threshold of knowledge, the point of sublimation.

The echoes of 'Burnt Norton' seem part of an effort to revoke the kind of use Eliot subsequently made of it, implanting it in *Four Quartets* where it must be read with reference to a religious arrival at the point 'where we started' in order to 'know the place for the first time'.[27] With *Caught*, we revert to the true effects of 'what might have been', the trajectory of a compulsion, the infinite memory of the unconscious.

In an essay entitled 'The Lotus and the Rose', Giorgio Melchiori has shown how dependent the imagery of 'Burnt Norton' is upon the Preface of the American edition of *New Poems* (1920) by D. H. Lawrence:[28]

The perfect rose is only a running flame, emerging and flowing off, and never in any sense at rest, static, finished. Herein lies its transcendent loveliness. The whole tide of all life and all time suddenly heaves, and appears before us as an apparition, a revelation. We look at the very white quick of nascent creation. A water-lily heaves herself from the flood, looks around, gleams, and is gone. We have seen the incarnation, the quick of the ever-swirling flood. We have seen the invisible. We have seen, we have touched, we have partaken of the very substance of creative change, creative mutation.

If you tell me about the lotus, tell me of nothing changeless or eternal. Tell me of the mystery of the inexhaustible, forever-unfolding spark. Tell me of the incarnate disclosure of the flux, mutation in blossom, laughter and decay perfectly open in their transit, nude in their movement before us.[29]

Although ideologically opposed to him, Eliot held that Lawrence was able 'to communicate, in visionary flashes, the sensuous fullness of the moment'. As Melchiori points out, it was natural that he should turn to Lawrence when seeking to present 'the moment in and out of time' in sensuous images. On his part, Green has separate recourse to this same Preface: the final sentence of the quoted passage surfaces in particular details in *Caught*:[30] 'he thought he saw the hot, lazy, luxuriance of a rose, the curling disclosure of the heart of a rose that, as for a hornet, was his for its honey, for the asking, open for him to pierce inside, this heavy, creamy, girl turned woman' (p. 64). These points of verbal contact tend to release the scene from the hold of Eliot's religious mysticism. Elsewhere in the text, religious terms are used pejoratively, linked with self-deception: 'He had forgotten that he used to take office worries home at night. He remembered only the beatitude of those evenings' (p. 93); 'In a sort of holy falseness he bade them farewell' (p. 43). The entire rose garden scene is also visually reminiscent of Lawrence's 'The Shadow in the Rose Garden', where the garden provides the essential memory of a past love-affair. *Caught* tries to contain the shadows of both versions of time in order to maintain their difference and to superimpose the claims of its own obsession with 'what might have been'. At this point, the syntax has an irresolute quality, as if to support an awareness of the alternative form it might have assumed: 'The afternoon, it had been before tea, was hot, swallows darted low at the level of her thighs, a blackbird, against three blooms bent to the height of its yellow beak, seemed enchanted by terror into immobility as the two of them halted, brought to a full stop at the corner round which this impermanence caught them fast' (p. 64). It forms itself around several features which seem incidental to one another, preferring a sense of improvidence, as if the experience was barely 'caught' by a certain sentence-formation and 'brought to a full stop'. The writing eschews both the instantaneous yield of meaning, and

the promise of a fixed meaning; it remains permanently provisional, as evidence of an improvised world prolonged in
memory for which the rose, with its verbal occurrence throughout the book, is an emblem, after the fashion of Proust's
Japanese paper flowers:

And just as the Japanese amuse themselves by filling a porcelain
bowl with water and steeping in it little crumbs of paper which
until then are without character or form, but, the moment they
become wet, stretch themselves and bend, take on colour and dis-
tinctive shape, become flowers or houses or people, permanent and
recognizable, so in that moment all the flowers in our garden and
in M. Swann's park, and the water-lilies on the Vivonne and the
good folk of the village and their little dwellings and the parish
church and the whole of Combray and of its surroundings, taking
their proper shapes and growing solid, sprang into being, town and
gardens alike, from my cup of tea.[31]

In one respect the whole novel resembles the dehiscent form
of a flower when it seems to open itself with the treatment of
these events which anchor the memory – pretending to reveal
its secret meaning at moments of great internal pressure, in
passages remarkable for a pictorial intensity: 'Roses had come
above her bare knees under the fluted skirt she wore, and the
swallows flying so low made her, in his recollection, much
taller than she had ever been' (p. 64). This image underlies
the first serious jolt to Roe's fantasy, once it has been transmuted into another skirt in another setting: 'This light,
reflected up the bell of her skirt, made her translucent to the
waist' (p. 50). In the flat shared by Prudence and Ilse, sensuous
plants like the rose are supplanted by alien, metallic forms:
'in a scarlet bowl, was a cactus, painted white' (p. 50). Ilse
makes artificial flowers out of sardine tins. The mellow light
of the garden is obliterated by the relentless white of 'an
acetylene lamp triangle of sunlight' (p. 50). Roe's fingers 'like
strings of raw pork faggots', his 'sweat-charged clothes',
'vinegar-coloured palm', and 'four-day growth of bristle'
combine to expel him from the garden; he begins to imagine
a different picture of himself: 'he thought he recognized that
he was now a labourer' (p. 51).

Prudence and Ilse are wintry girls, almost inhuman in their
distinct hardness and coldness. Prudence is 'knife sharp com-

pared to the opulence his darling had carried about in her skin' (p. 65), and even in laughter her eyes are 'lapped with melted ice' (p. 71). Ilse is a Swede 'whose cold country could have given her, so he thought, no such memories as his own' (p. 69). Roe connects his wife with spring, although this is another example of disremembering: 'It seemed to him it had been in April, but the afternoon she asked to be shewn round his parents' country place was in July' (p. 64). The summer and autumn are reserved for association with Hilly: 'the bloom, as he said to himself, of a thousand moist evenings in August on her soft skin and, on the inner side of her lips, where the rouge had worn off, opened figs wet on a wall'.[32] Motifs of autumn, often of fruition, stand also for a more general burgeoning of sexual availability; when Pye is returning on the bus from his first visit to the asylum where his sister is being held, he is aroused by a girl passenger, and this attraction is relayed through images of harvest: 'he *caught* sight of one protuberant, half-transparent eye, sideways, blue, hedged with long lashes that might have been scythes to mow his upstanding corn' (p. 142, my emphasis).

Mistaking summer for spring, Roe converts the past into a season of infinite promise. In effect, he dissimulates the kind of paradisiacal innocence which Pye finds it natural to recall: 'When I was a lad, me and my sister used to go out in the kingcups, soft of an evening after supper, and make gold chains we put about the other's neck' (p. 77). Pye frames his sister in a 'prospect' of flowers that suggest innocence, as opposed to the rose with its erotic associations. But a submerged recognition that this innocence does imply a fall is in the verbal reflection of Hilly's mouth, offering itself to be kissed: 'She thought she made her mouth a sort of loving cup' (p. 112).

The incest scene embodies Pye in the image he takes to represent his true self. It is a strong projection, an attempt to suspend all claims of the 'system we live under' (p. 38). But the system is invested in him; because it operates through his own conscience, the extent to which he depends on the image in some measure determines the severity of his breakdown – once he has convinced himself that the image disguises a fact of incest. Richard Roe knowingly indulges in a self-deception, so that his roses remain blooms. But for Pye, they turn into the counterpart, the 'twining briars' which afflict his sister. Unlike the corners in paths which represent a critical stage in Roe's construction of his own identity, and which cause him – and the syntax – an amount of fluctuation, Pye's 'winding lane' always leads back to the same place, 'in colour blue' (p. 40). Only when the image has been de-sublimated is the conceit of a threshold of meaning – now a vertiginous abruptness – reassumed: 'He thought he was going to come on it any minute round the next corner, as he was' (p. 132). Before that, the crisis remains sublimated in the picture infused with blue – a colour which generates a sense of infantile security; several passages are filtered through this connotation. The situation in which Christopher gets lost is drenched with a play of colour dissolving his problems ('He enjoyed teasing and was careful no-one should know what he felt', p. 5) with an interlacing series of references to the sea, to lakes, and to the boats upon them. He is 'lost in feelings', immersed in the 'Aegean', anxiety dispelled by the immobile permanence of 'those boats fishing in the senses' (p. 13), which in the manuscript are 'those ships of the senses, *becalmed forever*' (MS, p. 9, my emphasis).[33] Father and son are both fascinated by a veil of colour whose projection in any circumstances induces this comatose effect: 'For both it was the deep colour spilled over these objects that, by evoking memories they would not name, and which they could not place, held them, and then led both to a loch-deep unconsciousness of all else' (p. 12). In this diffusion of any awareness, they can empty themselves of all personal history, all co-ordinates.

This state of willing captivity submits to a condition like the fetish, which is instituted to relinquish unwanted information in a form that reproduces the circumstances of the information first coming to light. In such a way, Christopher is 'held to ransom by the cupidity of boys' as much as by any cupidity on the part of Pye's sister; the abduction is successful when he accepts her because she is captured by 'the world his need had made':

But when she pulled at his jacket, he did look up and saw nothing strange in how she was, *caught* full by the light from those windows, so that her skin was blue and her orbs, already sapphire, a sea

flashing at hot sunset as, uneasy, she glanced left, then right . . .
Caught in another patch of colour . . . Furtively she glanced right,
then left, but when, to make him do as she wanted, she *caught* full
at him with her eyes that, by the ocean in which they were steeped,
were so much a part of the world his need had made, and so much
more a part of it by being alive, then he felt anything must be
natural, and was ready to do whatever she asked. (p. 14, my
emphasis)

The night which includes a parallel to this abduction, when Pye
encounters a prostitute and then a lost boy whom he takes to
the Fire Station, is saturated with the same shifting variants
of blue and red: 'on the other side, were triangular dark
sapphire shadows . . . out of the blue . . . the milk moon
stripped deep gentian cracker paper shadows off his uniform
. . . he ogled the dark purple nipple, the moon full globe
that was red Indian tinted by the bulb . . . he spoke suggestively to gentian hooded doorways . . . the mucus reappeared,
almost Eton blue . . .' (pp. 162–6).

The way in which the characters are affected by colour
patterns equal to 'the world his need had made' offers a model
for reading a text whose title would seem to privilege the
hermeneutics of being 'caught' – a mode of rendering the novel
by which any substance built up is nothing but a shadow cast
by the need to substantiate.

Correspondingly, the absence of colour is confounding;
Ilse has an intractable presence in the book which stems from
her lack of colour: 'Declining light, in which there was no sun,
reduced her body. She lay dim, like a worm with a thin
skeleton, back from a window, pallid, rasher thin, her breasts,
as she lay on her back, pointing different ways' (p. 142). She
is not metamorphosed by coloured light but uncovered by
lamps 'in their logic', with no subjective associations: sterile,
devoid of any meaning.

The revelation of Ilse's body as meaningless because the
colour has been washed out of it – it is bleached like the
'objects thrown up on a beach' – diverts Prudence from her
own fascination with firemen: 'So it came about that Prudence
went off Pye' (p. 143). And Christopher rejects a toy boat
because it is uncoloured, 'a tanker, painted tropic white, that
Christopher hurled away from him not three weeks later' (p. 17).

This detail is a refinement on the typescript version, where the tanker remains blue.

In short, the book is not motivated in the way we expect of a novel, if the kind of measures by which a novel is enclosed in the sense familiar to Elizabeth Bowen can only operate on the understanding that some forms of writing are pressed into service while others are not. The unwritten literary history of the period is dominated by the question of legitimate practice, of the indirect resistance to change. The Second World War was a total war, directly involving the whole of society, civilian population as well as the armed forces; social change was rapid and total. Among many practising novelists there was an unformulated commitment to the novel as a surrogate for social stability. Where the work was directly addressed to contemporary life, more often than not the war was a back-cloth for inveterate attitudes. The social upheaval of evacuation merely enhances the comedy of Evelyn Waugh's *Put Out More Flags*, which does little to adjust the class-consciousness prevalent before it. A novel like Nancy Mitford's *Pigeon Pie* could be written precisely because its attitude to the Blitz was so flippant. As long as the novel is understood as being *informative*, it can represent society without having to interpret the modes of its formation. *Caught* proceeds to resolve the fixed representations that impound the novel with the fixed representations that impound society. It provokes a disunity in the self constituted by both novel and social world in a consideration of incestuous activity – illegitimate practice to a full extent.

According to Freud, the barrier against incest is 'essentially a cultural demand made by society. Society must defend itself against the danger that the interests which it needs for the establishment of higher social units may be swallowed up.'[34]

Wilhelm Reich, in his 1932 study (enlarged in 1935) *The Invasion of Compulsory Sex-Morality*, concluded that a dynamically excessive incest wish is found where there is too great an interest in the incestuous object because of a general restriction of instinctual life.

And in their subsequent findings, Claude Lévi-Strauss and Jacques Lacan agree that, in its ordering of sexual relations according to laws of preferential marriage alliances and forbidden relations, incest prompts the exchange of women between nominal lineages, 'in order to develop in an exchange of gifts and in an exchange of master-words the fundamental commerce and concrete discourse on which human societies are based'.[35]

Incest is prohibited because it is unserviceable: it does not allow the exchange which is crucial to society, just as the difficulty of *Caught* lies in its contravention of the novel as a mutual grant of equal interests between reader and text – the reader's ability is not equal to the strange intensities of the writing. Incest is a powerful force which society is unable to employ in the pursuit of its own logic. Incest becomes unthinkable. There is a parallel moment in the reading of a novel, caught up in an accustomed equilibrium of forces, where adaptation is unconditional – transgression is literally meaningless.

But this was a total war; in 1940, professional observers were relaying acute misgivings as to how society would be seen to have justified its specific encroachments:

The average person surrenders part of his cultural individuality with every new act of integration into a functionally rationalized complex of activities. He becomes increasingly accustomed to being led by others, and gradually gives up his own interpretation of events for those which others give him. When the rationalized mechanism of social life collapses in times of crisis the individual cannot repair it by his own insight. Instead his own impotence reduces him to a state of terrifying helplessness . . . It seems to me that the more slavishly subjected to the will of the state the individual has been, the greater the collapse is likely to be either into panic or into apathy.[36]

Virginia Woolf, taking aerial bombardment as her pretext, and writing of the way that women are ideologically placed within a rationalized mechanism of social life, makes it her purpose to supply an awareness of how such political liabilities are fully sexualized: 'Let us try to drag up into consciousness the subconscious Hitlerism that holds us down. It is the desire for aggression; the desire to dominate and enslave . . . If we could free ourselves from slavery we should free men from tyranny. Hitlers are bred by slaves.'[37] At the same time, recognition of the dependence on specific representations took the form of frantic solicitation for reliable sources of information.

In his comic extravaganza *Shaving through the Blitz* (which was published serially in *Penguin New Writing*), George Stonier makes this the basis of a farcical indirection:

People say in these times it doesn't matter what newspaper you read, but that is a mistake; you should always read the same newspaper, through thick and thin, so as to be able to read between the lines.

In the Tube carriage, for example, where I am wedged between intruding elbows, every man has a paper spread on his lap or held up in front of him. And nearly every one is squinting over his neighbour's sheet for the news he doesn't find in his own. Somewhere, these hungry eyes seem to say, if only one could put one's hand on it, there is news, real news, the whole story.[38]

Because the 'whole story' was withheld, 'wishful thinking' and, grossly inflated, rumour took hold. A striking example occurred on 7 May 1941, after the last big Blitz on Liverpool when the city centre was temporarily sealed off to ease traffic congestion; within hours the rumour was running in London that martial law had been enforced.

In a climate of such apprehension, there is a faintly bridling tone to the very first sentence of *Caught*: 'When war broke out in September *we were told* to expect raids' (my emphasis). The first person plural pronoun invites the reader to decide whether to assent to, or dissent from, an account which claims to be able to speak for him. As its first consideration, the book appeals to a memory that can be shared and so regulated. This is of course to read the rest of the book into the first sentence: in its subsequent practice the book does give rise to a definite impression of the novel as a form providing the reader with the shape of his own history in return for obedience, a filial dependence – an impression which is being constantly translated into glimpses of a separate form by writing as a diverting technique which cites its own material in a kind of forbidden, or incestuous, union. It is as if the novel-form were bounded by a horizon beyond which writing begins to lose its meaning, and this horizon is what *Caught* dissolves in its reorientation of the reader. It demonstrates how the subject is caught up in a formation which necessitates his captive presence for its own survival: 'We are fascinated by the growth of freedom from powers *outside* ourselves and are blinded to the fact of *inner* restraints, compulsions, and fears, which tend to undermine the meaning of the victories freedom has won against its traditional enemies.'[39] 'Freedom' is reactivated as a concept that depends on the subject assimilating himself to a unified image of his own co-ordination. All the emphasis is on a consistency of the subject for which the prototype is the strong visual image he fixes upon himself.

This developed sense in which the individual is present to himself only operates in a fixed context. The prolonged dislocation of normal living conditions provides an interval in which this context can be seen to have sustained itself with a spurious momentum:

If he (the civilian) is threatened with air-raids he is at a disadvantage in picturing what this threat means. The soldier can form a tolerably accurate picture which is drawn from experience of related phenomena; the novice tends to be flooded with emotions which arise from phantasies that are set in motion by the threat, and which he cannot check by appeals to fact. Therefore there is a danger that the aggressive component of these emotions will be towards his own side rather than towards the enemy or towards hostile objects in reality, as would be the case if it were a conscious aggression.[40]

With the lapse of an authorizing context, it was in fact the case that 'juvenile delinquency increased, which increase can be largely attributed to the break-up of family life'.[41] At one point in *Caught*, the Auxiliaries discuss a newspaper report of a case of theft by a Regular's sister. In fact, several references in the typescript to thieving by members of the Fire Service have been suppressed in the published version. In the typescript, the two Regulars, Wal and Chopper, who 'were always in the bar' (p. 47), steal glasses from it (TS, p. 79). And when Hilly has left some silk stockings at the Station, Roe reports 'they'll have gone by now'. She assures him that in the event of fire in her own home, 'I'm going to lock everything up before I put through my firecall' (TS, p. 96). More significant were the growing signs of what the editors of Mass-Observation described as 'considerable moral abandon'! There was, at the least in the minds of observers, an atmosphere of sexual availability which clings to *Caught*. The general feeling of dissociation is siphoned through this into an aptly indiscriminate grammar:

This was a time when girls, taken out to night clubs by men in uniform, if he was a pilot she died in his arms . . .

Limp, dancing as never before entirely to his movements, long-haired sheaved heads too heavy for their bodies collapsed on pilots' blue shoulders . . . (p. 49)

The undetermined agency of these sentences is mechanical; moral abandon is automatic, a candle to the girls who are 'moth deathly gay, in a daze of giving' (p. 49). Richard Roe has to 'prompt' his feeling, reminding himself of the part he has to play, '*caught* up in what he understood to be the way other people acted at this time' (p. 50, my emphasis). The new sense of independence is compulsory: the outcome of a morality-machine driven by the logic of its own dynamism and turned into its opposite – a compulsive immorality. In its night-club setting, this aura of sexual freedom is a 'forced communion, this hyacinthine, grape dark fellowship of longing'.[42]

The seduction of the will by expert discoloration begins to suggest the utter blankness of a putative ideal subject, origin of his own actions: 'The music floated her, the beat was even more of all she had to say, the colour became a part, alive and deep, making what they told each other, with her but in silence, simply repeatedly plain, the truth, over and over again' (p. 112). The night-club is steeped in various shades of blue, 'violet shades . . . steep purple . . . intense blue . . . dark blue' (p. 107). With the additional lulling of music, the familiar submersion becomes a volatile surrender. The editors of Mass-Observation, summing up reactions to the increased popularity of jazz, concluded that it 'reaffirms, reassures, in the soft, enveloping arms of the Mother or (now) Motherland'.[43] Again and again the writing disinters those compulsions the reader would localize and secure, scattering what he would concentrate, allowing a desultory recourse to the same accretions of colour and image. Hence the women are imbued with marine characteristics: 'with sea flower fingered hands' (p. 108); 'dressed as if she was in diamonds fathoms under the sea' (p. 110). And a studied eroticism is assigned to the sensuous fig, the fruit that was kept alive in the dead of winter through artistry – in the glass-house that Roe and Christopher had strayed into: 'Her lips' answer, he felt, was of opened figs, wet at dead of night in a hothouse' (p. 111). The description is overbalanced by the metaphor; the text is always fastened in knots using the same threads and fibres found elsewhere.

At the same time, the prevailing colour is modified by a comparison with 'stained glass window light' (p. 111) recalling the abduction scene. The 'storied glass' of the department store is echoed by the spotlight which 'spread a story over her body'. These are attenuations of a narrative mediation such as Proust's magic lantern hints at, with the story of Golo which 'transubstantiates' the mundane.

There is a constant sensation of phantasmagoria in *Caught*, of the indistinct survival of other parts of the text, coalescing and flaking away again:

She had been wafted off, was enchanted not entirely by all she had had to drink and which was released inside her in a glow of earth chilled above a river at the noisy night harvest of vines, not altogether by this music, which, literally, was her honey, her feeling's tongue, but as much by sweet comfort and the compulsion she felt here to gentleness that was put on her by these couples, by the blues, by wine, and now by this murmuring, night haunted, softness shared. (p. 108)

This stylistic contraband includes that 'honey' which is the gift Roe exacts from his wife ('his for its honey, for the asking'); the glowing earth at a night harvest of vines which, along with the 'grape dark fellowship of longing', recalls Christopher's 'pink cheeks grape dark in the glow' (p. 13) when he is abducted; and a closeness to the earth which Pye broods over in his recollection of the incest scene, and which Roe mentions in his attempt to 'get the whole thing' (p. 180). It amounts to no more than a Lawrentian notion of natural desire, which only requires the lifting of restrictions, but the powerless image seems to be proof that even a perverse desire is preconditioned. A direct connection is made with the anonymity of the dark incest scene; Roe can make out the audience 'only as the less dark', and he tries making love to Hilly by 'toying with her arm' which he cannot see. There are the same opportunities for mistaken identity: 'he thought it wild that the touch of the unseen inside of her arm should have been so, and saw her not as she was' (p. 112).

With its strange conflations, the book is haunted by the

thought of being open to a specific form of interpretation; the unnatural intensities are meant as points of departure from this configuration, attempts to release the writing that 'might have been' but for the memory of how a novel is ordinarily read.

Sibling incest tries to erase the memory of a sexuality of reproduction, a sexuality based on the family as prototype of social, sexual and other relations. Sex between siblings does the most violence to a sexuality measured by the degree of success in identifying inner restraints with external laws:

Analysis shows that conscience rules with a harshness as great as external authorities, and furthermore that frequently the contents of the orders issued by man's conscience are ultimately not governed by demands of the individual self but by social demands which have assumed the dignity of ethical norms. The rulership of conscience can be even harsher than that of external authorities, since the individual feels its orders to be his own; how can he rebel against himself?[44]

If the self is unable to escape its familiar inhibitions, it can only protect the integrity of its own designs at its own expense in a negative gesture. Thus, in Faulkner's *The Sound and the Fury*, Quentin Compson commits suicide from the same moral disposition which forces Pye to gas himself. Pye's death *before* the Blitz implies that socially conditioned anxiety is a more potent force than unconditioned fear. In *Hangover Square*, George Harvey Bone accounts the murder of Netta a necessary preliminary to infantile reunion with his sister, who is in fact dead. The book finishes with his arrival in Maidenhead, associated with his sister, where he gasses himself after war is declared.

The alternative to suicide is to seal off the moral universe by an abdication of will – the self inflicting on itself the punishment of estrangement from a consciousness that still retains its assent. Pye's sister incurs the guilt of having perverted her child-bearing role, and shelters the offended moral system by inverting external blame into the obsession which insulates her, by which she is 'caught'. ('Being caught is the word for having a child, sometimes.')[45] She tries to retrieve 'her child' by abducting Christopher; she reproduces the darkness of the incest scene – 'She did not turn on the light' (p. 15) – and hides her face as if trying to conceal her identity in a re-enactment of that night: 'She snatched away her hands which, outspread before her face, wrists against mouth, fingers pointing at him, shook with urgency' (p. 16); 'She put both hands over her mouth, which was wide open, and so left, in the shadow, a dark hole between firelit fingers over a dark face' (p. 16). She covers her mouth, as if there was an opening that should have remained closed; in this attitude, she gives a 'sly smirk' at the entrance of Pye. The relation of 'mother' to 'child' is given a sudden erotic charge: Christopher's face is 'round, red and so round that both eyes disappeared in his frown. His pointed tongue curled up, dull red' (p. 16). It becomes a permutation of the rose, a curling disclosure, red, round and furrowed, a projection of the sexuality 'caught' in the Oedipal vendetta.

Brid, the daughter of Mary Howells, is mentally unbalanced precisely because she is called Brid – because she is a bride; her derangement focusses on the neglect of her child, and this reverses the obsession of Pye's sister – both cases are subject to the same moral pressures.[46] In one sense, Brid is also a child who has been abducted. Her repeated 'don't' when she suspects her mother of poisoning her is the same interdiction used by Christopher. Equally, when Pye tries to quell the lost boy excited by his display of temper, he repeats the interdiction used by his sister to pacify Christopher: 'For Christ's sake, hush' (p. 169).

The selfhood is abject, contracted to a morality that threatens eviction as the penalty for default, reduction to an uninventive lack. Pye observes his sister 'creeping as he was but lower, more like a wild animal' (p. 41); her cringing matches the antics of the deranged hound bitch that 'crouched with love' (p. 31).

The intelligence that can be reconstructed on the basis of this evidence has, therefore, definable limits most explicitly described not in *Caught* itself but in the short story 'Mr Jonas', which was written at the same time and which preserves the organizing imagery of *Caught*:

Accustomed, as all were, to sights of this kind, there was not one amongst us who did not now feel withdrawn into himself, as though he had come upon a place foreign to him but which he was aware he had to visit, as if it were a region the conditions in which he knew would be something between living and dying, not, that is, a web of dreams, but rather such a frontier of hopes or mostly fears as it may be in the destiny of each, or almost all, to find, betwixt coma and the giving up of living.[47]

Coma is an unconscious manoeuvre, suspending a contrariety that seems to actuate the environment, while it leaves the self still within the horizon of a certain set of moral imperatives – a horizon which is merely obscured by the neurotic web of dreams. Suicide affords the only final means to surpass such a frontier of hopes or mostly fears.

This analysis has maintained the reference to an historical moment when the self was overtly represented as being critically aware of its own alienability, of a threat to its unity – the general sense in which 'there was not one amongst us who did not now feel withdrawn into himself, as though he had come upon a place foreign to him but which he was aware he had to visit'. This awareness may be traced further in the imaginative writing of the time.

In *The Ministry of Fear*, published in 1943 – the same year as *Caught* – the chief character is curiously but appropriately named Rowe (and the author is named Greene). Rowe is pre-occupied with the dead wife he killed out of pity; he suffers an amnesia, in effect a resourceful metaphor for suicide, allowing him to erase the self adapted to condone the appeasement of a pitiless Fascism:

'. . . this is rather a dingy hole. We've come to terms with it of course.'
'What frightens me,' Rowe said, 'is knowing how I came to terms with it before my memory went . . .'[48]

His new persona is 'the kind of man the boy he remembered would have become'.[49] As with Pye and Roe both, 'what might have been' is entirely successful in captivating the self because what has been is inadmissible.

This dualism affected the composition of Spender's 'September Journal', where a first-person account of his support for Chamberlain is contradicted in a switch to the second person: 'There you are, you analyse your hatred of fascism and it comes to a desire to be left alone.'[50]

In *Hangover Square*, the protagonist is schizophrenic, alter-
nating between a state of complete docility and the compulsion
to murder Netta, 'the net', and her Fascist lover. This intention
is paradoxically the vehicle of 'natural' feelings, and specifically
of the same kind of pity which motivates Rowe: 'He would
never forgive himself if he hurt them. In fact the whole thing
would be off if there was any question of doing so.'[51] The
murder coincides with the radio transmission of Chamberlain's
declaration of war against Hitler.

It is in common with all this attention to a disjunction in
the self that *Caught* insinuates into the character of Richard Roe
a basic mutual repulsion of instinct and reason: 'He had never
felt war was possible, although *in his mind* he could not see
how it could be avoided' (p. 28, my emphasis). Roe equates
feeling with an unquestioned falsity: 'He kept on saying,
falsely, and over and over, that he was to rejoin his wife'
(p. 28). This nervous insistence, his conscious difficulty in
maintaining one image of himself, is ultimately in collusion
with the unitary idea of the self:

It was he who had changed, who dreaded now, with a hemlock
loss of will, to evoke how once he shared these scenes with no one,
for he had played alone, who had then no inkling of the insecurity
the war would put him in, and who found, when confronted by
each turning of a path he knew by heart but which he could never
call to mind when he closed his eyes, that the presence, the disclosure again of so much that had not changed and shewed no
immediate signs of changing, bore him down back to the state he
wished to forget, when he was his son's age and had no more than
a son's responsibility to a father. (p. 32)

His need to regain the consistency of 'the presence, the disclosure' which he has had constantly to improvise through his
obsession with 'the curling disclosure of the heart of a rose' is
a conscious subterfuge. He thinks that he understands how he
plays himself false and why; but the sentence has an introverted side in which falsity is re-located. The 'hemlock loss of
will' is a textual rumour of Pye's suicide, an implicit recognition
that the dictates of conscience are an artificial frontier, and
this is represented once more as the 'turning of a path he knew
by heart but which he could never call *to mind*' (my emphasis).

The syntax is accordingly eccentric; it seems to proceed by driving out the will to provide a centre, it falters 'when confronted by each turning of a path' and re-forms.

The text is subversively alert to the presence of a frontier of 'hopes or mostly fears' which Roe's neurosis attempts to obscure. In direct contrast, it is the clarity with which he suddenly perceives this frontier that destroys Pye: 'In a surge of blood, it was made *clear, false,* that it might have been his own sister he was with that night' (p. 40, my emphasis). The immediate corrective, 'false', interrogates the dense clarity of an assumption, questions the meaning of a prohibition of incest; as the unanswered challenge, it acts as a pivot balancing the alibi of unproblematized innocence against a survival of incestuous desire. This desire is secreted in the 'unconscious' of the text, where it is almost visible in the ambiguities of grammar: 'Yes, he had been close to the earth then, and it led him back to the first girl he had known, not long before his father took them away from the village in which their childhood was passed, for that too was of the earth' (p. 40). 'Them' is intended to refer to Pye and his sister, but it conveys this sense only very weakly in the face of a rhapsodical insistence on Pye and his first girl. He is indeed 'close to the earth' in *both* relationships, but the nature of such congruency is only unconsciously acknowledged – it is not at the disposal of his 'wishful thinking' self; his dilemma is precisely that 'he had always known, and never realized' (p. 40).

More often than not, incestuous desire survives in its negative counterpart of guilt. Pye's own vision is 'warped by his need' (p. 40), but the moonlight is 'blind' as well because it is like a potential witness, and must be disarmed.[52] The dream which anticipates his first visit to the asylum is critically disturbed by the demand for Pye's family history:

'Is there any history in your family, Mr. Pye?'
"Istory, what d'you mean, 'istory?' (p. 86)

When the same demand is actually made on the second visit, his self-possession ebbs away: ' "Now I understand," Pye said slowly, with dread' (p. 138). On the first visit, he makes his sister a present of 'a comb with rose briars painted on the top' ('rose briars' is a manuscript alteration to the typescript which has 'little roses') (MS, p. 152/p. 87). Afterwards, he suppresses the interview with her because she pleads with him to 'bring her child. But it had all been so strange that he was ready next day to reject any version left him of what she may have said' (p. 87). At the same time, his own dreadful suspicions assume the image of a child of a forbidden union, 'suckling on an ulcer the sickly, sore-covered infant of his fears' (p. 169).

The residual presence of desire is most striking in the account of the asylum dream. The words 'dry' and 'wet' are absent from the manuscript; their subsequent addition, and their conjunction, instance a kind of Freudian 'postscript' that gives the real meaning. In the typescript and published version, Pye, having entered the asylum, passes 'dry striped men' and 'the dry yellow man' (in the manuscript there is a 'whitecoated attendant'). The surroundings change abruptly with the demand for 'history', from dry to wet. The superintendent, 'wet through, in full rig, dripping water', had been simply 'in full rig' in the manuscript.

The modifications may be attuned to a biblical canon – 'Hortus conclusus soror mea, sponsa, hortus conclusus, fons signatus' – and if so, could be on the true path to explain it. The same dictum, with the same proviso, intercepts the orbit of imagery pertaining to the garden secluded in the memory. It seems pertinent that depriving Roe of his wife puts him in a special relationship with his sister-in-law.

The second visit to the asylum coincides with the height of public hostility to the Fire Service; the revelation of incest augments a generalized paranoia. (In his official account *Ordeal by Fire* (1941), Michael Wassey's chapter on the Phoney War – 'Waiting, waiting, waiting' – is obsessed with this public contempt.)

Incest is not the absolute cause of Pye's breakdown, which is first conceived in the conflicts arising from his promotion; it is as a result of his first official disgrace that 'Pye was never the same' (p. 80). He rationalizes his sister's madness as the penalty demanded by 'the system we live under', which he feels is crudely bent on destruction: 'but the instinct in the 'uman animal to save itself is stronger than the ruling class can credit' (pp. 22–3). He obviates a sense of his own guilt through resentment of the ruling class. In consequence, his own promotion is critical because the bad external object is introjected, and he is 'caught' in a demoralizing ambivalence, torn between class loyalty and official duty: ' "The moment they get the report from hospital to say she's been admitted then I'm *caught*" ' (p. 89, my emphasis); 'Pye was *caught* if he was detected' (p. 90, my emphasis); ' "If old Pye's a man 'e'll take 'is punishment when 'e's *caught*" ' (p. 126, my emphasis). This excessive consternation strains the popular conception of everyone pulling together; on this view, the unrestrained mixing of classes during the Blitz would have served to disunite as much as it seemed to harmonize the relations between them. Another contemporary writer certainly exposes a definite antagonism:

For the first time in our neighbourhood's history the landlord did not show up – whether through fear of the bombs or the tenants' possible wrath in the face of rent demands for homes they were scarcely occupying, it is difficult to say. What is notable is the sinister effect his absence lent to the daily happenings; it intensified the feeling that a place from which the landlord did not even think it worthwhile to collect his rent, was indeed beyond salvation . . . One aspect of it, I would say, was the discovery of the inflexibility of the existing class distinctions here in England.[53]

This tension was in fact exacerbated by the first propaganda poster issued by the Government after the declaration of war:

YOUR COURAGE
YOUR CHEERFULNESS
YOUR RESOLUTION
WILL BRING US VICTORY

Intended to unite the nation, the wording was felt to be divisive; Mass-Observation, conducting a survey to monitor reactions to its publication, discovered that a majority of the public read the poster in this light: 'The courage, cheerfulness, and resolution of you workers will bring victory to us capitalists.'

But this interpretation of events has barely survived. Tom Harrisson, one of the editors of Mass-Observation, has demonstrated the transformation of attitude in his own observers, comparing their recollection of events with the original records of thirty years before. In every case, memory distorts and does not corroborate the evidence:

For most surviving citizens the major effect has been (as often) in two opposite directions, both processes in 'reality obliteration': either to be unable to remember anything much (with no wish to do so), or, more usually, to see those nights as glorious. There is not much in between. But in between is where most of the unpublished evidence points – the evidence, that is, written down and filed immediately, without any intention of publication.[54]

The process of 'glossification' as Harrisson calls it, the impulse to mythologize the blitz, 'has largely determined the public record since'. The myth of solidarity has usurped the uneasy proximity of two classes, casually yoked together in the textual gadgetry of *Caught*: the names Pye and Roe combine as the two syllables of *pyro*, the root for Greek words connected with fire. Similarly, the names Pye and Piper together suggest 'Pied Piper' – the fairy-tale figure who abducts the children of Hamelin. (Initially, Piper, whose skin is 'dry and pied' (p. 21), is the only person in the Station who shares with Pye and Roe the knowledge of the abduction.) But these relationships are *symbiotic* in the sense which Erich Fromm, in a contemporaneous analysis, gives to that term:

[Symbiosis] in this psychological sense, means the union of one individual self with another self (or any other power outside of the own self) in such a way as to make each lose the integrity of its own self and to make them completely dependent on each other. The sadistic person needs his object just as much as the masochistic needs his. Only instead of seeking security by being swallowed, he gains it by swallowing somebody else. In both cases the integrity of the individual self is lost. In one case I dissolve myself in an outside power: I lose myself. In the other case I enlarge myself by making another being part of myself and thereby I gain the strength I lack as an independent self.[55]

The constituency of the self which has come to appear natural predominates by subduing otherness to its own pattern, obscuring the frontier of hopes and mostly fears, retarding otherness by conducting its uncommitted energy into predetermined forms – by *rationalizing* its own demands. Roe's uncontrolled outburst –

He felt a flash of anger. It spread.
'I know this,' he announced in what, to him, was direct answer, 'you've always been most unfair to Pye.' (p. 194)

– is the articulation of his own guilt, struggling to re-establish Pye in a prescribed condition, working to standardize his otherness. No distance at all has been crossed between his early self-righteousness at Pye's assault on the class system – 'It's sheer provocation' (p. 57) – and his final distaste for 'that awful local school' (p. 185). This is mere squeamishness compared to Pye's deep vulnerability – 'Her educated accents cut him' (p. 151). Pye's symbiotic relationship with Piper is characterized by the old man's echoing of his words: a confounding, hollow repeat of his own isolation.

Glossification, or rationalizing, is the terminus of a process in which the self is governed by the promise of meaning after the event. As Fromm expressed it, 'rationalizing is not a tool for penetration of reality, but a post-factum attempt to harmonize one's own wishes with existing reality'.[56] In other words, 'when today has become yesterday, it will have integrated';[57] the obsolescent self is driven by a need to rationalize. The object of formal experimentation in *Caught* is to dismantle the type of novel constructed by an obsolescent self to satisfy that need.

Caught does have an element of pure recreation, in passages that resist integration by the production of excess material:

And the sails, motionless, might have been stretched above a deeper patch of fathomless sea in the shade of foothills as though covered with hyacinths in that imagined light of evening, and round which, laden, was to come the wind that would give them power to move the purple shade they cast beside the painted boat they were to drive.[58]

The extravagance of this writing is *optative* (nothing happens, but it all 'might have'); by choice it avoids the laws of exchange basic to the composure of reader and writer, the synthetic values which determine whether a narrative unit is justified; by desire it hypothesizes a separate form, which can erase the memory of this value apparatus in an intense otherness. The circuit of meaning produced in a novel is broken with the presence of recurrent intensities, which have the quality of affects: sometimes strictly predictable, at other times they seem freakish and illegitimate. Thus, the pub where Richard and Hilly meet is called The Rose and Crown; Mrs Howells's teapot is 'covered with pink roses', and fires are inevitably depicted as showers of rose petals ('a flickering reddish light, as though in a shower of rose petals', p. 16); 'the light of his coal fire from which rose petals showered' (p. 120). The obsession with marine imagery slips a knife into the hands of the psychiatrist which is 'carved at one end like the figure head beneath a bowsprit' (p. 138). Hilly croons to herself, 'This man's my gondola' (p. 120). And on her trip to Doncaster, Mrs Howells strikes up an acquaintance with a man who 'was white-haired, and lived with a sister' (p. 114). The sister is distinctly introverted: 'The sister was next him, she hardly spoke' (p. 114). Successive revisions to manuscript and typescript were often made on this pattern: eyes that were 'brown, grey or green' in the typescript, became 'blue, and blue, and blue' (p. 49) in the published version.

Green has explained his procedure in an interview: 'I have to make my opening statement and for the remaining seven-eighths of the novel revolve around it.'[59] It will be remembered that *Party Going* required nine or ten beginnings. In a later interview, the construction of a novel is seen as a process of re-writing:

INTERVIEWER: How much do you usually write before you begin re-writing?
GREEN: The first twenty pages over and over again – because in my idea you have to get everything into them. So as I go along and the book develops, I have to go back to that beginning again and again . . . It's all a question of length; that is, of proportion. How much you allow to this or that is what makes a book now. It was not so in the days of the old three-decker novel. As to plotting or thinking ahead, I don't in a novel. I let it come page by page, one a day, and carry it in my head. When I say carry I mean the *proportions* . . .[60]

This process of reconciling the text to its otherness is an unbroken sequence of coadjustments, a chain reaction which skims over the coagulations of narrative. The phrase 'under which, on sunny days' (TS, p. 16) becomes 'under which, on sun-laden evenings' (p. 12). Similarly, 'a rose, held close, smells of those heavy, sun-laden evenings after tea' (TS, p. 21) becomes 'a rose, held close, holds summer, sun-laden evenings at six o'clock' (p. 15). 'The half seen tower at dusk' (TS, p. 16) becomes 'the half seen tower at six o'clock' (p. 12). In the excursion of re-writing, what would be the production of immoderate waste in the economy of a novel is the assertion of different size, the book carrying its own proportions which are not those of a novel. In the first eighth of the book, Christopher takes charge of a bonfire, emulating his father. He insists on taking along a scarlet handcart that resembles a fire engine. Correspondingly, Roe is given charge of a ship in the Blitz on the docks. The bonfire, which is 'glancing rose in places with the wind' (p. 26) is in the 'pied garden' ('pied' is an addition to the typescript). It can be seen that the text is not occupied with symbols but *symptoms*, organized intensive states whose meaning is inaccessible to the rationalizing self.

The text has a reserve material, of images, textures, colours, which is the only origin of its recurrent intensities:

(What he did not know was the year after year after year of entanglement before her, the senseless nightingale, the whining dog, repeating the same phrase over and over in the twining briars of her sense.) (p. 42)

Every inch of the path they followed slowly through the wild garden, which was no longer tended, would, at any time before this, have reminded him of so many small events he had forgotten out of his youth, of the wounded starling here, the nightingale there one night, the dog whining across the river one morning, while he stood, motionless behind that elm, to watch two cats from the stables. (p. 178)

This reappearance gives an outrageous frisson. The first sentence refers to Pye and his sister, the second to Roe; shortly after this, 'the air caught at his wind passage as though briars and their red roses were being dragged up from his lungs' (pp. 178–9). The use of imagery as appliqué seems aimless. Revolving around an opening statement, the writing aims at every possible resort.

The generation of a text through textural equivalences, and not equivalences of sense, is practised on every level. The name Roe is phonetically linked with 'rose', but also with the deer which, both in the wild and in the department store – 'the light *caught* red in their bead eyes' (p. 13) – are 'heraldic'. The epithet, which in both cases is added to the typescript, pronounces their over-determination. In the interests of proportion, the cousin with whom Christopher is so preoccupied becomes *Rose*mary, where in the manuscript she had been Josephine. And, in the 'winding lane' of the incest scene, the girl whom Pye imagined to be the first he had known was 'Mrs. Lane's little girl' (p. 42).

The writing is neither wholly transitive, nor wholly intransitive. The functional movement of the text is a principle of citation through and across its own material; to borrow a term from Joyce, it is 'trancitive',[61] carrying the reader *through* the history of a representation.

While he was writing *Caught*, Green published an essay on Doughty's *Arabia Deserta*. What he means to bring to light in this is the style, because it is 'not clear': that is, impervious to methods of elucidation applied by the rationalizing self, a self which the true contemporary idiom has to embarrass: 'Doughty without doubt wrote in the idiom of the real Arabia, and not of Araby.'[62] The essay's ulterior motive is to give a prospectus for contemporary writing at a moment when the need for an 'idiom of the time' has been given a special impetus:

Now that we are at war, is not the advantage for writers, and for those who read them, that they will be forced, by the need they have to fight, to go out into territories, it may well be at home, which they would never otherwise have visited, and that they will be forced, by way of their own selves, towards a style which, by the impact of a life strange to them and by their honest acceptance of this, will be pure as Doughty's was, so that they will reach each one his own style that shall be his monument?[63]

Although Green traps himself into an ornamental flourish, this does not efface an impressive grasp of the fact that writing is pressed 'by way of their own selves' to articulate a mutation in the self – both in writers and those who read them – which can only be expressed in something other than story. But the 'idiom of the real Arabia' has to multiply *inside* the 'idiom of Araby' so as to expose it as a form inadequate to the self shifting through the history of its own realization – forcing itself into the idiom of the time.

In *Caught* itself, the first description of a blitz (pp. 95–8) is virtually a tableau of these complementary pressures on the narrative. The Black-out is shattered by a lighted gas main, which fills the scene with unreal clarity of detail: 'he was able to pick out details of brickwork and stone facings more easily, and in colours more natural, than would have been possible on a spring morning, in early sunlight' (p. 95). But the extreme precision is given a certain remoteness by insertions of a fairy-tale atmosphere – a straightforward appeal to the tone of Araby. The wrecked buildings are like 'a palace in a story, the story of ruin' (p. 95). A flare is 'dropped by magic' (p. 96). (In the typescript, it is 'dropped by magic in the Thousand and One Nights' TS, p. 167.) Roe stumbles into an air-raid shelter: 'And in the near corner a girl stood between a soldier's legs . . . Man and girl were motionless, forgotten, as though they had been drugged in order to forget, as though he had turned over a stone and climbed down stairs revealed in the echoing desert, these two were so alone' (p. 97). When Chopper emerges from the same shelter, 'he might have come from seeing a Prince and a Princess' (p. 97). This combination of precision and remoteness is typical of the way in which character has been defined through the mechanisms of fixation; the impulse to disremember, to rationalize threats to an established sense of order, engenders a system of floating over the present with an effective delusion, avoiding the necessity to realize a situation in which 'He had been kissing her mouth, so that it was now a blotch of red' (pp. 96–7). The idea that Prudence has – 'War, she thought, was sex' (p. 19) – is given a scenario in the transformation of this red blotch:

At that moment two ambulance men carried a stretcher up. They laid it down. The twisted creature under a blanket coughed a last gushing, gout of blood.
   Two police brought past a looter, most of his clothes torn off, heels dragging, drooling blood at the mouth, out on his feet from the bashing he had been given. (p. 97)

The red blotch is also found across Pye's mouth: 'And a smear of jam must have been across one corner of his mouth, for the first he knew was when she mouthed it off' (p. 141). The scene is transfigured by separate chains of association, and by separate forms of organization that occupy the same space: the idiom of

Araby, which encourages the idea of consistent, tenable meaning, and the idiom of the real Arabia, which subtracts that meaning, since it is always found bearing the reader off without explanation to other parts of the text. The one idiom is forced to recognize the other which suddenly and literally materializes within it as a countermand.

The true contemporary idiom has an essential readiness, in a situation where the widespread depreciation of the novel is a result of flagrant unreadiness – nowhere more evident than in those features from which the novel derives its authority, its claim to be able to *know* more than the reader who, on contact with the text, finds himself already caught in a web, held in position where he depends on the novel as a source of information about society, a portrayal of 'the way we live now'. *Caught* parodies the informative accents of a novel: the circumspect tone of an author is brought to bear on trivial items – 'It is possible that he was confused by the amount [of sweets] he was getting' (p. 7) – or is used pointlessly: 'It is unnecessary to say how Christopher spent the days' (p. 33). The text is punctuated with a series of crass intimations of an omniscient author:

How utterly harmless you are, thought Richard, sleepless, and how wrong he was. (p. 42)

Later on he carried out his promise. He was to regret it. (p. 47)

But in this he was wrong twice, both times. (p. 66)

But he was wrong. (p. 105)

'Yes,' he went on, speaking as refined as he knew how and with an utter lack of interest that she shared, the bed was all they had, and were not to have much longer, in common . . . (p. 119)

But the peril was drawing closer and heavier about Pye . . . (p. 122)

It was the beginning of the end. (p. 132)

These inflexions of a privileged acquaintance with a range of information extend to the recall of historical events:

He was too disturbed to notice the invasion of Norway. (p. 153)

The invasion of the Low Countries had begun. (p. 154)

But the Germans were to be quicker than that. (p. 155)

Although it was hardly mentioned, each man in this group outside was aghast at the news, for the evacuation of Dunkirk was on. (p. 163)

In its more blatant manifestation, the text resolves a sense of its own proportions *as a novel* with the social consensus regarding the pattern of events: 'This was how the story got around, in bits and pieces, and it was in this way that it grew, and grew in a short time, *for there was not much time left*' (p. 150, my emphasis). The imagination is seen to be captivated by a guarantee of meaning. In his own attempt to 'get the whole thing', Roe admits to the way in which the self is orientated towards the recapitulation of its experience:

'The extraordinary thing is,' he said, 'that one's imagination is so literary. What will go on up there to-night in London, every night, is more like a film, or that's what it seems like at the time. Then afterwards, when you go over it, everything seems unreal, probably because you were so tired, as you begin building again to describe to yourself some experience you've had.' (p. 174)

The constant activity of 'picturing' reunites the self with the framework it needs to function within a horizon of imperatives, normally obscured by the webs of neurosis, of rationalizing – a whole repertoire of attempts to empty the self of its history; a history which can be restored when the disruption of this web allows a breach through which to release desire running counter to the inertia of the self, clarifying the frontier of hopes or mostly fears. With regard to the binding power of representations, this opposition of obscurity and clarity is stated in a short story of Elizabeth Bowen's, published while *Caught* was being written: ' "We can no longer express ourselves: what we say doesn't even approximate to reality; it only approximates to what's been said. I say, this war's an awful illumination; it's destroyed our dark; we have to see where we are." '[64] Stephen Spender includes the identical theme – the fireman relating his own experience of the Blitz – in his autobiography *World Within World*, and 'literary' description is seen as the most inherent means the self has of formulating its congruity to the world:

One man, Ned, had a secret cause of shame. He could not read or write. For this reason, he was never asked to keep the log. Ned had an energetic face full of expression, particularly in the large brown eyes and the mouth like a tense bow. Because of his illiteracy he was the only man in the station who told the truth about his fire-fighting experiences. The others had almost completely substituted descriptions which they read in the newspapers or heard on the wireless for their own impressions. 'Cor mate, at the docks it was a bleeding inferno,' or 'Just then Jerry let hell loose on us,' were the formulae into which experiences such as wading through streams of molten sugar, or being stung by a storm of sparks from burning pepper, or inundated with boiling tea at the dock fires, had been reduced. But Ned had read no accounts of his experiences and so he could describe them vividly.[65]

'Literary' descriptions are modes of representation that can avail themselves of stereotypes, among which the novel is only the most fully comprehensive source of order: 'With the closing down of football – a leading peace-time talk topic – the war was also much talked about in terms of the sports news.'[66]

Despite his bid for a hard-won sagacity, Roe's own attempt to 'get the whole thing' is a self-conscious move toward accuracy that only reverts to another stereotype, the supposititious faith-fulness of documentary. With its first-person directness, it is unavoidably reminiscent of the multitude of testimonials pub-lished in a hurry only months after the first Blitz. Dy considers the result is a rather sedentary performance: 'how very dull his description was . . . this inadequate description . . . there was nothing in what he had spoken to catch her imagination' (pp. 177–8). What her imagination is 'caught' by is a commonplace 'literary' image: ' "Our taxi was like a pink beetle drawing a peppercorn" . . . the bit about the beetle had drawn her attention because she thought it vivid' (p. 179).

According to the omniscient author, 'It had not been like that at all' (pp. 176 and 180). But the scheduled account of what it had been like is drenched with a violent assortment of colour that the text can barely hold:

This fan, a roaring red gold, pulsed rose at the outside edge, the perimeter round which the heavens, set with stars before fading into utter blackness, were for a space a trembling green. (p. 177)

What he had seen was a broken, torn-up dark mosaic aglow with rose where square after square of timber had been burned down to embers, while beyond the distant yellow flames toyed joyfully with the next black stacks which softly merged into the pink of that night. (p. 180)

This polychromatic density is a systematic derangement of the perspicuousness of an *eye-witness* account:

A barge, overloaded with planks, drifted in flames across the black, green, then mushroom skin river water under an upthrusting mountain of fox-dyed smoke that pushed up towards the green pulsing fringe of heaven. (p. 182)

The prismatic style exceeds the range of 'literary' description by the sheer exorbitance of its effects, disconcerting the ambition of clear reportage. Its intensity is girded in with brackets, which aggravate the discordancy between two competing idioms. This element of discomposure was reinforced by an extensive strain of violent abuse and obscenity in the dialogue, lost to the published version but unadulterated in the typescript.

Although Roe can lay claim to some shrewdness in his recognition that 'one's imagination is so literary', he only alleges this; in fact his perceptiveness is obscuring another kind of misapprehension: 'He had been talking to her as though she was her dead sister' (p. 174). He is evidently still trying to create a future memory, re-adapting the image of his wife, so that the past 'will have integrated'. Unconscious of his own manoeuvre, he stalks up and down the length of the garden, even though Dy has planned a walk beyond it: 'Now they were coming to that stile again. She wondered if she could get him out of this beastly decaying place' (p. 184).[67] In the typescript, Dy the wife appreciates that 'the garden was not the proper place. She made up her mind that if he seemed to be getting upset she would take him off to bed at once' (TS, p. 335). He becomes aware of the garden, and of the fact that it no longer affects him in the same way, once he has effectively misconstrued the past by alternative means:

He had forgotten his wife.

Even when, twelve months later, he had begun to forget raids, and when, in the substation, they went over their experiences from an unconscious wish to recreate, night after night in the wet canteen, even then he found he could not go back to his old daydreams about this place. It had come to seem out of date. (p. 178)

This is a further example of disremembering – the other side of 'glossification': 'to be unable to remember anything much (with no wish to do so)'. Roe is only converting his memory into a different form on the same level of tolerance. The narrative culminates in a display of damaging aggression:

> 'God damn you,' he shouted, releasing everything, 'you get on my bloody nerves, all you bloody women with all your talk.'
> It was as though he had gone for her with a hatchet. She went off without a word, rigid.
> He felt a fool at once and, in spite of it, that he had got away at last. Then his son came up, gravely looked at him.
> He said to Christopher, for the first time:
> 'Get out,' and he added,
> 'Well, anyway, leave me alone till after tea, can't you?' (p. 196)

In this aspect, Roe's character illustrates how the self is regulated on the axis described with a rather sinister pragmatism by the editors of Mass-Observation: 'In order to conduct a war thoroughly, we must then turn certain passive feelings into active feelings, and externalize violent hatreds which are ordinarily turned inwards within civilized individuals in this country.'[68] Roe does understand that something is lacking, that despite his avowed intentions, he is simply unable to *know* any means of communicating the truth of his experience:

> 'Yet I suppose it was not like that at all really. One changes everything after by going over it.'
> 'But the real thing . . . is the picture you carry in your eye afterwards, surely? It can't be what you can't remember, can it?'
> 'I don't know,' he said, 'only the point about a blitz is this, there's always something you can't describe, and it's not the blitz alone that's true of. Ever since it happened I feel I've been trying to express all sorts of things.' (pp. 179–80)

What he needs, and what is at work in the text, is a method of *historization*, a practice which gives him charge of his own history by de-rationalizing the environment from within which he is unable to countenance any reformation of the self by a perverse activity. Historization disperses the fog of 'wishful thinking'. It is the reverse of those practices governed by the provision of meaning after the event, materially exceeding the integrity of such forms in the effort to forget them. The 'idiom of the time', instead of directing the self to be paralysed by a fixed memory of past turning points, reintroduces these to the creative life of the self by its future purpose of freedom, the intense desire of otherness. It actuates a theoretically limitless chain of recurrent intensities, sets up a 'trancitive' movement of reading which allows for the constant possibility of a historization.

5 *Loving:*
a fabulous apparatus

After the London Blitz of *Caught*, *Loving* is set in a country house in Ireland; the contrast between the two locales – which is virtually that of the difference between pastoral and anti-pastoral – is almost immediately established: 'For this was in Eire where there is no blackout' (p. 5). This is the first indication of an unseen, but not unheard, background of war against which the conduct of affairs inside Kinalty is called in question. When Raunce's Albert struggles over his options during a picnic by the sea, a very precise alterity makes him see the landscape not in terms of natural features but bluntly as 'Ireland', conceptually opposed to 'England': 'For answer he rolled over onto his stomach and faced inland, all Ireland flat on a level with his clouded eyes' (p. 131); 'He turned over onto his stomach again, facing Ireland' (p. 135). The principal challenge to the Irish life is the implied duty of each member of the household to return to England for war-work: a challenge which is doubly intrusive since nearly all the servants are English.

But a duty towards what, exactly, or to whom? However winning its ways as a novel, however lustrous its texture and cunning its narrative shifts, *Loving* is unignorably set in a household which is organized along certain lines, which has certain relations of power. Does the implied duty of each member of the household involve preserving, or changing, the kinds of social relations which it represents?

The new and energetic commitment on a national level is lacking in definition unless it bears with it an understanding of the distribution of interests in society, and a key to that understanding is found through examining the Country House; as one investigator of the 'Country House Ideal' in the literary tradition has it: 'All but the largest provincial cities were under the wing of the lord of the manor. The network of such families and houses, spread over the face of England, might be thought to represent the greater part of English society.'[1] The network survived, and in one respect, the Irish Country House was a more uncompromising version of the English case, since the isolating of an English household had the effect of allowing its peculiar structure to become more prominent and vivid. Elizabeth Bowen, who was born into the landed gentry of Ireland, describes the 'intense, centripetal life' of the Irish house: 'Come on round the last turn of its avenue, or unexpectedly seen down a stretch of lawn, any one of these houses – with its rows of dark windows set in the light façade against dark trees – has the startling meaning and abstract clearness of a house in a print.'[2] This is a visual impression of self-declaration, but the same characteristics apply in a description of the social abstractness of the same house:

The land around Bowen's Court, even under its windows, has an unhumanized air the house does nothing to change. Here are, even, no natural features, view or valley, to which the house may be felt to relate itself. It has set, simply, its pattern of trees and avenues on the virgin, anonymous countryside. Like Flaubert's ideal book about nothing, it sustains itself on itself by the inner force of its style.[3]

The force of style is never enough in *Loving*. Kinalty Castle is filled with the results of an excessive pretension to a Poynton-like project of self-sustainment. The effect is one of overweight:

'Why my cluster ring Violet,' she said going over to an imitation pint measure also in gilded wood and in which peacock's feathers were arranged. She lifted this off the white marble mantelpiece that was a triumph of sculptured reliefs depicting on small plaques various unlikely animals, even in one instance a snake, sucking milk out of full udders and then she blew at it delicately through pursed lips. (p. 205)

The snake is singled out, and it certainly could be emblematic of the unnatural, even parasitic vainglory of the decoration. Actual physical contact with the artefacts seems to produce ever more bizarre instances of 'the magnificence and the gilt':

Edith . . . steadied herself round a turn of the Grand Staircase by holding the black hand of a life-sized negro boy of cast iron in a great red turban and in gold-painted clothes. (p. 112)

Then she reached for the latch which was a bullock's horn bound in bronze. (p. 169)

She replaced into its niche a fly-whisk carved out of a block of sandalwood, the handle enamelled with a reddish silver. (p. 207)

There is a virtual abuse of natural materials in displays of pointless artifice; organic materials, surrounded by this over-ripe decoration, can only achieve diminished growth: 'Charley went straight over to a red mahogany sideboard that was decorated with a swan at either end to support the top on each long curved neck. In the centre three ferns were niggardly growing in gold Worcester vases' (p. 14). The rose, which had been transformed almost into flesh in *Caught*, is present here in the shrivelled petals of a pot-pourri, 'the dry bones of roses' (p. 61). The disharmony is finally grotesque in a counterpoint between needless ostentation and what is literally the call of nature: 'Michael ran forward to catch Punch's droppings before these could fall on the gravel which he had raked over that very morning' (p. 31). Even the owner of the house is like a display item or curio, remarkable for gaudy plumage like the two hundred or more peacocks (status symbols since antiquity)[4] which stalk through the grounds: 'She had moved over to the open window with this man's wife and stuck her rather astounding head with its blue-washed silver hair out into the day, as though she were a parrot embarrassed at finding itself not tied to a perch and which had turned its back on the cage' (p. 187). The dovecote which is a model of the Leaning Tower of Pisa, and the ludicrous reproduction in 'jagged cement' of a ruined classical temple give the extravagance a visual association of precariousness, perhaps hubris, easily disposed to co-ordinate with a moral flimsiness.

The house has neither the aura of style, nor the humanized aura of a Howards End. In the terms of the Country House Ideal, specifically of Ben Jonson's poem 'To Penshurst', it is an example of 'envious show'. Its neglect of the culture from which it stands aloof is not easily offset by the kind of self-absorption which is so attractive to Evelyn Waugh: 'More even than the work of the great architects, I loved buildings that

grew silently with the centuries, catching and keeping the best
of each generation, while time curbed the artist's pride and the
Philistine's vulgarity, and repaired the clumsiness of the dull
workman.'[5] Waugh adds a touch of antagonism to the aura
which comes from patrician continuity. Elizabeth Bowen
silently neglects the question of community in order to preserve
the wistful appeal of this idea: 'What runs on most through a
family living in one place is a continuous, semi-physical dream.'[6]
But in the Country House Ideal this continuity is the prior
basis for direct involvement with the community; it is a social
role, not an unproblematical aura, that emerges from 'the
succession of the title from holder to holder while the property
each is steward of remains the same. The effect of Jonson's
powerful imagination is to turn the material basis, as the
Marxists would say, into a spiritual idea, an image of the good
life.'[7]

Without this continuity, the Tennants hold their position by
an empty prerogative. As the name suggests, there is no profound link between the family and the estate, and their tenure
is of the most superficial kind; they are interested in the
material basis to the precise detriment of the spiritual idea:

'Did Jack's stepfather live here much before he died?'
'Edward would never be away from the place when he first
rented it,' Mrs. Tennant replied. 'But once he bought outright he
seemed to tire.' (p. 187)

Within the family itself the line of succession (from stepfather
to stepson) is not absolutely clear, and there seems barely a
chance of its security in future: ' "I look on myself simply as a
steward. We could shut Kinalty up tomorrow and go and live in
one of the cottages. But if I once did that would your darlings
ever be able to live here again? I wonder" ' (pp. 186–7). A
handful of narrative indiscretions give us the ultimate fate of the
house – destruction by fire, like Poynton – but the heritage on
offer is in any case no more than merely property, without the
greater privileges and responsibilities of the role that Jonson
almost hallows by its tenure of 'the mysteries of manners,
armes, and arts': 'Jonson . . . sees the country house as
performing an integrating service in society, as the focus of a
culture based on the countryside.'[8] The centre-piece of Kinalty's

spectacular vacuousness is a complete travesty of this culture based on the countryside, a 'fabulous dairy of a drawing room'. Under a vaulted roof, 'painted to represent the evening sky at dusk', articles of everyday farmyard use are translated into priceless bric-à-brac: 'As she rubbed the shoulder of her husband's mother she was surrounded by milking stools, pails, clogs, the cow byre furniture all in gilded wood which was disposed around to create the most celebrated eighteenth-century folly in Eire that had still to be burned down' (p. 203). The house itself stands metaphorically for the spoliation of a culture based on the surrounding countryside. In this same 'fabulous dairy', the plaque of a snake sucking milk out of full udders suggests a spiritually toxic return for material drains on the community. The workmanship is not even indigenous ' "It's all French you know." '[9] An article like the hammock 'fashioned out of gold wire' or the pitchfork, 'a gold instrument . . . a museum piece', is the symbolic token of sucking gain from the host body of peasant life, an extreme parody of the ideal coexistence found in poems of the Country House tradition: 'These poets see the country house as accommodating a cross-section of the whole community. Society is hierarchically conceived, but in the country house this stratification seems to mean not segregation, but familiar contact between different levels of an ostensibly integrated community.'[10] Far from being integrated, the Kinalty community is absolutely divided: ' "We're really in enemy country here you know" ' (p. 11). The Tennants see themselves as on a war-footing, but opposed to the element with which they ought to be maintaining familiar contact: ' "But in a way I regard this as my war work, maintaining the place I mean. Because we're practically in enemy country here you know and I do consider it so important from the morale point of view to keep up appearances" ' (p. 186). The 'morale' endorsed here rides on the general sense of an appeal for solidarity but its application is narrower than that. Mrs Tennant interprets her duty to be 'keeping up appearances'; in the context of a nationally invoked defence of a way of life, war-work is seen as the upkeep of envious show in danger from a lack of the right sort of education. Familiar contact is replaced by a violent disassociation from enforced ignorance; the real threat is the invasion of the ramshackle,

and the defence which is down is the 'ruined wall which shut
this demesne from tumble-down country outside' (p. 29). The
Tennants are equally remote from their own servants – ' "What
do we know about the servants?" ' (p. 187) – whom they
regard with the same degree of contempt: ' "Whether it's never
having been educated or whether it's just plain downright
stupidity I don't know" ' (p. 183). But the English servants
themselves are hostile to their native counterparts: ' "Gawd
save us from 'em, they're foreigners after all" ' (p. 177). And
in fact their phobic rejection of the Irish is a good deal more
hysterical; an Irishman will live in a 'pig sty of a hovel' (p.
141), the instrument of an altogether unacceptable religion:

> 'No Roman Catholics thank you,' Miss Swift said sharp.
> 'Yes,' Miss Burch agreed, 'we don't want those fat priests about
> confessin' people or taking snuff.' (p. 123)

Neither servants nor employers can interpret the Irish accent of
'sibilants and gutturals' (only Kate bridges the gap – only
through affection for Paddy). The situation is virtually colonial,
social disparity being governed by the conflict between a
language of dominance and a language of subjection, and Mrs
Tennant's detachment from the Irish – ' "But my dear it's not
for us to understand O'Conor" ' (p. 207) – is simply a more
acute degree of the exclusion practised on her own servants.

The inequality of English-speakers and Irish-speakers is
blatant; and the social order is maintained through generaliza-
tions of the same prejudicial principle, being geared by an
unwilled consensus to the knowledge of certain practices with
the limits set upon them – demanding the possession of an
elected language where the acquisition of (limited) power is
the outcome of learning to read it. This is taken quite literally
when Raunce captures the black and red notebooks which
reveal how to operate the system of fiddles and perks: 'By
keeping open a Cellar Diary which had also to be shown each
month to Mrs. Tennant and by comparing the two, he was
able to refer from one to the other. Thus much that would
otherwise have been obscure became plain' (p. 42). The Irish
themselves – especially those with an inside view – are soon
adepts in the same manner of exploiting the Tennants:

One hundred donkey cart loads of washed gravel from Michael's brother's pit had been ordered at Michael's suggestion to freshen the rutted drive where this turned inward across the ha-ha. Gravel sold by Michael's brother Patrick and carted by Danny his mother's other son who had thought to stop at the seventy ninth load the donkey being tired after it was understood that Mrs. Tennant would be charged for the full hundred. (p. 31)

Social transactions are in the worst faith. Eldon, whom Raunce succeeds as butler, had had his greatest success in blackmail, having 'touched the Captain for larger and larger amounts'. The free exchange of products common to the Country House poems is replaced by outright extortion: ' "She's been over to lunch many a time since and he'll have had the old dropsy out of her" ' (p. 34). From within a circuit of unnatural retention – 'dropsy' – Raunce is notably aggressive as he forwards the gains to his mother: 'As he licked the envelope after putting in the Money Order he squinted a bit wild, and this was shocking with his two different-coloured eyes' (p. 35).

A reciprocity of greed is the illustration of a concern not to inculpate a particular agent, but to uncover the institutional basis. The house itself is a vast, impersonal monitor in which everyone is under surveillance, and Eldon's blackmail is only the most obvious exercise of betrayal when it requires no effort for any member of the household to inform on all the others.

There is an atmosphere of oppressive perspicuousness, a general recognition of being exposed to scrutiny: 'The passage carpet was so thick you never could hear anyone coming' (p. 19). The house could have been planned for a maximum ease of surveillance, and its inhabitants always consider how audible they are: 'Before going on Miss Burch waited until Raunce, who was leaving Mrs. Jack's room, should be out of earshot' (p. 21); ' "The old cow," Charley remarked once she was out of earshot' (p. 69). Ruled by a pretence of the uncounted moment, they will drop the voice or soften its tone, creating a climate of hugger-mugger. Edith is typically obsessed, with her repeated enjoinder to 'Hush . . . someone'll hear.'

It is as if each person is subject to an irresistible, invisible gaze coming from an unspecified coign of vantage. When one is not being physically watched one still behaves as if one is: 'He paused to look over his shoulder with his hand on a leaping salmon trout in gilt before pressing this lever to go in. There was no one. Nevertheless he spoke back the way he had come. "They'll break it," he said aloud as though in explanation . . .' (p. 62). This is evidence of an unbroken submission to the controlling gaze. Raunce has to answer for his every movement: ' "It was about your ring Madam," he went on taking his time. He gazed at her as though hypnotized' (p. 170). Mrs Tennant exercises that kind of power, but the ultimate power of the eye is in the hypnosis of institutions. Under supervision, the only means of self-assertion is to establish a vantage-point of one's own: 'Mrs. Welch moved over to perforated iron which formed a wall of the larder, advanced one eye to a hole and grimly watched' (p. 50). The household regulates itself on the principle of trying to see and hear without being seen or heard, (' "with that mad Irishman with his ear to every keyhole" '). Everyone adopts a superintendent role in the hope of transferring suspicion from himself to another: ' "Yes," she went on dark, "I've watched their thievin'. Raunce an' that Edith. Not to mention Kate with what she gets up to . . . As I've witnessed times without number from me larder windows" ' (p. 168). Mrs Welch (whose name is indicative of treachery)[11] provides the most active examples of a common need to inform on others. This need is almost openly competitive:

'It was Albert told my young ladies. That little bastard had it from Mrs. Welch. There's no other word to describe the lad.' (p. 195)

'It was young Albert again who else? I promise I never told 'im nothin'. I wouldn't do such a thing. And then in addition Mr. Raunce went and informed about that peacock Mrs. Welch had in the larder . . .' (p. 196)

The mutual treachery is not serving special interests; there is no advantage to the ruling class, and in fact the most spectacular failure in survivorship is Mrs Jack: 'Hearing this from inside the room Mrs. Jack cowered, put a trembling hand over her lips, and pushed the tray to one side' (p. 84). If she is indeed the most thoroughly demoralized person in the book, this is not entirely due to fear of concerted action by the servants; she is equally apprehensive about the manoeuvres of Mrs

Tennant, whose assumption of the overseeing role is certainly the most self-conscious to be found: ' "I shall get to the bottom of it," Mrs. Tennant announced. For an instant she sent a grim smile at her daughter-in-law's back. "I shall bide my time though," she said, then quietly left that chamber the walls of which were hung with blue silk. Mrs. Jack swung round but the room was empty' (p. 207). But in spite of her sinister faculty for having the edge on everyone else, Mrs Tennant is prone to the same anxieties herself: ' "That is to say what I really came for was to ask your advice," Mrs. Tennant countered, looking again to make sure the kitchen door was shut' (p. 178). And of course her suspicions are well-founded because on the far side of the door 'Jane and Mary went crimson outside, began to giggle' (p. 180).

It is clearly impossible – for members of either class – to infiltrate to anything like sanctioned power. And in fact there is no essential potency that could be obtained and directed; at best one can negotiate a position of advantage within the apparatus that maintains itself without respect for office. Specific agents are even occasionally obscured, as if to dilate a sense of menacing impersonality: ' "Now you girls hurry with that washing up," said the dreadful voice . . .' (p. 37). This minatory premonition is disembodied, out of nowhere. In fact it stems from the pathetic and farcical alcoholism of Mrs Welch.

The most forceful image of pre-emptive surveillance is provided by the weathervane: 'This was fixed on top of the tower and turned with a wind in the usual way. Where it differed from similar appliances was that Mr. Tennant had had it connected to a pointer which was set to swing over a large map of the country round about elaborately painted over the mantelpiece' (p. 43). This is the remaining sense in which the house is a focus for the surrounding countryside; the weathervane with its map is like a symbolic panopticon – it suggests an absolute capability of observation which nothing escapes: 'As Charley stood there it so happened that the pointer was fixed unwavering E.S.E. with the arrow tip exactly on Clancarty, Clancarty which was indicated by two nude figures male and female recumbent in gold crowns' (p. 43). Charley is surprised in this attitude by Mrs Jack, disadvantaged by the conditions which make for ease of surveillance: 'The carpets were so deep Raunce did not hear her.' But Mrs Jack does not keep the advantage, she is in turn the victim of surveillance by her supposition that the two nude figures represent her lover and herself. The subject is exposed to the point of nakedness; Raunce later refers to the Army Detention Barracks as a 'glass 'ouse' and this term projects the sense of total visibility into a frankly penal context. The function of one institution is liable to bear directly on that of another through the conspicuousness of its subjects:

'It's wicked the way they spy on you.'
'They've been raised in a good school,' he remarked. (p. 223)

Any aptitude recognized by an institution is one that will ensure the reproduction of its own forms of containment and superintendence; it is worth remembering the controlled regimes of the schools in *Pack my Bag* and *Concluding*.

Of course, the strongest point of surveillance is in its connection with property; the servants are taken aback by the arrival of Mike Mathewson, an 'enquiry agent' for the Irish Regina Assurance. Raunce mistakes the initial letters of this company for those of the Irish Republican Army, but it's all the same – the methods of coercion and manipulation are transposable from one organization to another. Meanwhile, not even the professional operative can avoid the usual discomfort: 'He came quiet and Mike Mathewson did not hear him' (p. 148). Much play is later made of the 'inthinuations' made by Mathewson; his lisp is an attempt at guilelessness which fails to conceal a clear implication of the word, that all surveillance is inherently deceitful: indirect, devious, winding, it is like the treacherous serpent in the Garden of Eden, linked with the original crime of 'loving'.

Surveillance intends a systematic coverage of eventualities: ' "Holy Moses look at the clock," he went on, "ten to three and me not on me bed. Come on look slippy" ' (p. 8). The characters are obsessed with the strict observance of a code of conduct by which experience is completely covered. Raunce adheres to this system with a paranoid determination: ' "I'm going to get the old head down, it's me siesta. And don't forget to give us a call sharp on four thirty" ' (p. 9). The success of coverage depends on a segregation of functions;

emphasis is laid on the cellular structure of the household. It is divided into 'kingdoms', with dominant characters holding sway in each 'kingdom'.

One and all, they are sensitive to the conflicting spheres of influence, and to the 'no man's land' in between: 'He went out, shutting the mahogany door without a sound. After twenty trained paces he closed a green baize door behind him. As it clicked he called out . . .' (p. 8). Among the servants, a premium is set on having 'a place you can call your own' (p. 121). On the ocular model offered by surveillance, the household is organized along the lines of perspective within which nothing has meaning or presence except with regard to fixed co-ordinates. In effect, the moment surveillance makes itself felt, the subject adapts to the line of sight: 'Right to the last meal Mr. Eldon had taken in this room it had been his part to speak, to wind up as it were, almost to leave the impress of a bishop on his flock. This may have been what led Charley to echo in a serious tone . . .' (p. 34). Raunce is accepted once he adapts himself to a fixed point, within the perspective, known as 'butler': 'In this way for the first time she seemed to recognize his place' (p. 34).

The vital irrelevance to these concerns is the love-affair between Raunce and Edith; but even here, Edith's seduction is bound up with a capitulation to 'place':

'Well even if you can't tell whether you're comin' or goin' I know the way I'm placed thank you.'
'Look dear I could fall for you in a big way,' he said and he saw her back stiffen as though she had begun to hear with intense attention . . .
'You tell that to them all Charley.' (p. 110)

The first thing Edith wants when love has been declared is to make it improve her standing with the others. Despite her obvious concern for Raunce's health, she encourages him to sit in the Red Library, out of a hankering for 'place': 'She seemed to have no thought to the draught' (p. 141). It is the proper setting to stage a married scene.

The Raunce and Edith affair is secretive and improper, a misalliance in terms of the dispensation that supports itself by methodically reconnoitring. The ruling perspective will only prevail by conferring on its subjects the visibility of 'place'. The institution has first to attract the imagination it needs to restrain:[12]

> 'I've got no hold on your old imagination, not yet I haven't.'
> 'What d'you mean not yet?'
> 'I mean after we're married,' she whispered, her voice gone husky. 'After we're married I'll see to it that you don't have no imagination. I'll make everything you want of me now so much more than you ever dreamed that you'll be quit imaginin' for the rest of your life.' (p. 191)

With the marriage threshold crossed, the expanding horizon of promise will contract; and this re-definition of boundaries means that passion is outlawed. At first encouraged to speak, it is now enjoined to silence, within the same co-ordinates of moral blackmail that will tolerate a mutual exploitation of classes. Legality becomes a function of discretion: ' "But there's no place for valuables like this object," he went on. "You've got to see that dear. Why you'd gum up the whole works" ' (p. 128). The absolute priority is always the *efficiency* of a system. It simplifies the running of the household if Raunce is dubbed 'Arthur', 'as every footman from the first had been called' (p. 8). Once he is promoted to butler he regains his own name, but the very facility of the change emphasizes how a servant's being given a new name is a form of recognizing only his function, which arrogates his real self. The whole business is a matter of caprice to Mrs Tennant: ' "I don't like that name." Her voice had taken a teasing note. "I think we shall have to change it don't you?" ' (p. 21). On the other side, the servants find some revenge in reducing her to a cipher: 'Mrs. T'.

Points of unease occur to withstand the efficiency mandate when Raunce's Albert periodically gives way to fits of shaking and trembling. Where demeanour is so fully circumscribed, evident resistance like this seems forestalled; critical excitement is glossed as the admission of guilt, but not only that – it is also the effect of actually suffering it. Mrs Jack demonstrates the working of this double bind in her blatant diversions and displacements, trying to counter the supervision of Mrs Tennant:

> 'Was it the beginning or the end of June Jack wrote that he expected to get leave? . . . I'm so glad for you both. It's been such a long time. I expect you'll go to London of course.'

'Simply look at the daffodils,' her daughter-in-law exclaimed. (p. 24)

'When d'you think he'll let you know dear?'
Mrs. Jack showed irritation. 'No Badger no,' she said. On being spoken to the dog made as if to leap up at her. 'Down damn you,' she said. (p. 25)

Under these conditions of knowledge – the cult of accountability – no offered resistance would be possible except in the role of scapegoat. The consequential, foreshortened action has to resort to subterfuges like the conspicuously blank face: exchanges take place 'with no change in expression', 'without a flicker', 'from an expressionless face', 'without a sign of any kind'. The self-effacing is intended to prove an adaptation to the controlling gaze; it is the alibi for efficiency, and as such is singled out by Mrs Tennant, ironically in praise of Mrs Jack: ' "your contemporaries have all got this amazing control of yourselves. Never showing I mean. So I just wanted to say once more if I never say it again. Violet dear I think you are perfectly wonderful and Jack's a very lucky man" ' (p. 203).

But there is no easily made distinction between a tactical self-negation and the full identification with a conferred role; as long as the self must answer to a constantly required adaptability along the lines of ruling perspectives, the most 'efficient' activity is going to be *mimicry*.

There are very few situations in which one character does not imitate another: Moira and Kate 'quote' Nanny Swift while Edith 'quotes' Miss Burch; towards the end of the book, Edith is 'beginning to speak like' Raunce (p. 219) while he 'quotes' the mannerisms of Mathewson; Raunce even mimics himself: ' "You leave all the brainwork to your old man. Lucky Charley they call him," he said in a threadbare return to his usual manner' (p. 224). This example confirms that the aim of mimicry is not the projection of a counterfeit image but the retroactive insertion of the mimic in a given situation or function:

The boy looked speechless at him.
'Oh get on with your work,' Raunce quoted from another context. (p. 58)

Albert's speechless look is an accusation, the model of surveillance; against it Raunce repeats the form of Mrs Jack's resistance
to his own surveillance: ' "Oh get on with your work," she
said appearing to lose control and half ran out.' (p. 44)

Mimicry is the systematic extension of the 'picturing'
exposed in *Caught*; it is even more easily the guarantee of cheap
meaning, abandoning the personalized image, conceding everything for the sake of coming to terms with a disjointed self. It is
rooted in the principle of coverage; no matter what the outcome, mimicry provides a safe transition in terms of knowledge
from one coverage to another. Edith imitates Miss Burch in
her aspiration to 'place':

And because Miss Burch was still indisposed Edith as though by
right took this woman's place at table.
'Well what are we waiting for?' she asked quite natural in
Agatha's manner. (p. 208)

The function by which Miss Burch can be expressed is given
as a language which it is possible to master. Correspondingly,
Miss Burch can be imagined apart from her function when its
language is dropped: ' "'E's puttin' 'is shirt on," was all Miss
Burch said, shocked into dropping her aitches' (p. 76). The
same is true for Miss Tancy; it only needs Raunce to overhear
her 'momentary brogue' (p. 31) for Albert to be told on her
next visit to 'Put 'er in the Red Library an' don't leave till I
come or something might go missing' (p. 144).

Nearly all the characters join in the imitation of Mike
Mathewson; but his mode of delivery is already a form of
camouflage. The dialogue in general proceeds by substituting
one language for another out of the many distributed throughout
the text. By deliberately lisping, Mathewson proposes that his
character is readable – he asks to be included in a function of
harmlessness: ' "Jutht had a tooth out that'th why I thpeak
like thith" ' (p. 146). But although he is suggesting his potency
has been removed (his bark is worse than his bite), he is also
the official 'enquiry agent' and strongly reminiscent of the
'house-detective' with a fluctuating accent in *Party Going*. The
house-detective had seemed to have a special relationship with
death, and Mathewson certainly interrupts the proposal of
marriage like a symbolic interdiction of desire. His arrival is
timed to reflect on Edith's later assumption of the lisp:

'Oh give us a kiss do,' he begged.

'If you behave yourthelf,' she said. (p. 192)

This is the occasion when she tantalizes Raunce with the idea of exhausting his imagination; simply by lisping she inserts herself in a function of manipulation.

Edith provides the most forcible outlet for 'loving', but she can also be the means of 'loving's' degeneration into a social attitude which presupposes the existence of 'calf love', a sedative function marked by association with 'indifference': 'She seemed altogether indifferent' (p. 132); ' "Now Albert," Edith remarked indifferent' (p. 133); ' "Just let 'im be," Edith said indifferent' (p. 136). Kate is on hand to reinstate the erotic imperative: ' "Calf love you call that? Why you talk like you was your young lady. We got no time for calf love dear as you call it. We're ordinary workin' folk . . ." ' (p. 139). An implicit violence of feeling is at odds here with its own conversion into a standard excitement and a moderate betrayal of 'reasonable' behaviour. The same corruption makes Mrs Welch behave 'like an established favourite' (p. 116). And Mrs Jack regains the favour of Mrs Tennant with the act of 'a spoiled child' (p. 185).

The most protean exponent of mimicry is Raunce (his variability is reflected in his differently coloured eyes), but his repertoire seems anchored by the accents of Mrs Welch's Albert: ' "I tell you this won't do," he answered. "Put'm back where you found'm" ' (p. 127). When Raunce senses he might be placed in a 'criminal' situation, he resorts to imitating Albert. Just as the name 'Arthur' is synonymous with 'footman', so 'Albert' is absorbed into a definite meaning; Mrs Welch and Mrs Tennant can discuss 'Albert's' crimes referring to two different boys because they are interchangeable in a function of criminality for which 'Albert' is simply the name.

Albert the proletarian evacuee is also the 'invader': ' "Children is all little 'Itlers these days . . . the little storm trooper" ' (p. 47). Evacuation is the real threat to privilege; it brings the dissolution of boundaries between existing orders of society (Miss Evelyn begins to speak 'with a trace of cockney accent', p. 111).

The evacuee is regarded as the criminal counterpart of the guest made unwelcome in a situation deplored by the Country

House poems: ' "There's one thing about evacuees," he said. "No matter what the homes are they've come from they're like fiends straight up from hell honey after they've been a month or more down in the country districts . . ." ' (p. 174). Albert certainly does seem to portend the destruction of envious show, throttling 'one out of above two hundred' peacocks (p. 47).

But he is also the principal informer; and this makes the point that criminality is not tied to specific acts or agents, it is an effect produced by a generalized mechanism of surveillance of which there is no inside knowledge – the most effective informers are the innocent:

> 'I must tell Miss Evelyn and Miss Moira.'
> 'That's been the cause of half the trouble in this place. Once they get hold of something it's taken right out of control.'
> 'But it wouldn't be right. Why they're innocent.'
> "Ow d'you mean innocent?' he enquired. 'There's a lot we could lay to their door.' (p. 226)

Raunce, in describing Mrs Welch as a 'diabolical mason' (p. 218), pays tribute to the sense in which everyone is under suspicion, victimized simply through being in the line of sight of a masonic conspiracy to which there are no initiates: ' "But detethtable's right. It is detestable and distasteful if you like, to have been put through what we've been as if we were criminals," he said' (p. 210). Raunce employs the words of Mathewson, but mimicking the accents of power to ridicule its hold over them immediately removes him to a defensive stance, that of 'criminal'.

The text itself appears to be organized in terms of 'efficiency'. At least, it requires the author to efface himself, and this destitute figure is the blank face of writing; the narrative inserts itself directly in the language of the characters, giving the adverb an adjectival form, substituting for a proper noun the argot usage (a cup of 'you-and-me'). The viewpoint of 'author' is merely incidental to an overall perspective: 'So she sat down alongside him although this must have seemed rather noticeable, seeing that it was nearly time to start work' (p. 161). Apart from the author, who is not entirely sure, 'it' in this context can only be 'noticeable' to a general function of surveillance.

When the stance of an author *can* be identified, it is under the aspect of a *locum tenens* – of a callow deputy who overvalues the badge of office: ' "I'm fed up with you," Mrs. Welch said to her Albert at this precise moment . . .' (p. 91); 'At this precise moment out of the dovecote . . .' (p. 146). This pedantic assertiveness alternates with a sense of lame authority, marked by frequent interpolations of the qualifiers 'perhaps' and 'probably'. Self-confidence reverts to insipidity – or fatuous certainty (with qualifiers like 'obviously'). Narrative abandons its power of registration; although 'Raunce looked for the person Edith said she had heard' (p. 46), it is a fact that Edith *said* no such thing, she only behaved 'as though she could hear somebody'. The account only awkwardly determines the extent of its own self-knowledge: 'So nobody saw this car drive up but Edith. She noted in it *not the lady above referred to* but a stranger, a man, a grey homburg hat' (p. 144, my emphasis).

The authorial function is largely taken up with the labour of deduction: 'On which she must have recognized that he was naked' (p. 76); 'It must have been she could not help herself' (p. 86); 'But she must have understood' (p. 89); 'This must have been a reference to the fact . . .' (p. 201). It is as though the author will only risk himself in interpretation based on the accruements of surveillance, of what is accountable because it can be *seen*: 'They stood looking down and from the droop of her shoulders it could be assumed that her rage had subsided' (p. 129). This paranoid cautiousness would suggest that some sort of reputation is at stake: 'Also there was a rainbow from the sun on a shower blowing in from the sea *but you could safely say* she took no notice' (p. 84, my emphasis). The author suffers to an equal degree the sense of insecurity which dogs the characters; he is enrolled in the text *where it is turned towards the light,* subject to a controlling gaze that will insert him in his function; what the text is producing is the *mimicry* of an author.

On the other side – what can be thought of as the dark side – of the text, there is a corresponding intensity of covert action. The characters themselves experience a clandestine urge:

Raunce put a finger to his lips . . . Then Miss Evelyn and Miss Moira each put a finger to their mouths, as they went on bowing to each other . . . They saw Kate and Edith in long purple uniforms bow swaying towards them in soft sunlight through the white budding branches, fingers over lips. Even little Albert copied the gesture back this time . . . (pp. 53–5)

The purpose of this conspiracy is to escape the attention of Miss Swift; as she recites a fairy-tale she represents the narratorial function, but she is deaf, with closed eyes – a retrograde image of the oppressively candid. Secrecy is dependent on the cover of darkness: 'But at the mention of a name and as though they had entered on a conspiracy Edith blocked even more light from that window by climbing on the sill' (p. 22).

Throughout the work of Green, the panoramic aspect of the novel is recognized as a type of despotism; the generation of viewpoints will impound the reader in the stance of 'master of all you see'. It follows that disengagement from the practice of the overbearing text involves confusion of the line of sight, the angle of vision; freedom is synonymous with diffusion or diffraction, or even deliberate obfuscation.

In the schools of *Pack my Bag* and *Concluding* the only resort is sleep, away from the treachery of light coincident with power. *Loving* stresses the position even below the level of its own ability: ' "Miss Swift she come down to have a chat and Jane and me gets out of the light thinking there will be ructions but not a sound come past that closed door not one" ' (p. 36). To be inconspicuous is specifically to be 'out of the light'. The game of blind man's buff, which is after all a mimicry of 'loving', takes place in conditions of 'another darker daylight' and 'before witnesses in bronze in marble and plaster' (p. 117). The writing is slightly out of the way to emphasize a positive advantage – 'witnesses' who do *not* see. In the same order, windows may be disarmed, made 'blind' or 'muted', to demote them from their panoptic role.

In the game of blind man's buff, Edith 'moved her arms as though swimming toward them' (p. 117), and covert action is commonly associated with a sort of watery environment: 'The sky was overcast so that the light was dark as though under water' (p. 38); 'Edith lay still with closed eyes. The room was dark as long weed in the lake' (p. 40); ' "Ah but she's deep our Edith, deep as the lake there" ' (p. 90). These hints add up to a problem; simply retiring from the light is no real opposition, it ultimately inclines to the absolute repose of the inorganic – 'But there were two humps of body, turf over graves under those pink bedclothes' (p. 76) – because absorption with the inorganic offers the only lasting means of resolving what seems an incontrovertible tension: 'Her arm that was stretched white palm upwards along deep green moss struggled to lift itself as though caught on the surface of a morass' (p. 135). This moves in the vicinity of *Party Going*'s equation (after Marvell) of greenness with unity: a nostalgia, moreover, in which one is liable to get 'caught'. Fragments of the image of a drowned girl recur, and are repossessed by the text of *Concluding* (equally reminiscent of Ophelia and of the imagined death by water of Stephen Dedalus's sister).[13] *Loving* is suffused with a measure of fatalism; it succeeds the failure of opposition in kind to surveillance and its debasement of the self. The first page of the text is filled with instances of a regressive decay. The butler, whose name 'Eldon' connotes the sere and antiquated, takes to his deathbed murmuring the name 'Ellen'; this wish for reunification is slyly reinforced by the approximation of the two names. In a similar fashion Kate mutters the name 'Paddy' in her drowsiness connected with inorganic repose ('as though caught on the surface of a morass'). Raunce, whose name connotes the stale and rancid, is described on this first page as a 'pale individual, paler now', having withdrawn to the extent of staying indoors for three years; his pantry boy is 'yellow' and 'looked sick'. At the end of the book, Raunce is reproducing Eldon's symptoms; he is 'noticeably paler even', and 'weak with exhaustion', starting to vomit and to move like an old man. The mimicry is so complete he even calls out Edith's name, using 'exactly that tone Mr. Eldon had employed at the last when calling his Ellen. "Edie" he moaned' (p. 229). There is finally a progressive concentration on his shutting eyes: 'he squinted terribly . . . in a weak voice, with closed eyes . . . He closed his eyes . . . He let his eyelids shut down over his eyes . . .' (pp. 223–8). This form of retreat is the ostrich's answer to surveillance.

Nanny Swift, narrator of the fairy-tale, indulges in the same delusion. Besides being rheumatic she is deaf, and she frequently exploits her deafness; her condition is interesting in view of the personal history of *Jonathan* Swift, another narrator, also based

in Ireland. Swift had Ménière's disease, an affliction of the
inner ear which produces deafness and faulty balance; a connection between the two symptoms is made strongly in *Caught*.
Both Nanny Swift and Richard Roc deploy a sort of veil to
obscure that transparency felt as oppressive. But the infiltration
of decay is general. We are told that Albert's father died of a
cancer, and both Miss Swift and Miss Burch take to their beds;
neither appears except by allusion during the course of the last
fifty pages of the book.

If these massive deteriorations are the symptoms of a retreat
from exposure and control, they are also sheltering under a
more symbolic purpose. Nanny Swift's anecdote of little
Lancelot offers to identify a seat of corruption – Lancelot was
a child of privilege who had something stuck in his gullet: 'It
was as black as pitch' (p. 119).[14] If this is unduly grotesque,
then the peacock's corpse 'swarming with maggots' is even
more demonstrative of a hidden decay that could be linked to
the upkeep of envious show.

The corpse is disinterred by the greyhound 'Badger'; and
this canine retribution borrows the sense of Eliot's figure in
The Waste Land:

> 'That corpse you planted last year in your garden,
> 'Has it begun to sprout? Will it bloom this year?
> 'Or has the sudden frost disturbed its bed?
> 'O keep the Dog far hence, that's friend to men,
> 'Or with his nails he'll dig it up again!'[15]

The peacock is furtively buried, it has sufficient backing as a
symbol of moral declension and as in Eliot, the dog will bring
this to account; the resulting text can give the cliché the
strength of its own concerns:

> 'Would you advise me to have Raunce in and get to the bottom
> of things I mean?' . . .
> 'Not if I were you,' she said. 'Let sleeping dogs lie.' (p. 184)

> 'Then Violet you don't really consider I need do any more?'
> 'Well I don't see why. I'd let sleeping dogs rest.' (p. 185)

Mrs Jack has more to fear from a final reckoning. And there is
every appearance of a final reckoning – closing the book is the
sudden, ominous return of the dog: 'He opened his eyes and
found Badger wagging his tail so hard that he was screwed

right round into a crescent' (p. 228). The writing at this point
is more conducive to Eliot's other, more rhetorical association
of the dog with death as a poetical figure ('Those who sharpen
the tooth of the dog, meaning Death').[16]

But the overwhelming retribution is the fire by which the
house is doomed to destruction: 'For this house that had yet
to be burned down, and in particular that greater part of it
which remained closed, was a shadowless castle of treasures'
(p. 61). The conflagration is augured with a reminder that
Kinalty is a partly disused warehouse of extravagance and
irrelevance. The seasonal drought would be a contributory
factor to fire, but it is noted more than once that 'huge fires
were kept stoked all day to condition the old masters' (p. 141).
If this were the cause of the house burning down, it would give
a physical dimension to the sense in which 'envious show'
leads directly to the extinction of the Country House and its
ideals.

Loving interrogates the residual role of the Country House; and
its implication of unfulfilled responsibilities is set in Ireland –
which is the actual setting of Green's interrogation of his own
responsibilities when faced with the prospect of war.

In the essay 'Before the Great Fire', not published until 1960
and originally intended as the prelude to a factual account of
the London Blitz, Green describes a visit made with his wife to
Ireland on the eve of war: 'My London at war in 1939 begins in
Eire in 1938.'[17] 'Before the Great Fire' opens with a beach
episode as dilatory as could be imagined, but its obliquities
concur with those of *Loving*; there is an erotic tableau provided
by a naked couple, and an old woman 'like a fairy story witch'
(it will be seen how largely a fairy-story element looms in the
earlier text). The presence of the naked couple means that the
beach is 'not this time *untenanted*' (my emphasis). This super-
charge – and its admittance here for casual work – is a good
example of the way Green writes through distending the
circumstantial, across long intervals, working out of a reserve of
textural points.

The essay is comprised of feelings of guilt as the other guests
at the hotel are recalled for active service. Green and his wife
'turn a blind eye, on officers leaving for home and mobilization'.

This voluntary myopia is of course a reaction to prolonged and supposedly hostile observation with the familiar, concomitant threat of betrayal: 'Indeed, as so often at such times, their being the wives of officers made it seem as though they guarded secrets with their virtue and that they might report one if, by ill chance, one asked any sort of a question which might seem to call for a knowledgeable answer.' The pronounced hesitance to identify with the war effort is fed by a disturbing evenness in the way these coercive expectations are found to inform opposite pretexts for war:

What between hope one week, despair the next, it was as if Hitler was at an end of the seesaw, with oneself at the other dominated by the eyes of this maniacal genius with a hypnotic stare out of every published photograph; one would be up one moment, down the next, and completely at the mercy of these ups and downs, with nothing to be done except join one of the Services.

This image concurs with *Party Going*'s see-saw imposition and removal of an obstruction to knowledge; knowledge of the history of the self; knowledge of previous ownership of the self revealed in the act of transference to other ownership, which has the possessiveness of a hypnotic stare. It is the ultimate reference for surveillance as the coefficient of 'duty'. On these terms, the assumption of civic responsibility is a form of mimicry, like opting into a function for which one has been chosen in the first place: 'Meanwhile, over in England, unbeknownst to us, Committees had already been sitting for years to decide what, in time of war, was to be done with and for civilians such as ourselves.' Foreshortening the range of action gives a plausibility of self-determination to what is effectively the lost resistance to a hypnotic stare.

The actual occasion of Green's self-debate bears on a decision whose issue is relatively trivial: 'So now we were torn two ways. We had our only child, a son, in London, and it did seem right to get back to him. On the other hand we had paid for the car in advance, and had a few days in hand.' But the basic sense of dilemma is over-dramatized to allow a consideration in broader terms of exactly what one is fighting *for*.

As co-operative writing, *Loving* projects back to this period of 'waiting for the worst', rehearsing the grounds of a decision.

The text is conceived as the answer to a question which its own practice will allow to emerge from a context of social and cultural constraints. The idiom of the time is made out of debris from closed forms (as with *Caught*) reviving the sense of 'what might have been' as the critical moment of the text itself; this moment reasserts a continuity between a certain perspective on events and a perspective within the novel which moves the reader to particular interpretative acts. Its own disordering of the novel liberates a pre-history of the same constraints that will relativize those interpretative acts; on one hand, there is a strategic impersonation of an entrant in the tradition of writing about the Country House; there is also a resumption of the position of 'Meditations in Time of Civil War'. Yeats's sequence of that title is headed by the poem 'Ancestral Houses', whose scenario is reproduced in *Loving* almost down to the last point: the gravelled ways, the straying peacocks, the invading mice all recur, together with a conviction that the glory which is merely inherited has no future:

> And maybe the great-grandson of that house,
> For all the bronze and marble, 's but a mouse.[18]

'But if I once did that would your darlings ever be able to live here again? I wonder.' (p. 186)

Yeats is of course concerned with an Irish setting; the life which the house represents (admittedly viewed more out of concern for a social charisma) has disappeared. In a time of war, what is behind the residuum men and women are meant to defend?

When *Loving* is read as a novel, the pre-history of conditions out of which it arises and which it articulates leads a very hidden life indeed. An effective break with the novel's hypnotic stare depends on confounding its line of sight, overwhelming the transparent medium for its steady and co-ordinated vision with an obliterating light which it is difficult to situate. This brilliant illegibility is identified with 'loving', as highly inefficacious in a system which calls to account whatever is productive of excess; the primary source for its emanations is Edith, the medium for 'brimming light' (p. 108): 'At this moment she flung round on him and his hangdog face was dazzled by the excitement and scorn which seemed to blaze from her' (p. 110). Raunce is the object of this rout; Albert is also overthrown by her radiance,

and his infatuation leads to a faint glimmer in response – 'His
weak eyes shone' (p. 41). The incontinent light is correlative
with the natural effulgence on which no limit or horizon can
be set: 'Against the everlastingly hurrying ocean with its bright
glare from the beginning of the world, he wandered with the
donkey dropped to his tracks as if he was a journeying choirboy'
(p. 138). With the suggested backing of infinite resource,
Edith can look 'straight up at that sky without wrinkling the
skin about her eyes' (p. 139) in a mutuality of resistless 'glares'.
Laughter, which abandons restraint as much as 'loving',
appears in 'a waste of giggling behind their eyes' (pp. 34 and
87), another expanse where no bearings are set; this aspect of
firmamental depth is continually taken up:

His white face was shot with green from the lawn.
'I haven't said yes have I?' she countered and looked straight at
him, her heart opening about her lips. Seated as she was back to
the light he could see only a blinding space for her head framed in
dark hair and inhabited by those great eyes on her, fathoms deep.
(p. 142)

The oceanic dimensions to Edith's eyes are like the 'other seas'
of Marvell's 'The Garden', and there is a distant infusion of
greenness here. As in *Party Going*, the mixture of greenness with
oceans buoys up the Empsonian dialectic of 'including everything because understanding it, and . . . including everything
because in harmony with it', inviting the passage from transitive to 'trancitive', following a collapse of representational
depth which is perspectival – based on the eyesight. The
obliterating, 'blinding' light further removes a sense of place
or any possibility of perspective: ' "No that's right," he mur-
mured obviously lost' (p. 143). Under the influence of 'loving',
Raunce is unable to 'picture' himself: ' "I can't properly see
myself these days," Raunce went on looking sideways past her
at the red eye of a deer's stuffed head' (p. 163). The deer's eye
could seem to retrieve his perspective – it reverts to the bead
eye of the heraldic deer in *Caught*; while the portentous phrase
'her heart opening about her lips' is a verbal mimicry of the
anterior 'the curling disclosure of the heart of a rose' (*Caught*,
p. 64). But the living eye is the instrument of irrefutable light.
In Edith's case it is invincibly 'shining', 'sparkling', or 'hot to

glowing', even 'dazzled dazzling' – its resourceful incidence empowering a text where the sense can refract, and enter a medium of different density (including the fatuous): ' "There's more in this than meets the eye," she suggested' (p. 157); ' "I'd've told within a second, like in the twinklin' of an eye . . ." ' (p. 158). Conversely, the eye as detective is like the stare of the novel, as piercing as a gimlet: 'she dropped her gimlet eyes' (p. 83); ' "How's that Edie?" Kate asked opening her gimlet eyes' (p. 137); 'Her gimlet eyes narrowed' (p. 208). Constant directions of penetrating light are abused with oblique and scintillant points; and the more influential image for the eye is of a compound organ whose facets hide surreptitious pin-pricks of desire: 'With no change in expression, without warning, she began to blush. The slow tide frosted her dark eyes, endowed them with facets' (p. 7). This is the functional movement of the text – an erotic flush: 'Her eyes left his face and with what seemed a quadrupling in depth came following his to rest on those rectangles of warmth alive like blood. From this peat light her great eyes became invested with rose incandescence that was soft and soft and soft' (p. 142). Edith's eyes are enlivened by rose incandescence spreading behind a faceted surface; it is the same light that Raunce is trying to exclude: 'Lying back he squinted into the blushing rose of that huge turf fire as it glowed, his bluer eye azure on which was a crescent rose reflection' (p. 142). Raunce habitually squints in the face of unyielding brilliance; the full splendour is treated like the first revelation of sex, and squinting is the anxious imposition of a screen: 'Then the wind sent her hair over her vast double-surfaced eyes with their two depths. As she watched him thus, he might have felt this was how she could wear herself in bed for him, screened but open, open terribly' (p. 131). For both Albert and Raunce, it is an unmanageable excess (on a less fraught level it makes Mathewson 'goggle'); the eyes are endued with forbidding harshness in a repercussion of the imagery of archaic menace familiar from the art and literature of the Nineties; when Mrs Tennant is portrayed as having jewel-like eyes, it is their hardness which is emphasized: 'There was something hard and glittering beyond the stone of age in that other pair below the blue waved tresses' (p. 205). This image, in counterpoint with Edith ('soft and soft and soft')

informs a direct contrast made between the loving gestures of
servants and employers. Edith's comfort for the weeping Kate
consists of 'stroking', while there is more abrasive contact
between Mrs Tennant and Mrs Jack; the latter rubs the point
of the older woman's shoulder, then grips it, and digs in her
nails: ' "Good heavens," the young woman exclaimed gazing
at the impression her nails had made on Mrs. Tennant's shirt
and with trembling lips' (p. 204). Although her own flirtation
with the Captain gives her a certain brilliance, this is subdued
to a damaged aspect: 'With a sort of cry and crossing her
lovely arms over that great brilliant upper part of her on
which, wayward, were two dark upraised dry wounds shaking
on her, she also slid entirely underneath' (p. 76). The 'wounds'
are inflicted by a brutal gaze; but the brilliant 'loving' which
surveillance seeks to oppress emerges in secret throughout. Its
surviving want of steadiness belongs to a Mallarméan text:

Les mots, d'eux-mêmes, s'exaltent à mainte facette reconnue
la plus rare ou valant pour l'esprit, centre de suspens vibratoire;
qui les perçoit indépendamment de la suite ordinaire, projetés, en
parois de grotte, tant que dure leur mobilité ou principe, étant
ce qui ne se dit pas du discours: prompts tous, avant extinction,
à une réciprocité de feux distante ou presentée de biais comme
contingence.[19]

Taken in isolation, this describes a text whose faceting insures it
against loss of meaning apart from its historical constraints –
a meaning in secession. But in *Loving*, it has a converse ability to
imply the motivation through which the writing derives
inflexions from historical circumstance; faceting is a mode of
alertness to political exigencies, which determines which
moments in the pre-history of the same constraints are reflected
in a present text:

The operation of meaning has its own internal side of which the
whole flow of words is only a wake, an indication of only its cross-
points. But established significations contain the new signification
only as a trace or a horizon. The new signification will later recognize itself in them, but even when it takes them up again it will
forget what was partial and naive in them. The new signification
only relights sudden flashes in the depths of past knowledge,
touching past knowledge only from a distance. From the past
knowledge to the new signification there is an invocation, and from

the new signification in turn there are a response to and acquiescence in past knowledge.[20]

Merleau-Ponty's description of 'a new system of expression' juxtaposes the Joycean practice of the 'wake' and a Mallarméan practice of reciprocal reflections in a strategy whose purpose can be read in the mutual concessions of text and pretext which hold one another in view, subject to a faceting which disconcerts the medium of an evenly maintained stare. As in the counterpoint of 'Araby' with 'real Arabia' in *Caught*, the uninterrupted donation of meaning from a given stance is the obverse action of a text which principally reverts to a side-slipped 'idiom of the time'. In *Loving*, the fairy-tale atmosphere is thicker, but is not this time in a measured opposition to internal dissent; fairy-tale motifs and procedures are explored instead as a means of extruding the torpid coherence of information which a conventional view of the novel accepts:

The fairy tale clearly does not refer to the outer world, although it may begin realistically enough and have everyday features woven into it. The unrealistic nature of these tales (which narrow-minded rationalists object to) is an important device, because it makes obvious that the fairy tales' concern is not useful information about the external world, but the inner processes taking place in an individual.[21]

This introversion is formalized and given a further twist by incorporating *another* fairy-tale in the body of the text: ' "Once upon a time there were six little doves lived in a nest . . ." ' (p. 53). The recitation is subsequently back-dated to 'that first afternoon of spring' (p. 188), which is traditionally the occasion on which romances are set. Even the 'outer world' of Ireland is suspended in a fairy-tale cocoon: 'Do they still believe the boys get carried off by fairies?' (p. 26). The house itself is partitioned into 'kingdoms'; the movement from one to another is described as the passage 'into yet another world' (p. 67). When Kate and Edith open the door into Paddy's 'kingdom', they admit light in the manner of Psyche illumining the sleeping Cupid. A period of inertia and preparation is a frequent component of fairy-tales – it appears in the figures of Sleeping Beauty and the 'once and future king'; Paddy's snoring frame is firmly associated with the 'old kings': 'the floor of cobbles reflected an old king's molten treasure from the bog' (p. 52). It is the same legendary past which attracts Captain Davenport, who 'Digs after the old kings in his bog' (p. 30) (he and Mrs Jack are the 'two humps of body, turf over graves'). Kate and Edith want to accoutre Paddy as an 'old king': ' "If I make a crown out of them ferns in the corner," Edith said, "will you fetch something he can hold?" ' (p. 52). There is a suggested past of equestrian action, compatible with Yeats's vision of the national heritage: 'What they saw was a saddleroom which dated back to the time when there had been guests out hunting from Kinalty' (p. 51).

But the opening and closing lines of *Loving* provide the shrewdest of collusions with the textuality of fairy tales: 'Once upon a day an old butler called Eldon lay dying in his room attended by the head housemaid, Miss Agatha Burch' (p. 5); 'Over in England they were married and lived happily ever after' (p. 229). According to Bettelheim, these neutral-sounding phrases are progressive, not regressive, means of reassuring an anxious child:

An uninformed view of the fairy tale sees in this type of ending an unrealistic wish-fulfillment, missing completely the important message it conveys to the child. These tales tell him that by forming a true interpersonal relation, one escapes the separation anxiety which haunts him (and which sets the stage for many fairy tales, but is always resolved at the story's ending). Furthermore, the story tells, this ending is not made possible, as the child wishes and believes, by holding onto his mother eternally. If we try to escape separation anxiety and death anxiety by desperately keeping our grasp on our parents, we will only be cruelly forced out, like Hansel and Gretel.[22]

In this context, the beginning and ending of *Loving* ironize a fairy-tale resolution of separation anxiety; at the end, Raunce is nearer to death than ever before, and he is literally returning to his mother: ' "We'll go straight to Peterboro' where my mum'll have a bed for you . . ." ' (p. 228). The book meticulously charts his regressive acts. Immediately after writing to his mother he curls up to sleep in a foetal position; his letters harp on about the desirability of an Anderson shelter – his need for a foetal security is so intense that he never strays out of doors: ' "Charley Raunce hasn't shoved his head into the air these three years it must be" ' (p. 24). His motivation for proposing marriage is explained by an anxiety to ' "get my old mother over out of the bombers" ' (p. 142). And his proposal is 'toneless' – the erotic is subtracted from it. An apt illustration of his insecurity is the over-cautious method used for actually writing letters home: first making a draft in pencil, then tracing this in with a pen. By contrast, Edith never writes to her mother; before the proposal she is keen to return to England but afterwards she is content to stay, regarding a proposal of marriage as the guarantee of her independence. And Kate is in Ireland solely because ' "I wanted to get away from 'ome" ' (p. 102).

Raunce's plan to retrieve his mother and install her in Ireland is rebuked by the mother herself: ' "She writes she reckons that would be cowardly or something" ' (p. 220). Her letter effectively awards him his independence, but on receipt of it he goes into a Groddeckian decline to abdicate the responsibility just given, reverting to the condition of an infant which relies on a mother's care. His eventual return to England is not a case of social commitment but an attempt to clear his honour in his mother's eyes. His own brand of 'loving' is socially immature, a failing betrayed in his prim distaste at the liaison of Paddy and Kate: ' "all I can say is that's disgusting, downright disgusting . . . why a big, grown girl like her an' that ape out of a zoo . . . Why it's unnatural" ' (p. 226).

Raunce's assumption of civic responsibility is only apparent; he is effectively resuming a filial dependence on every count. The distance from adulthood is marked by a self-conscious pretence of adulthood; he encourages Edith to more or less play at 'families': ' "Come to father beautiful" '; their habitual retreat to the fire in the Red Library is to the hearth which symbolizes the sanctity of the home. Raunce likes to imagine the domestic household as 'all one family' with himself at the head (p. 157). By mimicking the grown-up role, he prevents a legitimization of it in his own person; he is simply appended to his own mother, identifying so completely with her desire, it only remains to recreate himself as the object of it. This behaviour is linked by psychoanalysis to a stage of 'primary narcissism'; the child attempts to *be* the phallus (the complement of what is lacking in his mother) instead of assuming his

place in society through possessing a phallus (as the father
does). Raunce is given the unmistakable characteristics of a
phallic role; his preferred mode of action is to 'look slippy' or
to 'look sharp': 'He slipped inside like an eel into its drainpipe'
(p. 12); 'He appeared to ooze authority' (p. 34); 'he made his
way smooth' (p. 44); 'he whipped out' (p. 45); 'He slipped up
behind' (p. 45); 'He came smoothly out, automatic' (p. 46);
'he glided softly out' (p. 61); 'he said advancing smooth on
Edith' (p. 115). It is revealing that Mrs Welch bans Raunce
from her kitchen. The other characters suspect that Albert the
evacuee is her own illegitimate child; she herself calls him a
'bastard imp' immediately after observing that Edith is
' "runnin' in double 'arness with that Raunce" ' (p. 168). Her
sudden excitement (' "I'll tan the 'ide right off of you" ')
associates 'loving' with illegitimacy; her obsession with security
and 'double locking' and her prohibition of Raunce imply that
she identifies him with a phallic threat.

Phallic traits are more infrequent after Raunce's Albert
declares his intention to join up, because the assumption of
responsibility forces Raunce to assess his own position. But he
subsequently reverts, and at the end of the book the phallic
symbolism has a convulsive renewal: 'At this he began to flush.
The colour spread until his face had become an alarming
purple' (p. 228). In a state of advanced morbidity, on the verge
of regaining his mother, Raunce is 'stretched and tested' by
this event. His mimicry of the phallus is an extreme form of
adaptation to external power; his own choice of epithet –
' "Trust little Charley" ' (p. 105) – is the unconscious acceptance
of a dependent role. (Edith mimics the phrase – ' "Trust little
Edith" ', p. 137 – in a moment of submitting to Raunce's
will.) He deprives himself of his own self-presence, engrossing
the mother's desire in becoming a blank or lack; the unwilling-
ness to *have* a phallus (as opposed to *being* one) compounds the
fear of punitive action by the father into classic castration fear
– Raunce's illness focusses on the swelling at his neck, and this
affliction is constantly juxtaposed with images of decapitation
or of damage to the head or neck. He first appears with a
bandaged neck in a 'low room of antlered heads' (p. 95). His
phallic stealth embodies the same threat: 'He went so soft he
might have been a ghost without a head' (p. 14). At the dinner

table, the inverse image applies: 'He carved savagely like a head-hunter' (p. 31). This abrupt association of food and mutilation is continuous with an extensive strain of violent orality. Fear of the opposite sex as strange or threatening is exaggerated until the relationship between them is vampiric. After being kissed by Edith – 'her lips sucked at him warm and heady' – Raunce is found 'standing as he was like he had been drained of blood' (p. 201). Edith is replete with blood: ' "She should go and give one of them blood transfusions they are asking for, she's got too much" ' (p. 65). The same notion of primitive incorporation is behind the sexual ritual of the doves: 'the fat bird, grown thin now, had his head deep down the other's neck which was swallowing in frantic gulps that shook its crescent body' (p. 57). This spectacle is unnerving to Evelyn and Moira; oral incorporation of the head and neck is the violence proposed by Albert the evacuee (who also throttles a peacock), and his aggression offers to thrust sexual knowledge on the two little girls: ' "Tell you what," Albert said to Moira as they loitered to follow, "I'll bite 'is little 'ead off 'n" ' (p. 57). The inspiration for this act is a further example of decapitation: ' "There was a man there bit the 'eads off of mice for a pint" ' (p. 58).[23]

But while Edith seems to sexually engorge Raunce, his own oral response is severely conditioned. She remarks on the fact that he never takes the first opportunity of stealing a kiss when she brings him his early morning tea – a reserve that can be explained with reference to his tediously reiterated principle, ' "Clean your teeth before ever you have anything to do with a woman." ' For Raunce, sexuality is recovered by intense pre-occupation with the oral, and this is entirely consistent with the immersion in a phallic role; an excessive orality is the symbolic reversion to a state of dependence on the mother's breast (which is all-sufficient), it is an avid return to exemption from the need for individuation. Something of the same fixation is evident in Mike Mathewson, whose breath is scented with acid of violets; his and Raunce's fastidiousness invite a contrast with Paddy's 'great brown teeth' (p. 89).

Green himself has gone on record insisting that *Loving* sprang from an anecdote that vividly fused the voluptuousness of sex and food:

GREEN: I got the idea of *Loving* from a manservant in the Fire Service during the war. He was serving with me in the ranks and he told me he had once asked the elderly butler who was over him what the old boy most liked in the world. The reply was: 'Lying in bed on a summer morning, with the window open, listening to the church bells, eating buttered toast with cunty fingers.' I saw the book in a flash.[24]

In the finished work, the entire household succumbs to oral greediness: the closest reason for not returning to England is because ' "They're starving over there" ' (p. 48). When the peacock's corpse is found in the larder, Miss Burch condemns the sabotage in moral terms but what really distresses her is the thought of it ' "infecting all our food" ' (p. 122). Her own idea of a comfortable life is to sleep ' "in your own bed with a fresh joint down in the larder for dinner every day" ' (p. 124). When Edith steals a number of peacock's eggs to treat her skin with, Mrs Welch supposes that the real reason is because ' "they're starvin' over the other side the ordinary common people are begging your pardon mum" ' (p. 179).

Once again, the intestine motions of the book escape the postures of a novel, they elevate the haphazard; Mrs Tennant incidentally connects mutilation and food in her complaint that the servants are ' "simply eating their heads off" ' (p. 182), a remark that would bear translation as, 'Who is nibbling at my little house?' As a providential source of food, Kinalty Castle is like the Gingerbread House – a projection of oral craving – in the fairy-tale of Hansel and Gretel. The fairy-tale divulges the cannibalistic aspect of orality in the figure of the witch, and there are several parallels between it and *Loving*. The two children are guided to the Gingerbread House by a white dove (they are guided back by a white duck); although they do not cross an expanse of water on their way there, they do have to negotiate one on their return (as Edith and Raunce have to cross the Irish Sea); the episode may be understood as a kind of baptism, or transition to a higher state, ironized by *Loving*. The witch is eventually pushed into her own oven and burned to death; Kinalty Castle is burned down. Finally Hansel and Gretel inherit the witch's jewels; the persistent problem for Edith and Raunce is a question of what to do with Mrs Tennant's sapphire ring.

The ring is clearly intended as a symbol of female sexuality; Edith secretes it in the lining of a chair, giving it the status of a charm, like the complementary symbols of sex organs which Julia had buried in *Party Going*. According to Vladimir Propp, the exchange of a jewel or a ring is equivalent to the branding or marking of the hero in a folk-tale, and in *Loving* this equivalence is maintained; the bandage about Raunce's neck represents a ring around the finger, and the description of him tampering with the bandage carries a precise verbal reflection of Edith trying to retrieve the ring:

He hooked a finger into the bandage round his throat as though to ease himself. (p. 141)

He approached doltish while she hooked with her finger in the tear. (p. 143)

At the start of the text, Edith appears bearing further symbols of the female sex, 'a glove full of white unbroken eggs', which she also keeps to herself. And when Albert the evacuee acquires the ring, he conceals it *inside* the shell of an egg, an occultation increased by imposing an oath of secrecy on the two little girls; the symbol of female sexuality remains hidden as long as their 'lips is sealed' (p. 147). Meanwhile, Albert the pantry boy, who is besotted with Edith, tries to obtain the 'charms' for himself; he reminds Edith that 'she had still to return him that gauntlet glove' (p. 137); his pretence that he has stolen the ring is a symbolic means of claiming possession of her.

The ring (which is generally elusive) is a 'big sapphire cluster', an image of the faceting by which the text seeks to elude the official line of enquiry of a novel normally concerned with the security of strong points of meaning which from time to time go missing in *Loving* when the text effectively 'blinks'. The novel maintains a bearable light, the light of reason, which *Loving* dissociates through intermittence and excess; the ring is equally either a 'blaze of blue' (p. 146) or is seen to have 'winked and glittered' (p. 127), augmenting the sense in which it will 'gum up the whole works' (p. 128). Edith seems to reinforce the correspondence of 'loving' and 'brilliance' by throwing the ring into the fire – into the heat of passion.

But the ring is also a charm in the magical sense; Albert occults it with a bizarre ritual 'spell': ' "While I break a cock's egg over your mouth you say, My lips is sealed may I drop dead" ' (p. 147). For Raunce, 'loving' is specifically a form of enchantment which leaves him 'bewitched and bewildered'. His own proposal of marriage has the effect of a 'spell' under which the peacocks 'stood pat in the dry as though enchanted' (p. 141). By contrast, the married state itself evidently *dispels*: ' "now Raunce an' me's come to an understanding I got no time for charms" ' (p. 197). It is the veil before knowledge – seducing without disclosing – which is spell-binding. Edith teases Raunce with a black silk, transparent nightdress: 'She put a hand in at the neck so that he could see the veiled skin' (p. 199). Raunce is derogatory, but his abuse of the garment as a 'piece of cobweb' is an involuntary recognition of its power as a snare – he is aroused by its concealment which activates a sense of hidden knowledge. This 'spell' is like Albert's 'spell' a revocation of sexual difference (female sexuality is hidden by a contradiction in terms, a 'cock's egg'). The ambiguous response obscures the 'frontier of hopes or mostly fears' with a veil that stands for a hymeneal barrier removed when the bride has been carried over a threshold into marriage, breaking the spell of indistinct knowledge in order to 'come to an understanding':

'No,' she cried, 'you stop where you are. I'm goin' to punish you. What d'you say if we took this for when we are married. How would I look eh Charley?' And she held that nightdress before her face.
'Punishment eh?' he laughed. If it had been a spell then he seemed to be out of it for the moment. (p. 200)

The fascination with partial knowledge is also put into the form sustained in *Caught*, where the deflection of a path or the turning of a corner figuratively precludes a cognition or realization: 'With a swirl of the coloured skirt of her uniform she turned a corner in front along this high endless corridor. The tap of her shoes faded' (p. 14). Edith is again teasing Raunce; the glimpse of something fading from certain knowledge becomes the fulcrum of a desire on which no term is set (its trajectory is 'endless').

Seduction is unmistakably linked with a dispersion of focus, and *Loving* is a text whose own edges seem to blur when it is overlaid with images, words, and colours from other sources.

This veil of secretions from earlier texts acts as a kind of literary pretext for seduction and rape. The bed in which Mrs Jack and Captain Davenport are found is 'boat-shaped black and gold with a gold oar at the foot' (p. 33), like the barge at Cydnus – scene of Antony's seduction by Cleopatra.[25] The purple sails of Shakespeare's text reappear as 'pink silk sheets'; the silver oars and 'cloth of gold, of tissue' are transmuted into a gold oar and 'sheets like veils'; the 'strange invisible perfume' becomes the scent which clings to Mrs Jack's clothes. But there is also a funereal aspect to the scene in *Loving*; Edith handles the sheets, and lights the lamps 'softly gently as someone in devotion', so that the bed is also like a funereal barge, such as the one which carries Arthur (an 'old king') to Avalon. Shakespeare's 'pretty dimpled boys, like smiling cupids' form a constant inlay to the later text: 'In one of the malachite vases, filled with daffodils, which stood on tall pedestals of gold naked male children without wings, he had seen a withered trumpet' (p. 11). The indication of what is not there – male children *without* wings – is a negative inference of 'smiling cupids'; although the hieratic pedestals are perhaps even more closely reminiscent of their counterparts in *Cymbeline*:

> The roof o' th' chamber
> With golden cherubims is fretted. Her andirons
> (I had forgot them) were two winking cupids
> Of silver, each on one foot standing, nicely
> Depending on their brands.[26]

These are appointments of Imogen's bedchamber, which Jachimo describes to support his false claim that he has ravished her. They are part of another previous texture of seduction; Imogen's tapestry depicts

> Proud Cleopatra, when she met her Roman,
> And Cydnus swelled above the banks[27]

The 'gold naked male children without wings' are also matched by colour with the 'golden Cupidons' in 'A Game of Chess', also a seduction-text whose particular tableau of rape is 'The change of Philomel'; Eliot's own notes to *The Waste Land* confirm that *Antony and Cleopatra* is a strong presence behind a section of the poem that readmits the evasiveness of reflected

light, glittering jewels, synthetic perfumes, and lamplight. 'A
Game of Chess' individually complies with the texture of
Loving:

> Huge sea-wood fed with copper
> Burned green and orange, framed by the coloured stone,
> In which sad light a carvèd dolphin swam.[28]

She pushed the ashtray with one long lacquered nail across the
black slab of polished marble supported by a dolphin layered in
gold. (p. 11)

Loving's objet d'art has conceivably been forged from Shakespeare's prosopographical note: 'his delights / Were dolphin-
like, they showed his back above / The element they lived in'.[29]
In any case, the details of envious show transferred from earlier
seduction-texts are frequently revised in *Loving* by the addition
of gold, so that the presence of gold generally testifies to the
imminence of sex: ' "I got those sheets from the Gold Bedroom
to mend. I wish the people they have to stay would cut their
toenails or lie quiet one or the other" ' (p. 37). Mythic support
is delivered in the scene where Kate and Edith irrupt into
Paddy's 'kingdom' ('O'Conor's life was opened'); the light
they introduce is atomized like the golden shower in which
Zeus raped Danae: 'the shafted sun lay in a lengthened arch
of blazing sovereigns' (p. 51). Paddy is prone and passive by a
textual device which inclines towards the image of Gulliver,
bound by the hairs of his head: 'It might have been almost that
O'Conor's dreams were held by hairs of gold binding his head'
(p. 51). It is interesting to remember that in *The Battle of the
Books* by Swift the modern case is defended by the spider which
spins a web out of its own bowels, representing a text which
constantly draws on its own resources. As if to proclaim a
textual schematics, the cobweb here is 'caught' in a *reflection*
of *golden* light: 'Caught in the reflection of spring sunlight this
cobweb looked to be made of gold' (p. 51).

When these further texts are within sight, they are glimpsed
through details which only oscillate the imagery of *Antony and
Cleopatra*; the central permission for a texture with ready-made
overtones of seduction comes from this play, which is placed
under an obligation to *Loving* as a part of the pre-history of
Loving's own constraints. Just as Raunce is diverted from martial

duty in England by the enchantment of Edith, so Antony is distracted from a Roman perspective of martial achievement by 'this enchanting queen', 'this great fairy', 'my charm', 'thou spell'; he is 'the noble ruin of her magic'. The first six lines of the play announce that his line of sight has bent and turned from the business of war to Cleopatra's 'tawny front'. Rome is contrasted with Egypt as conceptually as England with Ireland. ('He was disposed to mirth; but on the sudden / A Roman thought hath struck him'). The oral greediness which blights the English in Ireland is parallel to 'gourmandizing' in Egypt, 'That sleep and feeding may prorogue his honour' (Raunce's obsessiveness is expressed through his religious observance of the siesta). Cleopatra herself is described as an 'Egyptian dish'. Raunce and Antony both have a tendency to bluster and expostulate, and both are superannuated lovers: Antony has grey and white hairs while the elopement of the forty-year-old ailing Raunce is preposterous. But each relationship has a 'brilliance' which induces 'oblivion'; and Mrs Welch derogates a certain grandeur in her dismissal of Raunce and Edith as 'the almighty lovers they make out they are but no more than fornicators when all's said and done' (p. 178).

Behind the preparatives for seduction there is also a threat of violent restraint; the fear of invasion is ultimately a fear of rape, contracted from a wider risk of oral attack: ' "They're famished like a lion out in the desert them fighting men" ' (p. 96). The bringing forward of sex entails a corresponding oral retreat: 'drawing a hand across her mouth' (p. 77). This suppressed violence is periodically released through bouts of screams, screeches and shrieks. The text is frequently punctuated by shrillness of one kind or another; Kate and Edith predominantly shriek when emboldening one another in discussions of sex. But equally vociferous are non-human objects like the squeaking door through which Raunce comes to interrupt the erotic tableau of blind man's buff. Another screamer is the mouse trapped in the mechanism of the weathervane; it responds in kind to Edith's alarm:

At this Edith let a shriek with the full force of her lungs. A silence of horror fell.

Then even over the rustle of Kate hurrying up a paper-thin scream came as if in answer from between the wheels. (p. 46)

The mouse is specifically *'caught* between those teeth' (p. 46, my emphasis) just as it is held by the interlocking correspondences of the text to allow an erotic influence on the way it 'gums up the whole works', literally – it impedes the operation of the symbolic panopticon. Edith afterwards refers to the incident in a gross exaggeration of the oral threat: ' "Just because when I see a mouse caught by its little leg in a wheel and he opens a great mouth at me . . ." ' (p. 139). But the decisive corollary of the human shriek is the call of the peacock: 'At some distance peacocks called to one another, shriek upon far shriek' (p. 188). Besides being aggressively oral – 'most greedy of all birds' (p. 222) – the peacock is already culturally linked with eroticism; the Ancients associated it with salaciousness;[30] in Flaubert's *Bouvard and Pécuchet* it provides the central erotic event:

A sudden gust of wind blew up the sheets, and they saw two peacocks, male and female. The hen was standing still, legs bent, rump in the air. The cock strutted round her, spreading out his tail, preening himself, gurgling, then jumped on her, dragging his feathers round her like an arbour, and the two great birds shook with a single shudder.

Bouvard felt it in Madame Bordin's palm. She loosed herself quickly. In front of them stood Victor, gaping and almost petrified as he watched; a little further away Victorine, stretched on her back in the sunshine, was sniffing at the flowers she had picked.[31]

Bouvard and Pécuchet inspects among many other things the residual role of the Country House; the two friends move out to a country district where they distinctly don't fit in, and take over a large estate which they proceed to ruin; their protégés, the mischievous Victor and 'innocent' Victorine might almost have been the models for Albert and Moira and Evelyn.

The mythical explanation for the multiple eyes on the peacock's tail is that they are the metamorphosed eyes of Argos *Panoptes*; even more remarkably, Argos was set to guard Io from one of Zeus's attempted rapes, and the form of his death was decapitation by the god Hermes. In *Loving*, the peacock is still in the service of surveillance, ' "It's wicked the way they spy on you" ' (p. 223), and Edith mimes the mythic defeat of Panoptes by her surreptitious theft of peacock's eggs and of the feather she wears in her hair: ' "Their eggs 've got to be lifted when there's not a soul to witness" ' (p. 22). Raunce gives her a pair of oculate feathers as 'charms', with the original panoptic purpose of keeping a jealous watch. But the peacock can also express the erotic 'brilliance' through its iridescent plumage and actual eyes, which are faceted: 'their eyes had changed to rubies, their plumage to orange' (p. 52). The same is true of the single eye of the dove, which is multiplied to increase the pavonine effect: 'The lad himself was shaded by that pierced tower of Pisa inside which a hundred ruby eyes were round' (p. 146). In the classical tradition, the peacock's plumage is a standard topic in the illustration of reflected light. In Pliny's *Historia Naturalis* it is also 'jewelled': 'gemmantes laudatus expandit colores adverso maxime sole, quia sic fulgentius radiant; simul umbrae quosdam repercussus ceteris, qui et in opaco clarius micant, conchata quaerit cauda, omnesque in acervum contrahit pinnarum quos spectari gaudet oculos.'[32] And in a distinction between 'use' and 'ornament', Cicero conducts an argument in which the peacock and the dove are interchangeable: 'alia autem nullam ob utilitatem quasi ad quendam ornatum, ut cauda pavoni, plumae versicolores columbis'.[33] The conjugation seems to be ready-made; and it probably does derive from a passage in Lucretius (to whom Cicero is elsewhere in debt) which approves the same examples in a description of the origin of colour which equally anticipates the *Historia Naturalis* with its 'repercussive' light:

> qualis enim caecis poterit color esse tenebris?
> lumine quin ipso mutatur propterea quod
> recta aut obliqua percussus luce refulget;
> pluma columbarum quo pacto in sole videtur,
> quae sita cervices circum collumque coronat;
> namque alias fit uti claro sit rubra pyropo,
> interdum quodam sensu fit uti videatur
> inter curalium viridis mescere zmaragdos.
> caudaque pavonis, larga cum luce repleta est,
> consimili mutat ratione obversa colores;
> qui quoniam quodam gignuntur luminis ictu,
> scire licet, sine eo fieri non posse putandum est.[34]

Colour depends on the incidence of light; it succeeds a change of perspective – the result of *clinamen*, which throughout the *De Rerum Natura* is the basis of generation. *Clinamen* is '*the inclination* or *turning aside* of a thing',[35] the mode of deflection in the path of atoms which leads to productive friction, a transaction which is practically convergent with *Loving* in its generation of a text through forms of faceting, refraction, brilliance, enchantment and disorientation. The insistent divorce from a straight line of evaluation is condensed in images of curvature:

They were wheeling wheeling in each other's arms heedless at the far end where they had drawn up one of the white blinds. Above from a rather low ceiling five great chandeliers swept one after the other almost to the waxed parquet floor reflecting in their hundred thousand drops the single sparkle of distant day, again and again red velvet panelled walls, and two girls, minute in purple, dancing multiplied to eternity in these trembling pears of glass. (p. 62)

The rotations of the waltz do not comprise a sequence of movements with start and finish but an open, self-perpetuating form which rebounds further in the faceting of the chandelier; it resists the textual aspect of the clear course with images of unmeasured depth: 'single sparkle' is 'multiplied to eternity'. The only level on which it can in fact be sounded is one of corroboration through the text, because the scene itself is a recurvation of the moment when Edith seductively gyrates in front of Raunce: 'With for her an altogether extraordinary animation she fairly danced up . . . She began once more to force her body on his notice, getting right up to him then away again, as though pretending to dance. Then she turned herself completely round in front of his very eyes' (p. 79). And this is on the same textual loop as the courting 'dance' of the doves, with the same advances and retreats; the airborne dove affects a flight of 'spiralling' and 'circling', a revolving ascent or descent which is the crucial image (along with the coiled valve of a seashell) in *Concluding*, a text which is more distinctly symmetrical – twisting itself around a number of motifs, tightening towards the centre, loosening towards the edge. The roundabout dance narrowly appears in the game of blind man's buff: 'She stumbled about in flat spirals' (p. 113). The dove is normally associated (especially in the Christian era) with superior benevolent powers, but its courting ceremony here consists of 'quarrelling, murdering and making love' (p. 57). This culminates in the engorging ritual mirrored by Edith's

vampiric effect on Raunce's neck; her own little ballet of
flirtation is in outline the dance of Salome (Dance of the Seven
Veils), the employment of a seductive means to achieve a
decapitating end.

The scene in the ballroom is one of a number of tableaux
marked with outstanding detail, a visual specificity that is
bathed in light. If the novel can be understood as a text that
is turned towards the light, these descriptive promontories seem
possessed of a luminosity, a textuality of glamour which is the
final product of a process of patiently eliminating extraneous
matter, the exhaustive coverage of a restricted field of vision
which is none other than the writing of *continuity* in the cine-
matographic sense:

In the morning room two days later Raunce stood before Mrs.
Tennant and showed part of his back to Violet her daughter-in-
law . . . She could not see Violet because he was in the way . . .
With her back to the light he could not see her mouth and nose.
(p. 10)

He cut off the head with a pair of nail clippers. He carried this
head away in cupped hand from above thick pile carpet in black
and white squares through onto linoleum which was bordered with
a purple key pattern on white until, when he had shut that green
door to open his kingdom, he punted the daffodil ahead like a
rugger ball. (p. 11)

The scrupulous recording of dispositions, the pacing and spacing
of an action, the itemization of stage properties – writing as
precise mensuration – creates an overestimation of the novel's
debt to engrossing observation; the writing of continuity is
already the intensification of a literary production in which the
novel is the radiance of information: that is its only interest. Its
ulterior purpose, of ensuring the means of revaluing a text, is
pursued by the characters themselves – always contriving to
inject the immediate circumstance with a stage value. Edith
can be seen manoeuvring Raunce into a position from which
to propose: 'She hardly *seemed* comfortable however . . . she let
out careless in a low voice . . . She *seemed* overexcited . . .
she echoed *as though* dumbfounded . . . she gave him a look as
if to say the sky always rained at weddings . . . she said *as
though* beside herself' (pp. 126–8, my emphasis). As a result,

social intercourse becomes a spectacle, ultimately constricted to the walk-on part, the 'extra' who is there in the first place as an exhibitionist: 'And while he heartily kissed Kate's mouth her right eye winked at Edith under one of his outstanding ears' (p. 46). In a saturated continuity, one that is absolutely unsparing of visual detail, human action is accountable to an extent which detaches it from the human agent; the animation of the body is an excuse for the parsimoniousness of expertise – an aggrandizement only of what may be *seen*, on a textual plane which does not care to elevate the human: 'He followed with his eyes and did not turn his head. As a result for a full minute one pupil was swivelled almost back of the nose he had on him whilst the other was nearly behind a temple but he grinned the while' (p. 89). Kate is the object or patient of this operation like the 'panning' of a camera for which Paddy is not the agent but the instrument, reduced to the vacuous function of swivelling eyes, under pressure of *another* panoptic scanning: that of the author as panoramist. The situation is doubled-up; it is the over-production of a novel, the over-exertion of a tendency towards the priority of panoramic effects – a long exposure during which everything has to behave itself, composing an optimum state of 'immeasurable stillness' (p. 12), a mimicry of the absolute repose of the dead. The desire of the panopticon is for the gratification of the fetish – it is easier to absorb its object in conditions of immobility; inertness will contract the field of interpretation, facilitate the authorization of a meaning under control: 'The girls stood transfixed as if by arrows between the Irishman dead motionless asleep and the other intent and quiet behind a division' (p. 53). This extinction of movement is the focal point of another tableau. Raunce is 'the other', actually in the next room, behind a glass-fronted cupboard against the dividing wall part of which has been cut away to allow an uninterrupted view. He is enclosed in a frame, effectively a show-case; the tableau seems to be mounted in the same way, cut out from the text surrounding it by a splendour of detail. It is a fragment like the fetish object, a morsel offered to the greed of continuity, which utterly consumes a confined space. It corresponds to a mode of key-hole surveillance which perfects the need to observe without being seen; when Mrs Welch spies on Kate and Edith through the per-

forated iron, a spotlight is trained upon them: 'the great shaft
of golden sun which lighted these girls through parted cloud'
(p. 50). Raunce confirms the voyeuristic aspect of the encased
regard: ' "Why there's all those stories you've had, openin' this
door and seeing that when you were in a place in Dorset and
lookin' through the bathroom window down in Wales . . ." '
(p. 79). The spectacle is always delimited by a surround: a
door, a window, or picture-frame. It is hardly surprising that
Raunce's own idea of envious show is to line his walls with
prints and photographs. The terms of his admiration for Edith
are those of a looker-on who evaluates his object, setting it
within a frame: ' "With those eyes you ought to be in pictures" '
(p. 13). He is referring colloquially, in the words of a popular
song of the period, to the motion picture, the film; which
makes Edith an even more likely subject for continuity:
mounted and imprisoned, brought into sharp focus, picked out
by exclusive light – it is all an attempt to harness the 'brilliance'
of 'those eyes' – pre-eminently in the tableau concluding the
book ('it made a picture'):

She began to feed the peacocks. They came forward until they had
her surrounded. Then a company of doves flew down on the seat
to be fed. They settled all over her. And their fluttering disturbed
Raunce who reopened his eyes. What he saw then he watched so
that it could be guessed that he was in pain with his great delight.
For what with the peacocks bowing at her purple skirts, the white
doves nodding on her shoulders round her brilliant cheeks and her
great eyes that blinked tears of happiness, it made a picture. (p. 229)

The passage appears to proclaim it is self-sufficient, it seems to
be part of a book that can afford to ignore the thought of any
depth by over-compensating for the loss with a surface textuality that is exceptionally well-lit and sumptuous. It has all the
virtues and failings of a purple passage, in fact it almost asks
to be excerpted from the novel as a representative, anthological
text. An initially 'unreadable' writing can of course be read
differently in the context of an anthology, where each excised
portion is picturesque, with newly emergent lines of force
adventurously curvilinear – the merest insinuations of newness
that introduce an acceptable modicum of challenge to the
rectilinear novel of the 'whole picture' kind.[36]

But on its darker side, the passage does have depth and it is

not an anthological text; although it is self-consciously projected as an image of bounty it thwarts the satiety required of a
peep-show text, dispersing its concentration and abducting it
elsewhere; it disesteems the tableau by giving an external
origin to every one of its parts, by means of a *clinamen* whose
warrant is the combination of peacocks and doves bowing and
nodding in the characteristic movement of the courting dance.
At what would be the vanishing point is a brimming light, the
faceting of tear-filled eyes and 'brilliant' cheeks. The visual
allure is a decoy, used to envelop the eye with a textuality that
blinks. The three-dimensional scene revealed in a beam of
light is superseded by a spectrum of words and particles of
phrasing, whose aggregation is the texture of the work. The
aperture of reading is not to review a scenography (through a
perspective-glass) but to diffract the light of a novel, breaking
it up into its constituent parts. This different textuality is
sporadic.

Loving has no clear and steady perspective on past knowledge;
its associations with other texts seem to be served up with more
or less indifference. Its writing prevaricates and dazzles; it does
not convince one of its methods but seduces one to them. In
narrative terms, it is irresolute, out of a commitment to its own
proportions – it is constantly tempted to cut corners, to redeploy
its own material. At one point Raunce is given a 'hangdog'
face on account of the greyhound which promptly appears
with the peacock's corpse; his idea of forestalling the rape they
connect with invasion – ' "What I had in mind was a cartridge
each for you ladies" ' (p. 97) – is precipitously used to add
piquancy to an unrelated claim: ' "Killed her it did as if she
had been blown in smithereens with a shotgun" ' (p. 98); the
metaphor designed for Edith's hair, 'bells without a note' (p.
113), is thoughtlessly counterbalanced in a description of red
fuchsias, whose 'bells swung without a note' (p. 130); and there
is no obvious justice in the visual accord between the statues
in the mock Greek temple and the windswept figures of Edith
and Kate (p. 131). All these detours are by way of texture
alone; they are without knowledge of the covert irritations of
meaning for which the writing sometimes does prepare itself.
What they specifically counteract is the sort of confidence
enjoyed by Edith: ' "Because I know Miss Evelyn and Miss

Moira like I've read them in a book" ' (p. 174). The glibness of
consorting with texture alone is measured against the coherence
in line with 'reading a book', an efficiency which is equally
gratuitous because it is over-insured; Mrs Tennant and Mrs
Jack provide a little drama of the fretfulness and alarm in a
situation which cannot be solved by reading it as a book:

> 'At all events you've got your ring back haven't you?'
> 'Yes but I don't like having things hang over me.'
> 'Hanging over you?'
> 'When there's something unexplained. Don't you ever feel
> somehow that you must get whatever it is cleared up? . . . Violet
> don't you find that everything now is the most frightful dilemma
> always? . . .' (pp. 184–5)

In *Loving*, it is precisely a dilemma by which the text regener-
ates itself; its wasted meanings (those which are not 'cleared
up') are conducted back as a kind of potential incoming
current of material whose availability for writing is what
sustains the work, continually producing these slight, material
assiduities which are extra and out of turn; their only meaning
is *to write*.

This practice of recycling is the eruption onto a written
surface of the poetics of the version: of the turning about of
material, the aggravation of detail with tried alternatives that
characterizes the reproduction of an anecdote: 'And he had to
listen to the whole thing again, and with embellishments that
he had never heard, that even he must have doubted' (p. 130).
Raunce is being subjected to another version of the Captain
Davenport—Mrs Jack scandal. What Edith departs from is the
impeccable finality of continuity; the value which continuity
undertakes, what it promises to reinstate and solidify is precisely
what her embroidery dissolves. The anecdotal material is like
the written material of *Loving* – repeatedly shaken into motion,
required or encouraged to run elsewhere, gaining solidity and
presence only when it is left to stand in a text which asseverates
by its practice the impossibility of transcribing what the eye can
see without creative interference by the process of writing it
down; the eye-witness account is a contradiction in terms, a
dilemma which *Loving* inflames by ratifying its own blindness,
writing inside-outwards rather than outside-inwards. Its

internal figure for the narratorial function is Nanny Swift, who
fabulates 'behind closed eyes and the wall of deafness' (p. 54),
'shuteyed and deaf' (p. 55). Myopia and deafness: on different
occasions, Green has ascribed to either a crucial role in the
composition of his work:

GREEN: 'Non-representational' was meant to represent a picture
which was not a photograph, nor a painting on a *photograph*, nor, in
dialogue, a tape recording. For instance, the very deaf, as I am,
hear the most astounding things all round them, which have not, in
fact, been said. This enlivens my replies until, through mishearing,
a new level of communication is reached. My characters misunder-
stand each other more than people do in real life, yet they do so
less than I. Thus when writing, I 'represent' very closely what I see
(and I'm not seeing so well now) and what I hear (which is little)
but I say it is 'non-representational' because it is not necessarily
what others see and hear.[37]

ALAN ROSS: Imperfect sight, it has recently been argued, affected
certain painters' view of colour. Do you think that imperfect hearing
has affected your view of character, and that the constant failure
in communication between your characters is a consequence – not
an entirely unhappy one – of it?
HENRY GREEN: Can't tell you. When you get very deaf you retire
into yourself. But as a writer it would be easy to pretend to hear,
wouldn't it? I have as I think short-circuited communication but
because I'm so deaf I don't know if I've done it well.[38]

These two interviews are roughly contemporaneous. In the first,
Green refers to a textuality which is the outcome of defective
naturalism – a procedure which he totally obviates in the second
interview with the contention that 'it would be easy to pretend
to hear, wouldn't it?'. This contrariness is of the kind he
relished both inside and outside his work. Earlier on in the
first interview, Green answers the charge that his writing is
unacceptable to an American audience because it is too
'subtle', by 'mishearing' it, converting subtlety into its opposite,
a particularly violent form of flagrancy:

GREEN: I don't follow. *Suttee*, as I understand it, is the suicide – now
forbidden – of a Hindu wife on her husband's flaming bier. I don't
want my wife to do that when my time comes – and with great
respect, as I know her, she won't –

INTERVIEWER: I'm sorry, you misheard me; I said 'subtle' – that the message was too subtle.
GREEN: Oh, *subtle*. How dull![39]

In both the written work and the work of producing Henry Green (quite different from the real Henry Yorke) deafness and blindness become the means of invention, ridiculing the assumption that the reproduction of data is never less than enough. Green presents either an excess or an insufficiency of data. With regard to the author of the work, it is a case of not enough; Green's public face is almost never seen – as a rule he declined to be photographed except from the rear three-quarters view.

Within the text of *Loving* itself, sensory data are forced into second place; description, which commonly defers to them, is dismissed into areas of what cannot be described: 'She was brilliant, she glowed as she rang her curls like bells without a note' (p. 113). The writing 'describes' what cannot be seen ('brilliance') in terms of what cannot be heard; its rejection of the novel as hearing-aid, surveillance device – a general perviousness to the means of being called to account – is discharged through a practice of 'loving' which deserts the powers of observation and deduction for those of seduction; the aperture through which it focusses the attention it aims to diffract is the game of blind man's buff. The clamorous game takes place in the mock Greek temple which ricochets with light and sound – there is no single source for either (the skylights are 'empty', and the walls produce an echo effect). The condition of 'loving' is that of one who does not see; the victim is blindfolded with the scarf printed with the words 'I love you I love you', a sensory deprivation more confident of success *without* the privilege of 'witnessing': 'Blinded as he was by those words knotted wet on his eyes he must have more than witnessed her as his head without direction went nuzzling to where hers came at him in a short contact, and in spite of being so short more brilliant more soft and warm perhaps than his thousand dreams' (pp. 114–15). The 'brilliance' of 'loving' is completely independent of visibility: 'He seemed absolutely dazzled although it had become almost too dark to see his face' (p. 115). In a sense, the textuality of *Loving* is that of one who neither sees nor hears, of a reader who is frequently 'in the dark'; it is a novel deprived of all regulatory functions, courting the disaster of unreadability, of unacceptability because it is too 'subtle' (the inadequacy of the term reveals the degree of helplessness). Green is alert to the possibility that 'Any work of art if it is alive, carries the germs of its death, like any live thing, around with it'; the more closely it interrogates the residual role of a literary form – the more it enlivens it – the closer it removes to a subcutaneous abyss of silence, 'the black cap on the whole projected work inexorably pronounced for a total lack of sympathy or communication with the reader'.[40] *Loving* has to seduce this reader, by distracting the trained eye and ear; the perspective within the form which advances a perspective on events – the apparatus by which the novel is something to look *through*, from a given point, in a limited scope of interpretation – is surprised by a brilliant connivance, the exhilaration of the nondescript, a *clinamen* or faceting, which sends the writing back to itself.

6 *Back:*
the prosthetic art

If *Loving* works by turning back in a curve upon its own material, the same is even more true of *Back*, which is incurably addicted to the sense and sound of the word 'rose'. This one-word refrain overturns the subtle biases of *Loving* – *Back*'s central character, Charley Summers, is psychotically fixated on the image of his dead girlfriend, Rose, and the resultant blind spots in his perception of the world endorse the writing's specialization. Its reconditioned idiom is unanimous with the time – Charley's instability, resembling Pye's in *Caught*, augments an already-existing, general disorientation, which bears on the demobilization of troops; the idea of the text being 'back' originates with the soldier's return from war. Almost from the outbreak of hostilities, demobilization was one of the issues uppermost in the public mind; the troops would come back to a society they would not recognize, with more women working than ever before, replacing men in industries geared to a war effort whose cessation could lead to massive unemployment. There was the hotly disputed question of how rapid or protracted demobilization ought to be; if the process became unreasonably lengthy, the impatience of the troops would in all likelihood bring on a revolution. Demobilization was in many respects the keynote to uncertainty about the future.[1]

' "We all of us came back to what we didn't expect" ' (p. 26) is the reaction of Arthur Middlewitch. A peacetime analogy for repatriation is the rehabilitation of a prisoner, but in *Back* they form one and the same problem; the fact that both Middlewitch and Charley have been prisoners-of-war – Charley for the duration – concentrates their bewilderment, abstracted as the recognition of 'difference': ' "you'll find conditions very different to what you remember of when you went off" ' (p. 33).

Their alienation is almost hyperbolized in the shape of physical incapacity; both men are equipped with artificial limbs, which are themselves bad matches – Charley is a multiple misfit, 'a young man with a wooden leg that did not fit' (p. 7). This circumstance unsettles a routine figure of speech: 'There were plenty still over on the other side would give the cool moon to stand in his shoes' (p. 9). The remorseless irony accepts just how extreme was the bitterness involved in coming 'back'.

The recalcitrance of the new Home Front environment is dramatized in the confrontation with a mass of initial letters: E.N.Y.S., I.T., B.R.N.Q., V.B.S., P.M.V.O., C.E.C., P.B.H.R., H.R.O.N., A.R.B.S., E.P.T., S.E.C.O., S.E.V.E., M.A.P., A.E.P. C.E.G.S., C.A.B., O.C.A., M.O.L. . . . Britain in 1944 is literally *unreadable*; the crucial disadvantage for returning servicemen is the inability to identify and decipher the messages received. Almost invariably, Charley misreads the tenor of a conversation; his anxiety is compounded when the interlocutor deliberately misreads the messages sent by Charley himself: 'Naturally Summers had not refused to meet the man. Hearing this made him confused' (p. 136). Since the messages he thought he had sent appear not to have arrived, Charley begins to doubt having sent them in the first place; his abject taciturnity stems from a growing mistrust of his own competence at making any acceptable sense of the world: 'He felt and felt what to say. He said nothing' (p. 68). As he stumbles round the country church-yard, he exclaims inwardly, 'Oh, he was lost in this bloody graveyard' (p. 9). The silent outburst is actually stimulated by 'the coupon question'; Charley possesses only one suit of clothes, 'the rest was looted', and the management of his clothing coupons is a constant source of disquiet – coupons represent one more facet of being 'back' which he fails to understand. The Britain of 1944 is the 'bloody graveyard' of everything he had known and thought he could trust in.

According to Mass-Observation, the common approach to the problem of demobilization was in terms of its reflection on the past: 'the past is the only future on which they can build, the only future they can clearly visualize'.[2] At the start of the war, fear of the unknown had led to absorption in the past by way of 'wishful thinking', but as a means in the avoidance of the future, thinking about demobilization led to pessimism.

The precedent on everyone's mind was the end of the First
World War with its disastrous outcome of unemployment: 'the
underlying principle which most people want to be demobilization's aim, is the prevention of unemployment'.[3] The characters of *Back* refer automatically to the First War, and its
social casualties: ' "There were plenty like it after the last war.
Sat about and moped" ' (p. 34); ' "They're coming back
nervous cases, like they did out of the last war," he repeated to
himself, and thought that, in that case, then everything was
hopeless' (p. 111). Mr Grant, Rose's father, broaches the
subject in typically manipulative fashion; the situation which
redounds to his credit is somehow made reproachful in Charley's
case: ' "Because what you have to remember, Charley boy, is
that you're one of the lucky ones. You're back. I know I reminded myself of that, come the finish of the last war, when I
couldn't seem to understand at times, just after I got out of
France" ' (p. 79). Grant's wife is an amnesiac who believes
that Charley returning from the Second World War is in fact
her brother John returning from the First. Her condition is
traced to the shock of losing her daughter – she surmounts the
death of Rose by rejecting the memory of her life, but the
eliding of this episode of her own life involves disavowing the
relationship with her husband as well. This apparently cause-
less side to the amnesia seems to require further explanation:
'Charley noticed that she never seemed to address Mr. Grant
directly' (p. 18). So far only one thing is certain; whatever the
cause of the amnesia, its effect is to prevent any misinterpretations at the hands of Grant. Charley's own flight from the
unintelligibility of the world is an attempt to retard the hands
of the clock: 'all he was after was to turn them back, the fool,
only to find roses grown between the minutes and hours, and
so entwined that the hands were stuck' (p. 9). Rose is exactly
synonymous with the pre-war period, having died 'six years
back' (p. 47, my emphasis), and as such is a talisman for coherence; but the conditions of incoherence under which Charley
now suffers derive ultimately from his liaison with Rose. The
more general loss of bearings cannot disguise the special
intensity of his own decline, the threshold of which is identified
as the sudden and unexpected marriage of Rose to James; the
latter accepts that Charley and Rose ' "were old pals, knew

each other long before we ever met" ' (p. 128). The un-
accountable swap to James evidently excited a maladjustment
in Charley's conditions of knowledge: ' "I didn't trust her
quite the same" ' (p. 204). His inefficiency at reading human
behaviour is subject to the terms of trust and betrayal – his
sense of the opposition of these terms has been completely
atrophied by the duplicity, first of Rose, and then of her father,
Grant: ' "Never divulge a confidence . . . I tell you it pays
hand over fist, keeping a confidence. . . . You see I trusted you.
It's not everyone I'd give her address. And I trust you still,
if I may have been mistaken in one respect" ' (pp. 78–9). In a
situation where he is in the wrong, Grant pretends that he has
extracted a promise from Charley which Charley has broken;
and, although resistant at first, Charley is eventually persuaded
of this. The perverse disquisition on 'confidence' (a word
suggestive more of collusion than frankness) is distantly interrupted by Mrs Grant, as if in accusation of her husband's own
real treachery:

> 'And it's paid me. Many's the time, even when I couldn't see
> what value there might be. I still kept silent. For why? Because it
> was a trust.'
> A voice quavered from the house. 'Gerald,' it called twice, thin
> and fretful. (p. 78)

Both Grant and Rose are adepts in a form of manipulation
which recalls the 'double bind' of Gregory Bateson: 'the
individual is caught in a situation in which the other person in
the relationship is expressing two orders of message and one of
these denies the other'.[4] When Grant communicates with
Charley, the latter is forced into a position of weakness from
which any resistance is turned to the former's advantage;
Grant establishes conditions under which every piece of bad
behaviour on his part is reclassified – he is the wronger acting
like the wronged: 'He said this in such a way as to make it
appear that he blamed Charley for the last visit . . . "So I
presume you've come to apologize, my boy, eh?" . . . But
Charley, as usual, was some sentences behind . . . he mumbled,
to protect himself from the unexpected charge of its being his
fault that he had made Mrs. Grant so much worse' (p. 77).
Grant is a bigamist – he is necessarily inured to the demands of

meaning the opposite of what he says; James is correct in his
surmise that a genealogy of Grant's character would throw
light on the condition of his wife: ' "That man's always up to
some deadly work. Poor soul, it's really no wonder she's as she
is today, Mrs. Grant, you know" ' (p. 126). Their common
experience of being the victims in situations which are con-
geners of the 'double bind' is behind the peculiar intimacy of
Charley and Mrs Grant: 'he kept hold of her hand, as though
it was they who had been lovers' (p. 153). Both of them are
liable to work against their tribulations in physical symptoms;
Mrs Grant's susceptibility is entirely framed by her marriage
to Grant – ' "I wasn't at all in good health soon after we
married" ' (p. 155) – and she reminds Charley of his own
vulnerability with regard to Rose, ' "when you had mumps so
bad just before she married" ' (p. 154). Mrs Grant's disabilities
vanish when her husband suffers a stroke; the power of speech,
his instrument of power, is transferred to her. The new arrangement is a guileless revelation of the old, with reversed roles:
'In spite of the warning she had given, Mrs. Grant carried on
in front of her spouse as if he were deaf, and the man could give
no sign that he heard' (p. 157). But this is the only irregularity
in a ritual of paternalistic dominance which Grant safeguards
even in death: ' "Gerald darling, Father, where are you?";
then, in a sort of torn bellow, "Father" . . .' (p. 185). Rose
herself underlines the destructiveness of this milieu, insisting on
the withdrawal of her own child from it: ' "Well, she made me
promise, if anything should happen to her at the birth, that I'd
never let those Grants have the kid" ' (p. 129). But Rose's
character is also bigamous – she abuses both James and Charley,
humiliating the latter, 'perhaps on purpose' (p. 84), by casting
him wrongly as the father of her child; and Charley is shocked
to learn of Rose having confided to James her anticipation of a
daughter, 'when with him she had been so full of a son' (p. 130).
In spite of counteracting measures, Ridley shows every sign of
conforming to family type: ' "He's got just the way she had
when she didn't want to do something" ' (p. 85). What this all
amounts to is literally the *familiarization* of a certain language;
Charley is forced to take his chances in a world of revoked
meanings – the more familiar this world becomes, the less
capable he is of functioning beyond its requirements, until he is

ready to interpret anything and everything in terms of contradiction and threat.

The most critical misinterpretation of the book – Charley's delusion that Nancy Whitmore, Rose's half-sister, is Rose herself – is therefore grotesquely logical in its attempt to undo the conditions of knowledge; Nancy offers a way of recuperating Rose, of making up for everything that Rose had held cheap: 'there was something here he had never seen in Rose, that he hadn't ever known of her, and it was shame' (p. 54). Through Nancy, Rose's vindictive treatment of Charley can be deflected onto the rival James, and onto Grant himself: ' "You wouldn't deny him, Rose" ' (p. 54). 'Denial' is another of the book's key words; success or failure in revising Rose through Nancy depends on the presence or absence of denial: 'For she had denied him, and it was doing him in' (p. 56); 'She spoke as though she did not mean to deny him' (p. 68). 'Denial' is, of course, the cardinal sin against Rose, and in this respect Charley is the subject of a permanent lapse:

So Charley bowed his head, and felt, somehow, as if this was the first time that he had denied her by forgetting, denied one whom, he knew for sure, he was to deny again, then once more yet, yes thrice. (p. 13)

Then out it came. 'Had a child by her as a matter of fact,' he boasted, denying Rose a second time. (p. 26)

Then he denied his love for the third, and last, time.
    'Rose?' he said. 'Her? Oh, she was just a tale.' (p. 151)

This denial in triplicate is mirrored by Nancy's reactivating the memory of her own dead husband – as the illegitimate daughter of Grant, she is naturally subject to the same familiarizations as Charley: ' "That's all right then. For you know, no matter what others suffered, it was his life he gave." This was the third time she had said it, and it had been different each time' (p. 198). The pattern of three denials is obviously an implication of the gospel episode, of Jesus making things difficult for Peter:

And Jesus saith unto him, Verily I say unto thee, That this day, *even* in this night, before the cock crow twice, thou shalt deny me thrice.[5]

Back provides the 'sudden upthrusting cackle of geese' (p. 6) as an incidental parallel to the cock-crow; its specific effect is to implant in Charley 'an idea that he had been warned' (p. 6). But the point about the allusion is that Jesus's ultimatum is an archetypal 'double bind' – however Peter responds to it, he is going to be in the wrong. Either he rejects the authority of Jesus, and he does – 'If I should die with thee, I will not deny thee in any wise' – in which case he is guilty of a lapse of faith; or, he accepts the authority of the message, and so runs the risk of appearing half-hearted.

Elsewhere, the attempt to get the text acclimatized to a scriptural precedent takes on the bizarre form of Charley's almost allergenic reaction to the name of Grant: 'The next thing Charley knew he was by a church. He found himself reading a poster stuck up on the notice board outside, which went, "Grant O Lord," then said something about a faithful servant. The first word shook him. He cried again, "The bastard," right out loud' (p. 58). Apart from the sarcasm of its wording, the telling irony of this passage is that Charley's very refraction of the poster's meaning brings into focus the link between Grant's perfidiousness and Charley's own impulse to refract. When he fails to gauge the tone of Jordan's letter, unlike Corker and Mr Pike who recognize it as a 'try on', his resentment is unconsciously redirected: ' "The lying bastard," he cried, once more reading Mr. Jordan's letter, as if it had been a note from Mr. Grant' (p. 108). Unable to isolate the context in which the letter ought to be read, he deploys a surplus of contexts:

But Charley's feelings got the better of him. 'You don't consider someone may have forged it?' he asked, on impulse.
Mr. Pike stayed quite still. Charley blushed.
'Silly I know,' he said, 'but I just wondered. Noticed some strange things lately. One of those handwriting experts could tell.' (p. 110).

Charley is being distracted by the idea of proving through a test of handwriting that Nancy is in fact Rose. He has received a note from Nancy, but its script is unlike that of Rose's letters, so it is under suspicion of being a forgery. The letters themselves are quoted in full, exemplifying Rose's method of subtly

laying blame on Charley, of requiring constant proofs of his
loyalty: ' "Dear Stinker. I must say I think it's a bit lop-sided
your simply making up your mind you'd forget when I asked
you especially to get me those mules we saw in the advert.
Don't be a meanie darling. From Rose" ' (p. 120). In order to
produce a text for the handwriting expert, Charley cuts the
letters up, using the fragments in a collage symbolic of all
written communications, such as Jordan's letter, whose meaning has been 'scrambled'. The last physical vestiges of Rose
have now been destroyed, 'Yet that night he slept very well for
once, and did not dream' (p. 122); Charley has momentarily worked off the influence of the 'double bind' by turning it
inside out – *he* distorts Rose's message, for a change.

The other occasion on which he sleeps well, 'for once' (p.
139), is the night of his discovery that James and Dot Pitter
are in bed together. Their liaison is construed as 'treachery' on
Dot's part, despite the fact that James's rivalry asserts itself at
the outset, when he encounters Charley looking for Rose's
grave: ' "Well this is it, isn't it?" James asked. "I mean you're
really home for keeps, for better or worse, richer or poorer,
aren't you?" ' (p. 10). By evoking the words of the marriage
vow, James unconsciously notifies Charley of his claim over
Rose. But Charley is actually mollified by what he sees as
Dot's treachery, because *this time* he will be able to get his own
back; he ensures that she is sacked from her job, 'because she
had not gone to bed with him' (p. 149). The final confrontation
between them takes place against two simultaneous back-drops,
that of the office, and that of the scene of 'betrayal' ('Moonlight,
coming through a fake Tudor window, lay over her bed with
the clothes pushed back like a breaking wave'):

She stood just within the door, looking through him as if he was
moonlight.
    'Well, I'm off,' she said.
    He got up, pale as a bed, from behind his kitchen table desk.
    'How's that?' he asked. (p. 150)

For Charley, Dot is no more than a cypher, as her name
suggests; she can only be treacherous precisely because she is
a substitute for Rose – the invariability of Charley's fore-
bodings of trust and betrayal makes her, in effective terms, no

less of an 'impostor' than Nancy. Rose is all women; and all women are ambiguous, a mixture of promise and denial.

Women materialize in the text as a source of part-objects, which are either frictional or sleek; Dot is a composite of 'covered creepiness', with 'fingers terribly white, pointed into painted nails' (p. 43). But this corporeal weaponry is offset by 'smooth and oval . . . beautiful subdued fat . . . it was the softness there must be on the underside of her arms which caught his breath' (p. 43). The fetishizing of Dot's body is what enables Charley to read into it the contradictory meanings that would depreciate with a sense of the whole body individually animated. It is as if he is trying to unriddle the way that Rose has treated him – to anatomize it – in a series of transitions from promise to denial. Dot can appear threatening to the degree of excoriation: 'She'd treated herself to a manicure up in town. Its nail was enamelled to the colour of wet flesh' (p. 123); but she still bears traces of the qualities that Rose had negated: 'there were her breasts which she wore *as though ashamed*, like two soft nests of white mice, in front' (p. 43, my emphasis). The oddity of this image is equalled by its inevitability, because a mouse had been the only object of Charley's tenderness during his imprisonment: ' "I had it in a cage I made," he said' (p. 199). Dot is bracketed with a congenial form of life, whereas carnal knowledge of Rose herself is bracketed with insects and spiders; Charley remembers her as 'flitting mosquitoes', and 'as she had been one afternoon, a spider crawling across the palm of a hand, the hair hanging down over her nose, telling him how many legs they had' (pp. 56–7). In a world whose messages overlap onto several contexts, this computation of legs would arouse the suspicion of a secret knowledge of Charley's dismemberment. Charley's strongest aversion is to hornets: 'He had a horror of hornets' (p. 185). In *Caught*, hornets had been literally coupled to roses, in a passage that is one of the cynosures of that text: 'he thought he saw the hot, lazy, luxuriance of a rose, the heavy, weightless, luxuriance of a rose, the curling disclosure of the heart of a rose that, as for a hornet, was his for its honey, for the asking, open for him to pierce inside, this heavy, creamy, girl turned woman' (p. 64). The intensity of this pairing offers a hint that Charley's violent nausea is, at least obliquely, a sexual nausea. Certainly, in *Back,* Rose is associated with 'Honeysuckle Rose' – represented as an 'oozing' song (p. 57). But the nearest approach to revealing the female sex is a 'blind' description in which a nonexistent gaze travels over Dot's body:

Her arms built great thighs on her in his mind's eye, while she might be asking him, 'About those needle valves in stainless . . .', made her quite ordinary calves into slighter echoes of what he could not see between knee and hip, as she might be saying, 'Now those break vacuum cocks . . .', but which, so he thought, must be unimaginably full and slender, when she wanted to know where the 'accessible traps' came from, white, soft, curving and rounded with the unutterable question, the promise, the flowering of four years imprisonment with four thousand twirps. (p. 44)

'Accessible traps' – this phrase which preserves the co-agency of promise and denial, of invitation and danger, is deliberately made contiguous to the ultimate sexual 'promise' of woman, the 'flowering' of which helps to make it indistinguishable from Rose. Elsewhere, Charley's self-preservation depends on his being able to repress another 'unutterable': 'something in France which he knew, as he valued his reason, that he must always shut out' (p. 186). Charley's sense of horror is induced by the literally unspeakable, the unmentionable, what ought to remain hidden, and undisclosed. On the very first page of the book it is stressed that his leg has been lost through a hidden agency, 'the gun beneath a rose' (p. 5); 'beneath a rose' is a translation of *sub rosa,* which means 'in secret, secretly' – the gun is hiding in a hiddenness. Charley's mental and physical mutilation comes from the revelation of what needs to remain profoundly secret, the 'unutterable' part of Rose.

The fear of hidden meanings, the air of trepidation surrounding the entire book, is consistent with Bateson's profile of the individual under pressure from a 'double bind':

He might, for example, assume that behind every statement there is a concealed meaning which is detrimental to his welfare. He would then be excessively concerned with hidden meanings and determined to demonstrate that he could not be deceived – as he had been all his life. If he chooses this alternative, he will be continually searching for meanings behind what people say and behind chance occurrences in the environment, and he will be characteristically suspicious and defiant.[6]

In *Back*, when a major clerical error is ascribed to Dot, she is driven to despair, but Charley's response is to treat it as a threat to *his* position, not hers: 'This upset Charley, because he thought someone might be getting at him by tormenting her' (p. 46). His real Achilles' heel is of course the word 'rose', the talisman for coherence which is out of his control; its magic is endangered by every chance occurrence in the environment. When Mrs Frazier speaks of rising prices, ' "they rose, they've rose . . ." ', Charley automatically flinches: 'For he was as sure he would feel the ache as he had, on his one early holiday before the war, been certain that he would hear a cuckoo each walk he took, each occasion he passed an open window' (p. 35). This particular occurrence fails to produce the expected 'ache': the word gradually loses its effect as Charley moves towards investing everything in Nancy. Which is to say, the word is still there but made flesh – Nancy is as much the incarnation of 'rose', as a surrogate for Rose herself. The 'cuckoo' for which Charley had been so alert would connote sexual jealousy, since Rose might be deceiving him on the other side of an 'open window'. This sense of exclusion from intimations of a complicity is at the centre of Charley's acknowledgement of the whole world; he erects a theory of conspiracy embracing nearly every character in the book. When Nancy starts to differentiate herself from Rose – her hair, voice, and face don't fit – Charley has little trouble in resolving the anomaly; the obvious reason is the paranoiac's reason: 'Then he knew what it was. She was an enemy' (p. 49). The physical difference is easily brushed aside. But Charley had made an important concession in this respect at a very early stage of the work; although he is haunted by the idea of Rose, his memory of her appearance is by no means thoroughly accurate: 'Rose, whom he could call to mind, *though never all over at one time, or at all clearly*' (p. 7, my emphasis). Rose is in fact identifiable as 'rose' in being essentially disembodied, awaiting reincarnation in one or another appropriate form. And Charley's unconscious is actively seeking a recipient before he is ever cognizant of Nancy: 'When he got out at the other end he followed a strange girl with red hair the best part of three miles, back to what may have been her home, without trying to strike up an acquaintance' (p. 22). The sudden apparition of Nancy

marks the final, not the initial, stage in a meticulous replication of Rose. The account of the approach to Nancy's door is
resonant with predisposition:

So it was that he found himself, by chance, within a few yards of
the address Mr. Grant had given.
The door was open.
He went in. He climbed stairs. He began to regret it.
Then he was outside an inner door, on which was written her
name. Her name was there on a card. (p. 46)

The sequence of short sentences is almost completely devoid of
reflection, allowing a sense of automatism. And yet the isolation of the statement, 'The door was open', seems the result
of a compulsion to draw conclusions, as does the sustained
attention to the name on the card. The introductory qualifi-
cation, 'by chance', seems to be offered in the spirit of excuse;
Charley is trying urgently to provoke associations with Rose.
The passage continues, 'He read her name, Miss Nancy
Whitmore, in Gothic lettering as cut on tombstones.' This
detail successfully establishes a connection with the lettered
tombstone of Rose, and Charley goes on to a ponderous
scrutiny of every nuance in the decorations around Nancy's
door, to the extent of noticing that 'the top coat was wearing
thin'. He is rewarded with several convincing pieces of evidence;
the door 'was painted pink', the wallpaper 'was of wreathed
roses on a white ground', and her card 'was held in place by
two fresh bits of sticking plaster, pink'. Even his fainting-fit on
the appearance of Nancy is entirely predetermined; it is a
deferred enactment of the half-heard scenario which intro-
duces the mistaken identity theme: ' "So I said, 'it's the same
person,' " Mrs. Frazier was bringing the story to an end.
" 'Look out,' I said, 'I'm going to faint away,' I said, and she
came forward to take me by the arm. For they were as like as
two peas," she finished, with a glance of triumph at Summers'
(p. 34).
This enforcement of connections on the slightest pretext
meets the description by Freud of a paranoic delusion 'making
ingenious use of some accidental circumstances'.[7] Charley's
unconscious habitually makes forays of this kind. His paranoic
avidity is vividly suggested in the hypertrophy of his eyes,

generally specified as being 'great'. They even appear to 'grow from his head, and float in the air before your own' (p. 36) as if swelling from the desire to engross every possible scrap of evidence.

Under the terms of paranoia, Charley's world is not a chaos of misinterpretations, but an order of misinterpretations – all his distortions are systematic ones. They are no more, really, than extensions of the principle on which his 'visible system' of filing is based. The connection between this particular reduction to order and his obsessional fantasies is quite explicit; it was this indexing 'which had kept him sane throughout the first re-flowering of Rose' (p. 38). The 'visible' system is a super-imposition over an existing system; it is Charley's idea, and one which Corker does not approve of: ' "you can't just put one system over another, and then be satisfied to sit back and use the top one without any sort of a check" ' (p. 147). Charley's delusions of reference operate on the same principle; they are placed over the conditions of knowledge of 1944, proclaiming certain aspects, and disclaiming others. And they form a 'visible' system in the sense that Nancy can appear to be Rose as long as there is no cross-reference to Rose's actual physio-gnomy. The result is a dissociation of ideas which echoes the pattern of symptom-formation in schizophrenia:

Everything which opposes the affect is more deeply suppressed than normally, and whatever falls in line with the affect is abnormally facilitated. The result is that an abnormally charged idea cannot even be opposed in thought any more: the ambitious schizophrenic dreams only of his desires; obstacles simply do not exist for him. In this way, complexes which are joined together by a common affect rather than any logical connection are not only formed, but are also more firmly fixed in the patient. Due to the fact that the associational pathways which join such a complex to other ideas are not used, these associational pathways lose their effectiveness in respect of the more adequate associations. In other words, the affectively charged complex of ideas continues to become isolated and obtains an ever increasing independence.[8]

The independence of the 'affective complex' in *Back* can be measured by the incidence of the word 'rose', which is ubiqui-tous. It also appears metamorphosed, as in *Rhoda*; and takes on more approximate form as 'redness' – the Grant household is

situated in 'Redham' which in the typescript of the novel had
been 'Ruislip'.[9] But if the process were carried to its conclusion,
Back would go no further than to inscribe the single word; its
ambition would be to eternize the formula devised by Gertrude
Stein, 'a rose is a rose is a rose'. And indeed, this form of words
is secreted at both turning points of the text which involve
'rose garden' scenes: 'climbing around and up these trees of
mourning, was rose after rose after rose' (p. 5); 'briars that had
borne gay rose, after rose, after wild rose' (p. 177). The principle
of repetition is what isolates the word from other 'more adequate associations' – whenever it occurs as the past tense of the
verb 'to rise', it still has only one meaning for Charley, because
it is secured by affective connections and not logical ones. In the
same way, *The Sound and the Fury* starts with Benjy overhearing
the word 'caddie' spoken on the golf course near his home. He
understands it only as the name of his sister, and the 'more
adequate' association is discounted.

Somewhere in the middle of this over-subscription, the
'affective complex' ceases to be exclusive to Charley, where the
writing shows signs of an abnormal facility in making *its own*
connections, quite apart from his: 'His day to day sense of
being injured by everyone, by life itself, *rose* up and gagged
him' (p. 131, my emphasis). The automatic usage of the word,
even though it confirms the link between Rose and paranoia,
is all the same beyond the cognizance of Charley himself. The
most dramatic example of these covert equations undergone by
the text on its own is the over-determination of the number
three: 'He saw everything a third time' (p. 70); ' "I doubt if
she'd see me a third time," he said' (p. 81); 'James was saying
for the third time' (p. 85); 'In the next three weeks he called
thrice at Miss Whitmore's' (p. 163); 'He bounced once, then
twice, yes thrice, as he lay there' (p. 184); 'He smoked a
third cigarette' (p. 185). Whenever Charley is slow at making a
connection, the text is quick to seize the opportunity that he has
missed. Thus, Ernie Mandrew, who lives in the same village as
James, and who is an acquaintance of Arthur Middlewitch, is
finally and quite gratuitously linked to Nancy's dead husband,
Phil. There is, nonetheless, a degree to which the temerity of
these connections is realized – the text is at least nominally
aware of its own unlikelihood: 'and her name, *of all names*, was

Rose' (p. 6, my emphasis); 'For *of all people, of all imaginable men*, and fat as those geese, was James' (pp. 9–10, my emphasis).

There are, however, no second thoughts about the most schizophrenic excursion of the book – the interpolation, half-way through it, of a passage 'From the Souvenirs of Madame DE CRÉQUY (1710–1800) to her infant grandson Tancrede Raoul de Créquy, Prince de Montlaur' (p. 92). The preparations for this are typically fastidious and underhand; Charley uncovers the name of the heroine of the French passage in his search for Rose's grave: 'He had time to read the one word, "Sophie", cut with no name or date' (p. 8). Sophie's provenance in history is left carefully unspecified. This allusion is relatively straightforward, but rather more oblique is the description of Charley's own wooden leg as 'the long *souvenir* he had brought back from France' (p. 9, my emphasis).

The form of the 'souvenir' is anticipated by the anecdotal bravura of Middlewitch and Mrs Frazier; the former regales Charley with successive anecdotes about his sister-in-law, about the dockside blonde, and about the bereaved mother whose daughter had died of meningitis. Even his name seems to hint at the French passage which is in the middle, sandwiched by the rest of the text. Mrs Frazier provides the crucial anecdote of mistaken identity. And the firm which Charley works for is involved in the production of 'parabolam', which leads one to expect something along the lines of a parable which is like a parabola – on a trajectory which is curving and oblique.

The passage itself deals with a case of mistaken identity, which might be thought enough to justify its inclusion; but its real meaning is a wholly schizophrenic one, irrecoverable without special knowledge. In intra-textual terms this is *unknown* knowledge, and the meaning remains ostensibly hidden, quite precisely *sub rosa*. Not only does it lie outside the text of *Back*, it lies outside the text of the *Souvenirs* as well, in the history of its authorship. Because when the first two volumes of the *Souvenirs* were published in 1834, one anonymous critic in *The Quarterly Review* denounced the entire project as being a confidence trick:

We do not think that there is one genuine drop of Madame de Créqui in the whole publication: we are confident, and shall prove, that the 'Mémoires' are, in every point of view, *a complete forgery –*

the grossest and most impudent of impostures; for not only are the facts
false, and the work spurious, but the very person to whom they are
attributed is a *phantom* created by the ignorance of the fabricator,
who, having very ridiculously mistaken *one* lady of the family of
Créqui for *another*, builds his whole edifice on this fundamental
blunder. [10]

In other words, the account of a case of mistaken identity is in
itself the occasion for *another* case of the same mistake:

There have been TWO Marquises de Créqui – the *one* the lady
mentioned in the *Biographie*, whose maiden name was *Anne Louise
Lefevre d'Auxy*, and who was married in 1720, and whose husband
died in 1771; and the *other* – the lady to whom these Memoirs are
attributed – *Renée Charlotte de Froulay*, the wife of a gentleman of
another branch of the Créqui family, which, on the death of the
husband of *Anne*, in 1771, claimed the Marquisate of Créqui . . .
Anne Lefevre d'Auxy was the Aunt, *à la mode de Bretagne*, of Renée
de Froulay, who, in the Memoirs, usurps her age, her place, and
her honours. [11]

Suddenly, the passage from the *Souvenirs* becomes the way
through of a meaning in transit – a meaning which seems
always to be receding behind a series of alibis. The central gap
which it makes in the text of *Back* is consequently an image of
writing as schizophrenia. When everything is written over the
need to remain essentially hidden – when the motive for writing
is the unimaginable – the lengths to which it is possible to go
in covering up tracks are theoretically limitless. The writing of
Back follows a path of systematic deviations, of parabolic
meanings unable to dispense with the knowledge of what they
detour, even though that knowledge is always out of view. The
withdrawal from the meaning is compounded by the fact that
Back itself appears under a pseudonym, or mistaken identity.
The writing is a form of surplusage; it says far too little in a
direct sense, and far too much in an indirect sense. It is a
confidence trick of the kind which Grant practises on Charley;
the reader is caught in a 'double bind', aware that a proper way
of interpreting exists, but equally aware that this remains
private – any reading without it must, to a greater or lesser
extent, be a speculative one: 'He left the lodgings at his usual
hour for going to work so that Mrs. Frazier did not know; his
bed, which had been an unquiet grave all night, disclosed

nothing to the maid, Mary' (p. 56). This sentence includes the title of yet another pseudonymous work, *The Unquiet Grave* by Palinurus, whose actual author was Cyril Connolly.[12] The reader might be expected to have heard of Connolly's work, but the 'unknown' knowledge of its contents discloses another tormented preoccupation with an expired love-affair, in a text which also incorporates extracts from French literature, especially that of the period of Madame de Créquy.

Even more schizophrenic is the series of allusions to Keats's 'Ode on Melancholy'. The first positive injunction in the poem, after several negative injunctions, is to 'glut thy sorrow on a morning rose'.[13] A number of other images break surface in the novel; they are spread out over the entire text, and are given in the order in which they appear in the poem. The opening scene in which 'the rose softly thumped his forehead' (p. 8) mirrors that of the prohibition, 'Nor suffer thy pale forehead to be kissed / By nightshade' (ll. 3–4). Mr Pike is described as 'an owl in daylight' (p. 110) for no discernible reason other than to evoke 'the downy owl' (l. 7) which is deprecated as 'A partner in your sorrow's mysteries' (l. 8). Similarly, Dot's vacant bed has its 'clothes pushed back like a breaking wave' (p. 139), corresponding to Keats's 'salt sand-wave' (l. 16). The episode which terminates the second stanza of the ode,

> Or if thy mistress some rich anger shows,
>   Emprison her soft hand, and let her rave,
>   And feed deep, deep upon her peerless eyes. (ll.18–20)

is also the culmination of the second 'rose garden' scene, minus the incidental phrase, 'He fed his eyes on her' (p. 140):

She cruelly spoiled it. She took her sweet lips off his.

'Was it like that?' she asked, as though nothing had happened.

He made to grab her up to him once more. But she twisted away.

'Was it?' she repeated. He did not realise that she was aiming at Rose.

Then, in the position she held, half in, half out of his arms, and so close that the one eye in his line of vision was in the outer corner of its socket to watch him, he saw it catch the dying sunset light around, and glow, as if she had opened the eye hole to a furnace. (pp. 177–8)

Finally, and perhaps most convincingly, Charley's valediction to Ridley is a mimicry of Keats's 'Joy, whose hand is ever at his lips / Bidding adieu' (ll. 22–3): 'Charley managed to turn round, without attracting her attention, in order to make the child a sign. All he could think of, and he did not know why, was to put a finger to his lips. At that, Ridley turned, and ran off fast' (p. 207). The phrase, 'and he did not know why', speaks volumes about the coexistence of different orders of knowledge in the text.

The tone of the ode measures up to the morbidity of *Back*. But is it all going too far? The reader is worried about being deceived; perhaps the schizophrenia of writing has been outdone by the schizophrenia of analysis. The point is that it does not really matter whether the quotations from Keats are verifiable or not. What is important is that there should be some doubt either way. Because in order to be accurate about what it means to read Henry Green, there must be a strong sense of the *giddiness* of interpretation that this entails.

It is within the terms of reference of the book that every clue should be a 'red herring'; when Nancy comes out with the idea of the cat giving birth to 'two tabbies and two gingers', she is relieved to find that Charley and Mrs Grant 'were not making this a red herring' (p. 170). In a fully schizophrenic way, the text understands the metaphoric as literal, since the leading imagery of the book really is red. When the meaning begins to drift, there is always a possibility of its leading nowhere at all: ' "With me, it was Rose Grant,' he explained, and yet it was as though he could do this painlessly, as of a rib that had been removed' (p. 145). The disavowing of Rose is equated with the differentiation of the sexes, with Eve's creation from the rib of Adam; it means far too much to mean anything at all. Likewise, the rain in the graveyard has the sound 'of a man scything long grass' (p. 11) – like Death the Mower, a figure so absolute it resists integration into any other category of meaning. And the scene in a restaurant is as suddenly alchemized by 'the silence that had fallen, in a sighing covey of angels, above their table' (p. 30). These metaphors are not incarnated like the metaphor of 'rose'; they remain insubstantial, suspended, outside the flesh of the writing. The overflow of the writing *abstracts* the reading – withdraws it from the immediate context; and if the text is to be understood in terms of its profusion of contexts, the controlling sense will be of more contexts than can be coped with in one kind of reading. So that another critic of the same book is able to see it as being in the shadow of Faulkner's *Soldiers' Pay*, a novel about the home-coming of an amnesiac soldier.[14] One cannot begin to read *Back* without taking every meaning on probation and every movement of interpretation stands the hazard of the 'trancitive'. The knowledge is there, even if it is unknown; the writing remembers, even if the reading does not. And just as the conditions of knowledge of *Back* are such that 'the past is the only future on which they can build, the only future they can clearly visualize', so the novel itself comprises a resumé of Green's own past works. In a text whose affective connections are so unusually developed, the case history of its authorship, like that of the passage from the *Souvenirs*, plays a structuring role.

The recovery of an earlier work is often in proportion to its investment in the imagery of the rose, first apparent in *Blindness*: 'Roses on wallpaper, roses hung down in strips from the damp wall pointing' (*Blindness*, p. 105); the first novel even provides a reflection of roses growing outside a church. The blindness of its main character is what facilitates the ideation of his own mother: 'now she was *back*' (*Blindness*, p. 45, my emphasis) – as with Charley's desire for Rose, the word 'back' is the accessory of what ought to stay secret: 'She was like a dream, something so far away that came *back* sometimes' (*Blindness*, p. 156, my emphasis). Charley's wooden leg may bear some relation to the Oedipal lameness.

Caught is even more synoptically present; the conjunction of rose and hornet has already been mentioned. The most extraordinary correspondence is between Amy Grant and Amy Pye; apart from the coincidence of the name, both women suffer a form of mental relapse, and both share a characteristic gesture – Mrs Grant is endlessly repeating the hand-to-mouth attitude of Amy Pye: 'When she saw this she dropped her eyes quick, and put a hand on her mouth as though about to belch' (p. 18); 'Mrs. Grant objected, between her fingers' (p. 20); 'Then he was shocked to see that she was covering her mouth with a hand' (p. 173). Perhaps the refusal to be heard, ('she mumbled'), is a form of protection from being misunderstood. *Back* also features the seasonal balance of *Caught*; in fact the book ends on Christmas Day, which is the terminal date given for the actual composition of *Caught*.

The rest of the oeuvre makes a fleeting but impressive show. Charley's account of the discovery of parabolam is a vivid evocation of the foundry setting of *Living*. The relationship of Grant and his wife virtually reproduces that of Mr and Mrs Dupret, since Mrs Grant also comes into her own when her husband falls ill: ' "It's everything for her, his being like he is" ' (p. 174). Charley shares the degenerative tendency of his namesake in the previous novel, *Loving*. And on at least one occasion, his distrust of women is obscurely related to the condition of his neck: 'Charley asked himself if it was safe for them to be left together, and then for no particular reason remembered that he had forgotten to buy the tie he'd meant to get in the morning' (pp. 16–17). The text abounds with other less particular, more habitual, manoeuvres: 'his mind turning a corner' (p. 17); 'Her mouth on his palm had been like a bird in the hand' (p. 198). What they add up to is a *facile* abstract of the other work. Most of the citations have an element of the routine about them; the memory is only approximate, like that of Charley, and Mrs Grant; it does not consist of remembering, but of 'misremembering'; 'Mr. Grant continued. "I knew a man once, in the ordinary run of business, who started to mis-remember in that fashion. Wasn't long before he'd lost all his connections" ' (p. 14). Grant himself is the cause of 'mis-remembering' in others. And in this respect, Charley recognizes that 'he was back now, all right' (p. 14); or at least, 'he was back' in the published version, whereas in the typescript version 'he was *caught* again. Not for the first time he felt how false it could be, a summer evening' (TS, p. 17, my emphasis). The process of revision has concealed the perfect example of a delusional reference to the past, a postscript to the 'disremembering' of *Caught*. 'Historization' is impossible in the context of a schizophrenia whose condition is precisely that of not being in touch with all the facts. Green is not being simply facetious when he asserts that 'As far as I'm consciously aware I forget everything I read at once, including my own stuff.'[15] The position is the same as Faulkner's with regard to *The Sound and the Fury;* fifteen years after first publication of the novel, he added an 'Appendix. Compson 1899–1945' without bothering to re-read the book.[16] Green's recoupment of his own writing is after the fashion of a screen memory, a projection based not on what he had actually written, but on 'what might have been'.

The system of abridgement is intra-textual as well as inter-textual. The scene in the graveyard, and the later scene in the bombed suburban garden, come together as the epitome of the whole work; they are simulacra of an ideal 'rose garden' scene. Both passages overlied the Steinian phrase, 'a rose is a rose is a rose', and there are other parallels of imagery and diction:

Well the old days were gone for good, he supposed while standing by a cypress, holding a briar off his face. The rose, rocking from it, sprinkled held raindrops on his eyes . . . when his glance was held by a nest the walking stick uncovered, and which had been hidden by thick enamelled leaves that were as dark as the cypress, as his brown eyes under that great ivory pink rose. Changing hands with the stick so the rose softly thumped his forehead, he pushed past to lean, to feel with a hand. But the eggs were addled, blue cold as moonlight. (p. 8)

But when they got round the red garage . . . they had before them . . . a single line of dwarf cypresses, five feet high with brown trailing leafless briars looped from one to the other, from one black green foliage to its twin as green and black, briars that had borne gay rose, after rose, after wild rose, to sway under summer rain, to spatter the held drops, to touch a forehead, perhaps to wet the brown eyes of someone idly searching these cypresses for an abandoned nest whence fledglings, for they go before the coming of a rose, had long been gone, long ago now had flown. (pp. 176–7)

In the later scene, the nest is free of its addled eggs, but is abandoned all the same; there is a sense in which the writing's approach to the rose garden is always mis-timed or miscalculated. The dereliction of the nest is an image of the failure to synchronize: 'Nance was shocked to find him absent. For a moment she wondered if the bird was flown' (p. 182). In Charley's eyes, Nancy takes on flesh only as a compromise with the idea of Rose, and discrepancies are counted as betrayal. The earlier scene takes place in a graveyard, by extension a Garden of Remembrance, or Garden of Gethsemane, and is directly associated with the prediction of Peter's denial. The later scene reproduces the setting, but is focussed upon a more active betrayal:

Both instinctively looked back to find whether they were being followed, but all they saw was the red mound of light rubble, with the staircase and chimney lit a rosier red, and, as they turned again to themselves in the garden, the briars wreathed from one black cypress to another were aflame, as alive as live filaments in an electric light bulb, against this night's quick agony of the sun.

Then, before he knew what she was about, she had put her arms round his neck, and kissed him. (p. 177)

The unexampled description of sunset as 'this night's quick agony of the sun' is surely alluding to the Agony in the Garden. Nancy's disconcerting kiss, which is 'cruelly spoiled' immediately afterwards, is like the betraying kiss of Judas. (The gospel episode is preceded by the prediction of Peter's denial and terminated by the kiss of Judas.)[17] The briars here would symbolize the crown of thorns, in a way that is familiar from Renaissance treatments of the scene.[18] The interval between the initial embrace and its revocation has Nancy metamorphosing into a distinctly more alien form: 'her hair an animal over his eyes and alive, for he could see each rose glowing separate strand, then her dark body thrusting heavy at him, and her blood dark eel fingers that fumbled at his neck' (p. 177). It accentuates the usual pattern of promise giving way to denial. In spite of 'each rose glowing separate strand', Nancy has dark hair, not red hair – it is one of the ways in which she is physically different from Rose. It is, therefore, appropriate to recall the traditional belief that Judas's hair and beard had been red. And still in the same area of connotation, there may be a suggestion of Pilate's method of self-protection in Charley's compulsive washing of hands.

The fascination of the gospel episode lies in its seminal instance of contradiction, the idea of the Incarnation. The Incarnation takes for granted the coexistence of two different orders of meaning, the human and the divine. Peter's confusion arises from having to respond to both the literal presence of the man, and the metaphorical presence of God. The additional presence of metaphor is what creates a 'double bind' situation – is what induces a state of mind akin to schizophrenia. What this ambiguity calls into being is the need for interpretation; in a sense that is important for the reading of *Back*, Jesus stands for the origin of writing. Writing inherits the dilemma of Peter, since the Incarnation raises the spectre of a hypostatic language which fails at the outset; what is generated instead is a dissociated language, one that is at best only imperfectly reconciled to the bad faith of indivisible meaning. The scene which recaptures the Agony in the Garden is itself a brilliant example of dissociated language, because the description of the roses in the bombed suburban garden is an anachronous description: the season is autumn; the month is October; the setting is '*what had been* the rose garden', consisting of 'briars *that had borne* gay rose, after rose, after wild rose' (p. 177, my emphasis). The whole passage is a kind of paralipsis, the over-assertion of what isn't, in fact, there. The effect of this obsessive concentration on the roses is to amplify the conflict of different orders of knowledge. It is this conflict, heightened by the particular confusions of Britain in 1944, which distinguishes the 'idiom of the time'. The writing of *Back* is like an elaboration of Pascal's wager; it is the construction of a *working knowledge*, in the absence of what remains unknown and hidden.

The scene in the bombed garden culminates with an image of this absence, the 'eye hole to a furnace', an opening onto extinction which is the visual equivalent of the destructive 'something' that must always be closed off, 'which he knew, as he valued his reason, that he must always shut out' (p. 186). The avoidance of the unspeakable demands an overdraft on what it is safe to speak; the result is a nervous insistence on figures of speech which live out their entire existence on the surface in a series of makeshift satisfactions, such as the instantly assimilable oppositions of 'the *dead* spit, the *living* image' (p. 47, my emphasis), and 'over and *over under* his breath' (p. 6, my emphasis). The latency of what is suppressed gives itself away in this easy volubility: 'the new limb waiting there *numb* and *numbered* in a box' (p. 8, my emphasis). The most gratuitous diversion from the object of fear is wholly unviable on any foreseeable level of meaning: 'He was struck at once, by the absolute silence, the waiting quiet, as though something dirty was at work which might at any time come out in this darkness, *and be green*' (p. 184, my emphasis). The only point of reference for the greenness of what is to be feared is the name of Henry

Green and the occurrence of greenness in other texts written under that name. This paranoic closure can be set alongside Charley's monotonous reiteration of the phrase 'there it is', a pathetically ineffectual gesture of placement in a world exhausted by displacements. John Russell has recorded that Green used to punctuate his own speech with the phrase; so much so that Russell has made it the title of his memoir.[19]

This remarkable entrenchment intensifies the seriousness and urgency of the need for avoidance. Charley's moment of crisis is simultaneous with the death of Grant; it reaches its highest pitch when he suddenly comprehends the impassiveness of the family cat:

> Then, at the idea that this animal could ignore crude animal cries above, which he had shut out with his wet palms, he nearly let the horror get him, for the feelings he must never have again were summoned once more when he realized the cat, they came rumbling back, as though at a signal, from a moment at night in France. (p. 186)

The 'unutterable' experience has something to do with ignoring 'crude animal cries' – it is the ultimate misinterpretation, a downright inability to read the basic messages of human pity and fear. The feelings summoned up by the cat are appropriately antithetical to those summoned up by Charley's mouse, which is first heard of near the end of the book, when he mentions it to Nancy. He can at last afford to lay himself bare because the opposition of trust and betrayal is no longer so unstable; Charley is re-negotiating the meaning of trust: 'He was so trusting, she felt, that she came to trust him' (p. 200). Even so, he never elapses from being subject to different orders of knowledge, and almost the final observation of the book is to the effect that he cries out for Rose while embracing Nancy, '*not knowing he did so*' (p. 208, my emphasis). What is more, his conspiratorial valediction to Ridley is bound to perpetuate the familiar conditions of mistaken purpose, paranoia, secrecy, and guilt.

7   Concluding:
the sea-change

MIRANDA: You have often
Begun to tell me what I am, but stopp'd
And left me to a bootless inquisition,
Concluding 'Stay: not yet.'
Shakespeare, *The Tempest*, I.ii.33–6

Concluding may at first appear to react away from the increasing timeliness of Green's work; but its futuristic setting is already implicit in *Back*, where society is presented as being completely permeated with bureaucracy, with the uncontrollable logic of official forms and files. *Concluding*, set in the year 2,000, anticipates the fulfilment of the kind of prophecies made by James Burnham in *The Managerial Revolution*.[1] According to this widely discussed theorist, it was not socialism, but 'managerialism' that would prevail over capitalism; and it was the threat of such a development, or something like it, which obsessed the British intelligentsia at the end of the Second World War. The publication, both of Orwell's *Animal Farm*, and of Koestler's *The Yogi and the Commissar*, in the same year, 1945, testifies to the depth of a concern which had, of course, had nearly six years of state planning during war-time to weigh in the balance of its argument. As early as 1940, Mass-Observation was able to report a premature alarm of the sort that must have determined the attitude Green is closing with in his fiction of 1947–8: 'In this country now, the private interest is very deeply rooted; and many of the biggest private interests are terrified that the communal, public ethic should become so strong and collectivized that people would not naturally return to the private after the war.'[2]

Once the war was over, Green turned again to the Country House which had been the symbol of private interest in *Loving*, making it almost a synecdoche of the totalitarian state. The historical point is driven home by reproducing the 'old tumble down Park walls' (p. 93) of *Loving*, and by reviving the memory of a Banqueting Hall that had been 'burned down' (p. 125). The house, now an Institute, is an image of centralization; it stands in a concentric universe, its own peculiar sickle shape extended and completed by a 'ring of beechwoods planted in line with the crescent' (p. 15). Between the house and the surrounding woods – filled with cries and echoes which are reckoned to be either centripetal or centrifugal – there is a succession of terraces, encouraging the impression of a hierarchical structure. At the very heart of this complex is a 'sanctum'; as is usual with Green, power is seen to assert itself by the implication of a sacral, or even oracular, status. The new method of saying Grace before meals in the Institute dining hall involves a formula – a simple 'Thank you' – whose first effect is to recall the absent Deity it negatively refers to. A centre of power has not been obliterated but inevitably usurped. The two Principals of the establishment, Miss Baker and Miss Edge, go on weekly trips to central committee meetings in London; but these outward movements only confirm the tendency of power to nucleate itself. The Institute is the microcosmic image of a centralized, planned society.

As James Burnham might have insisted, the new regime is repetitive of the old, and only essentially differs by its increased efficiency. So far, the analysis works as well in respect of *Animal Farm* as it does with *Concluding*. That Green was aiming to write at variance with Orwell can be judged from the manner in which *Concluding* takes *Animal Farm* on board. The students and staff of the Institute (the latter group just including the woodman, Adams) share the scene with the aging scientist, Rock, his daughter, Elizabeth, and his three animals: a cat, a goose, and a pig. The third of these animals is nearer to the centre of the stage than the other two; Rock, his scientific research now honoured but obsolete, is concerned more than anything else with 'this filthy swine fever' (p. 82) which is always in congruity with 'managerialism': ' "Next to the system we live under each one of us nowadays, it's the curse of our time" ' (pp. 39–40). Half-way through the text, a series of 'conclusions' arrive from a 'Secretary's State Council' to the effect that all girls such as those at the Institute 'under tuition for State Service . . . should be provided with pig farms' (p. 124) – inviting the prospect of a farcically literal conversion into an Animal Farm State. The acerbic reference made by Sebastian Birt, the Economics tutor, to the obtuse interventions of the State – ' "We admit of no domestic animal as self sufficient under the State . . ." ' (p. 100) – might be a parodic epitaph on the failure of the original Animal Farm. But whereas the image of society in *Concluding* reproduces that failure, its writing comes to a different point.

Orwell's text is virtually the illustration of Koestler's bio-logistic observation in *The Yogi and the Commissar* that, in a world split up into a hierarchy of levels of organization, 'a thing will display different characteristics on different levels, according to the specific "organizing relations" to which it is exposed'.[3] Once the animals of Animal Farm expose them-selves to the 'organizing relations' of humans they inevitably start to display human characteristics, and their revolution degenerates. Koestler surveys contemporaneous biological theory as part of an attempt to supplement his lengthy con-demnation of the Soviet system with a theoretical summary of the history of 'destiny versus freedom (or explanation versus volition)'.[4] The survey commences with a differentiation between the Primitive's experience of a homogeneous world – based on ritual which is 'the bridge between freedom and destiny'[5] – and the Christian experience of dissociation, familiar from *Back*, wherein 'the laws of divine logic are im-penetrable by the human mind whereas the latter is an open book to divinity'.[6] A scientific determinism perpetuates this dissociation, in that 'the "destiny" of a level is its dependence on the laws of the next-higher-level – laws which it cannot predict nor reduce'.[7] In social reality, it is the principle on which surveillance operates. Scientific explanation effectively reverts to the same expedient as religious explanation – 'it renounces the idea of a homogeneous universe ruled by one comprehensive law, and replaces it by a hierarchy of "levels of organization" '.[8] This hierarchy is conceived as 'a series of terraces on an ascending slope, or as a broad ascending stair-case'.[9] What is obscure in the account, according to Koestler, is the jump from one level to another, the element of freedom, the suddenness of volition. This obscurity – it is precisely what is *left* obscure in *Animal Farm* – 'consists, as we saw, in the fact that specific organizing relations only operate on "horizontal" planes and that we cannot predict or reduce them; in other words, *we have no laws which operate in the vertical direction*'.[10] It is these hypothetical laws, these vertical tendencies, or 'transordinal' movements, as Koestler names them, which *Concluding* aims to put into effect by way of writing.

By constant recourse to metaphor and simile, the writing stages the presence of one level inside another. The method of combining the elements of a text in a 'trancitive' manoeuvre, of making violent forays across the texture of a work to recycle its material – an operation which becomes increasingly familiar in Green's practice – is therefore interconnected with the short-circuiting of a system of organizing relations which stratifies our knowledge of the world. The writing, as it were, cuts vertically not only through the text but also through the world, always understanding the world as the extrapolation of the particular text. Metaphor and simile are used to jump from one level to another – transposing the characteristics of one level onto another – so that men, women, and children are given the attributes of animals, vegetables, and minerals; and vice versa. Rock and George Adams, moving about the woods in the half-light of early morning are like 'slow suiciding moles' (p. 8), while Miss Baker, treading the same ground later on in the day, is alerted by a strange noise, and looks back 'like a hen, at night, watching behind for a fox' (p. 154). The pair comprising Baker and Edge resembles 'a couple of old black herons down in the meadow, over the daisies' (p. 219). Apart from individual predications – Miss Edge is said to whinny like a horse, while Sebastian Birt's porcine falsetto echoes the squealing of Daisy the pig – there are also transordinal epidemics such as the collective curiosity of the students, which is 'like the smell of a fox that has just slunk by, back of some bushes' (p. 24). The combined murmuring of these girls is like a 'susurration of feathers' to the partial deafness of Mr Rock. And there is a constantly repeated transmission of this sort between the confabulating of girls and of birds: 'The noise of their talking was a twitter of a thousand starlings' (p. 98). The girls *en masse* are all but merged into the evocations of starlings whose flocking at morning and evening provides the images of convergence and divergence upon which, as will later be seen, the reading of the book effectively pivots. If we follow the writing in an opposite direction, the non-human world can be seen behaving in a corresponding fashion; the sun breaks through the dawn mist 'like a woman letting down her mass of hair from a white towel in which she had bound it' (p. 6), while at its height during the day it is 'beating stretched earth as a brass hand on a tom tom' (p. 75). A mass of azalea bloom 'in full sunlight' is compared to 'the colour of Merode's hair in her bath' (p. 95), Merode being one of the two girls reported missing at the start of the day (which is also the start of the book). The fallen beech tree where Sebastian and Elizabeth subsequently discover Merode is regarded as 'a middle aged woman he'd seduced' (p. 55), while on another occasion beech trees are apparently equipped with 'pointing fingers' (p. 109). Rhododendrons (as a variation on the usual roses) have flowers 'the colour of blood, and the colour of the flesh of bathers in open air in sunless country' (p. 98). And while nature is not invariably anthropomorphic, it may otherwise obey vertical rather than horizontal laws, if it is non-human or non-animal, by performing actions distinctly animal-like or human-like; so that rhododendrons 'stared' (p. 168); while the light from an open window 'increased by strides' (p. 187).

This everywhere transordinal activity might be a demonstration of 'the naturalism of man and the humanism of nature both brought to fulfilment' proposed by Marx for a definition of society itself.[11] This brings us rapidly to the contention that *Concluding*'s writing figures a socializing process which is the contrary of that inferred by its image of a totalitarian society in the year 2,000. The aging scientist, Rock, represents a point of greatest resistance to this society, as much by name as by character. His reference to the Greek word for rock – 'he spoke out loud the name, "Petra"' (p. 245) – alludes to the rock-hewn Graeco-Roman city as a possible image of the harmony of nature and culture. Another 'rock', whose proximity is increased by the form of the Greek word, exists in Peter, rock of the Church. But if the name of Rock converts man into metaphor, it is not with the effect of dissociation. *Concluding* takes over from *Back* the figure of incarnation only to cut a

vertical path through religious explanation, so that a notion of
man as the incarnation of a godhead, with all that that entails,
gives way to a process of incarnating *the whole world*: not man
as god, but man as rock. Knowledge of the world becomes the
knowledge of what Merleau-Ponty has conveniently termed
'the universal flesh'. The body no longer rivals the world
beyond it, but is 'on the contrary the sole means I have to go
unto the heart of the things, by making myself a world and by
making them flesh'.[12] This unity of being resembles the
transordinal, vertical lawfulness which Koestler, quoting the
Marxist biologist Joseph Needham, finally identifies in *The
Yogi and the Commissar* as nothing more nor less than *loving*:
'From this point of view, the bonds of love and comradeship
are analagous to the various forces which hold particles together
at the colloidal, crystalline, molecular, and even sub-atomic
levels . . .'[13] What *Concluding* does is to put this 'symmetry,
harmony, love' to work in a textuality of the universal flesh.
As in *Loving* itself, 'loving' is what makes the world flexible, is
what loosens it up; Rock's daughter, Elizabeth, is completely
inarticulate and incoherent except with regard to her lover,
Sebastian Birt: 'It was noticeable when she spoke of this young
man, and even more so when in his presence, that she was
fairly collected in her talk' (p. 37); 'It was noticeable how,
when with her love, she no longer hesitated with her spoken
feelings' (p. 41). Elizabeth is effectively disconnected from the
world in which her love is outlawed not in word but in deed.
Sebastian, on the other hand, is efficient in adaptation: 'for he
was always in a part' (p. 29). As the reader of *Loving* might have
predicted, his particular expertise is in mimicry (he bears a
physical resemblance to Mike Mathewson); indeed, his
adjustment to the ruling perspective is such that he performs
his imitations 'unaware' (p. 56), and 'unconsciously' (p. 61).
Elizabeth realizes that this 'trick he had' is a method of accom-
modation, of bringing a conversation 'to what he considered
to be the level of the person he addressed . . . in other company, it was the impulse which led him to do his imitations. She
was aware of this' (pp. 44–5). Whether she adopts her own
protective vagueness as unconsciously as he resorts to mimicry
is less certain: 'She had at once put on her vagueness for
protection in the circumstances' (p. 56). Sebastian has in

reserve an 'own voice', occasionally for use with Elizabeth, but more often produced in the company of Mr Rock: ' "They've mislaid one of their girls" ', he mentioned as casual as could be, speaking in his own voice, as he almost always did to the old man'(p. 39). We are told that Elizabeth has had a breakdown, was unable to function as a servant of the State; Sebastian succumbs to 'managerialism', but not without some regret for his complicity with it.

'Loving' as the disrupter of 'managerialism' had also featured in the 1942 work of Erich Fromm:

Man, the more he gains freedom in the sense of emerging from the original oneness with man and nature and the more he becomes an 'individual', has no choice but to unite himself with the world in the spontaneity of love and productive work or else to seek a kind of security by such ties with the world as destroy his freedom and the integrity of his individual self.[14]

Fromm diagnoses a commitment to 'managerialism', or totalitarianism, as the result of a 'fear of freedom', the inse-curity which follows replacement of a homogeneous world with a hierarchy of different levels. But Fromm's alternative is too narrow; man can be united with the world by other means than love and productive work, as Gregory Bateson suggests in 'Form, Substance, and Difference'.[15] Bateson parallels Merleau-Ponty's argument in seeking to commute the rivalry of man and world – 'as when you arrogate all mind to yourself, so that you will see the world around you as mindless' – with the interanimation of the two: a process which can be achieved as much by *dying* as by loving: 'But if mind is immanent not only in those pathways of information which are located inside the body but also in external pathways, then death takes on a different aspect. The individual nexus of pathways which I call "me" is no longer so precious because that nexus is only part of a larger mind.'[16] Far from being pre-eminent in nature, man becomes effectively redundant with the emergence of an universal mind – homologous to what has already been des-cribed as the 'universal flesh'. It is time to reveal that *Con-cluding*'s working title was in fact *Dying*, and that Green re-tained it until the very last stage of revision.[17]

Almost from the start, the writing is drawn in the direction of vitiation and death. The two figures of Rock and Adams, it will be remembered, emerge as 'slow *suiciding* moles' (my emphasis). And the light of this waxing day is described in terms that make it appear to be on the wane: 'A light came through, so grey it was *doomed*, together with a wisp of mist' (p. 13, my emphasis). The lake in the Institute grounds, where it is supposed Mary's corpse might well be found, has an ominous smell of 'rotting, for perhaps all of three times seventy years' (p. 147); this multiple of human longevity immediately draws attention to Rock's own declining years, as he searches the lakeside for any sign of Mary. The naturalism of man and the humanism of nature are to be brought to fulfilment by this concurrence of 'loving' and 'dying':

'Hush, Gapa,' she said. But he walked away, they followed, and a second time that group of children opened, reclosed behind the couple trailing after, having parted as another vast bloom might that, torn by a wind in summer, lies collectedly *dying* on crushed fallen leaves, to be divided by one and then two walkers, only for a strain of wind to reassemble it, to be rolled back complete on the path once more, at the whim of autumnal airs again. (p. 231, my emphasis)

The couple mentioned is of course the pair of lovers, Sebastian and Elizabeth, while the children are like the azaleas and rhododendrons which, having been picked to decorate the hall for the Dance, must be going over by now; there is a general atmosphere of gradual deterioration. The text unites man and world by the desire, and decay, of the universal flesh; its project might be expressed as the re-integration of those tendencies excluded by the ego. In effect, one could almost substitute for the titles *Loving* and *Concluding*, the terms 'Eros' and 'Thanatos', the two Greek words used by Freud and his followers in demarcating the 'life instincts' and 'death instincts'. Both classes of instinct can be regarded as transordinal, since the life instincts show a progressive tendency to establish more organized forms, while the death instincts have a regressive tendency to restore less organized forms. To recognize the presence of the instincts within the psyche is to recognize a vertical law opposed to the horizontality of the ego, understood as the agency of adaptation. The 'point of view' from which

Joseph Needham, in the passage quoted by Koestler, is able to compare 'the bonds of love and comradeship' with 'the various forces which hold particles together' is in fact an explicitly Freudian view of 'the task of Eros'.[18] Among the characters of *Concluding*, Sebastian Birt seems as much attracted by Rock as by Elizabeth: as much by the 'dying' of the one, as by the 'loving' of the other.

The jump effected by metaphor or simile from one level to another is often by way of the decomposition, or even the mutilation, of the universal flesh. An outlandish example occurs when Elizabeth embraces Sebastian 'as though she were an octopus that had lost its arms to the propellers of a tug, and had only its mouth now with which, in a world of the hunted, to hang onto wrecked spars' (p. 55). The extreme violence of the mutation is like that of a vertical current passing between 'loving' and 'dying', via the universal flesh, with the force of an electric shock. The transordinal law seems to be characterized by the mutual influence of 'loving' and 'dying' tendencies: Miss Marchbanks finds herself affected by Moira's beauty at the same moment as she is suffering 'the drain on her resolution which this absence of the two girls had opened like an ulcer high under the ribs, where it fluttered, a blood stained dove with tearing claws' (p. 47). A comparison of the typescript with the published version of the text reveals a chief element in the revision to have been a planned increase in the amount of damage inflicted in this 'world of the hunted': it is obviously the criterion for changing this – 'a person's lipstick, when it was smudged half way to her nose, gave the whole face a most dissolute appearance' (TS, p. 143) – into this: 'a person's lipstick, when it was smudged half way to her nose, wounded the whole face like a bullet' (p. 96). In any event of revision, the writing becomes less of a medium of explanation in direct ratio to its growth as a medium of volition: 'it was not for all this' (TS, p. 110); 'it was not, say, for a sight of decapitated frogs' (p. 75). The extravagance of these ruptures of the universal flesh is what lies behind the 'vertical' damage to a 'horizontal' grammar; witness, for example, the account of Merode's discovery: she is the girl 'whose red hair was streaked across a white face and matted by salt tears, who was in pyjamas and had one leg torn to the knee' (p. 56). In terms of explanation, the second clause ought to give the impression of a torn pyjama-leg; but in terms of volition, the writing has inclined us toward the view of an injured leg. That this 'vertical' pressure is tendentious, not accidental, is clear from the typescript, where the second clause is purely explanatory: 'who was in pyjamas *that* had one leg torn to the knee' (TS, p. 80, my emphasis).

Both the text and its world are voluntarily defective: the chief opposition (in principle, at least) to a more efficient, 'managerialist', system comes from Rock, who is qualified at the outset as being '– Old and deaf, half blind' (p. 5), and this approximate deafness cum blindness is stressed again and again in the text. As in *Loving*, a defective sensory apparatus ridicules the idea of a text having to reproduce sensory data, of the novel as a text that is turned towards the light, co-ordinated by a line of vision, a panoramic scan. Delusions of reference have the effect of reducing a hierarchy of organizing relations to a not inevitable or, if you will, primordial state – antecedent to all forms and degrees of organization. In one sense the writing does this quite literally, because the text opens onto a primeval landscape of a dense, impenetrable fog, out of which looms a 'rock' (Mr Rock) and a single beam of light (from Rock's torch). It is a scene reminiscent of *Blindness*, of Entwhistle's cottage in the early morning mist, of the atmosphere itself refusing to be a medium for vision. Rock's relationship with Elizabeth is comparable to that of Entwhistle with Joan. Both old men occupy a position that is marginal to society, and both are possessed of a 'great theory'. Rock's character even copies the drunkenness of the unfrocked priest: 'The fact was, the old man might, on occasion, get muddled drunk' (p. 249).

The strategic obscurity of fog is matched at intervals in the text by other opaque atmospheres; a combination of mist and sunlight streaming into Mrs Blain's kitchen has an equal, if different, 'blinding' effect: 'She could not see this because it was beyond the sunlight' (p. 23); 'And in a moment the old and famous man was left alone at table, altogether blinded by increasing brightness' (p. 29). Excesses of light are deployed to the same end as in *Loving*; Miss Marchbanks, faced with Moira, is 'dazzled' by exactly the same kind of 'brilliance' (p. 50) associated with Edith in *Loving*. Some sort of ethical distinction between the teacher's 'weak eyes' and Moira's 'strong eyes' is attempted; Marchbanks is susceptible to the girl's 'loving' attributes only with the removal of her spectacles, so that the impression of Moira as a sexual being is dispelled by a restoration of focus which makes her into a child once more: ' – You could admire children when you were not in a position properly to focus them' (p. 50). Rock's is also a conspicuously *spectacled* vision, but with all the emphasis thrown onto his 'thick lenses' which are remarkable because they 'distorted *edges* of vision' (p. 204, my emphasis). The more authoritarian of the two Principals of the Institute is Miss Edge, because the ruling perspective is always in need of a frame, the delimitation of a surround: Edge is necessarily the guarantee of its stability, and a means of achieving a sharp focus.

The aural counterpart to all refractions of the visible world arises from Rock's deafness; rhyming is his principal mode of social intercourse, and when the dialogue involves him, it often follows a sequence of half-intentional, half-unintentional, agreements of sound not sense: ' "You and your sort" . . . "Lose the fort?" . . . "Booze the port" . . .' (p. 161). Rhyming is a transordinal activity because it subjects the horizontal organization of normal sentence structure to the vertical tension of an arbitrary, wilful relationship of consonance between words. The text itself does not employ rhymes, but it does use homonyms for a similar reason. If we approach the following sequence horizontally, the first, momentary, sense derived from our reading is of a logical contradiction, or else a farcical reverse: 'But Miss Edge would not budge. She was moved' (p. 15). The subtlest vertical shift of one word, whereby Miss Edge is emotionally moved, allows writing as explanation to blunder on its own terms. With the sequence, 'a sort of adolescent's smiling courtesy, out of place in a beak' (p. 41), horizontal priorities momentarily impel us to visualize a bird-like beak, because of the proximity of a smiling mouth. The other, schoolboy slang use of the word – to denote 'schoolmaster' – also has to struggle against the widespread transordinal project of the 'naturalism of man'.

But perhaps the most perverse distortions are those by which a sensory medium is made conspicuous precisely when it is redundant:

They did not speak at once, went on together down the ride in silence, between these still *invisible* tops of trees beneath which loomed *colourlessly* one mass of flowering rhododendron after another and then the azaleas, which, *without scent*, pale in the fresh of early morning, *had not yet begun*, as they would later, *to sway their sweetness* forwards, back, in *silent* church bells to the morning. (p. 6, my emphasis)

The total effect of various forms of sensory unadaptability is of a lack, or at least a hesitation, of central control. The senses are not straightforwardly co-ordinated by, or arrogated to, any single consciousness. In the world of Merleau-Ponty's universal flesh, ' "my consciousness" is not the synthetic, uncreated, centrifugal unity of a multitude of "consciousnesses of. . ." which would be centrifugal like it is', but is rather the condition of a body which 'assembles into a cluster the "consciousnesses" adherent to its hands, to its eyes, by an operation that is in relation to them lateral, transversal'.[19] The unity of man and world evoked here – Merleau-Ponty calls it a "prereflective and preobjective' unity – is homologous to the primordial state already mentioned, antecedent to all forms of organization. There is no basis for dividing man and world with the rivalries of subjectivity and objectivity; the senses are free to supplement their horizontal organization on the human level with a vertical ('transversal') organization which relates them universally to Visibility, Tactility, and the like. The centre-orientated consciousness produced by 'managerialism' is countered by a cluster of consciousnesses not subject to hierarchical organization. And the replacement of an individual (horizontal) Sentience by a general (vertical) Sensibility is furthered by yet another kind of transordinalism, in a process of synaesthetic combinations by which 'there is even an inscription of the touching in the visible, of the seeing in the tangible':[20] 'the fog bank . . . had made all *daylight deaf* beneath' (p. 5, my emphasis); 'a great shaft of early sunlight . . . *shone* so *loud*' (p. 21, my emphasis); 'The girl and the old man came together over this, in the *megaphone of light*' (p. 21, my emphasis); 'But the girl did no more than move her *blind hands*' (p. 65, my emphasis); 'So they haltingly crept down into *blinding silence*' (p. 203, my emphasis); 'the *moon* was so full and *loud*' (p. 244, my emphasis). The examples are countless, but

perhaps the *locus classicus* of synaesthetic transformations is the
episode in which Merode is fascinated by the black and white
squares of the dado in the 'Sanctum'. The girl is hardly the
subject perceiving an object, because the dado is more active
than she is – it thrusts its visibility on her attention: 'while her
horror at this interview increased, so the dado began to swell
and then recede, only to grow at once even larger, the square
in particular to get bigger and bigger till she felt she had it in
her mouth, a stifling furry rectangle' (p. 69). The dado plays a
game of touch and of taste with her vision; and in fact there is an
almost animal tactility about it:

The furry square on her tongue started to swell once more.
    'I'd like to help you but you won't let me,' the woman said.
Merode began to cry again. This cut her off from the growing
dado, but the rectangle was black with stiff hairs on her tongue.
(p. 71)

Once again, it is the transordinal motive that is set on edge
when the typescript is compared with the published version:
'the furry square' is 'the black square' in the typescript (TS,
p. 104), while 'black with stiff hairs on her tongue' is simply
'black on her tongue' (TS, p. 104). There is heavy irony in
Edge's adoption of a quasi-synaesthetic attitude – ' "at the
present glorious season, down here, *to see is to feel*, sergeant" '
(p. 92, my emphasis) – because nature only really exists for
her in what is visible from a given point; after the flowers have
been picked for the Dance,

'I had blamed myself for telling Marchbanks they were to take care,
when they robbed nature, that it should be where we could not see.
For you know how it is, Baker. Usually one has only to suggest what
must not be done to find it carried into practice far quicker than
any order, however sensible my dear, but there' (pp. 76–7)

Nature, in other words, is given an edge; it contracts to what
is visible to man, becomes an object for his use. This restrictive
view corresponds to Baker's regard of nature as interchangeable, *quid pro quo*, with a farm of black and white animals, as
if all she had to do was to extend the 'radiating perspective'
(p. 12) of the black and white dado beyond the Sanctum,
beyond the Institute, and out over the whole of the rest of
nature.

The antidote to this 'managerialist' perspective is a form of visibility in which there is no longer any question of *control*. It is rather an experience of the visible which Merleau-Ponty calls the 'art of interrogating it according to its own wishes'.[21] When Miss Edge looks 'with anguish about the great room in which they were to dance', she notices 'flat oak panelling eight foot up the walls, all of which, including a vast bow window over the Terraces, had been varnished a hot fox red, then, at some later date, treated with lime, until the wood turned to its present colour, the head of a ginger haired woman who was going white as her worries caught up, in the way these will' (p. 125). The subject becomes dissolved in the object; there is less reason for excluding that which sees from that which is seen, because the visible is no longer under the control of man at the imaginary centre of his universe but is immanent, a part of the sensibility of the universal flesh. The panelling turned into the head of a woman is like a reverse image, and man's redundancy is more or less settled by a series of mirror images, in the larger scale of the whole text. One of the more prominent examples concerns the reflection between the discovery of Merode wearing her pyjamas, on 'some nondescript overcoat' (p. 57) underneath the branches of the fallen beech tree, and the revelation of the doll 'dressed gaily in miniature Institute pyjamas, painted with a grotesque caricature of Mary's features on its own flat face, laid disgustingly on a bit of mackintosh, embowered by these blooms' (p. 140). The images are in effect rhymed, and like rhymes they add to the difference between vertical and horizontal the rhythm which opposes the recursive to the lineal. The principle involved is of a recession of images in a pair of facing mirrors; the relationship of the one with the other is stronger than the apposition in place of either. And it is the degree to which this reciprocity is adequate which determines the advancement or retirement of man in control. Reciprocity is nowhere more intense than in those passages which cover the flocking of starlings at morning and evening:

Because, except for what still hung over the water, the mist was evaporating fast, the first beech trees away to the right were quite freed, her Park itself was brilliantly clear, the sun up, a lovely day had opened and, as she watched, a cloud of starlings rose from the nearest of her Woods, they ascended in a spiral up into blue sky; a thousand dots revolving on a wave, the shape of a vast black sea-shell pointed to the morning; and she was about to exclaim in delight when, throughout the dormitories upstairs, with a sound of bees in this distant Sanctum, buzzers called her girls to rise so that two hundred and eighty nine turned over to that sound, stretched and yawned, opened blue eyes on their white sheets to this new day which would stretch on, clinging to its light, until at length, when night should fall at last, would be time for the violins and the dance. (p. 19)

They swarmed above the lonely elm, they circled a hundred feet above, until the leader, followed by ever greater numbers, in one broad spiral led the way down and so, as they descended through falling dusk in a soft roar, they made, as they had at dawn, a huge sea-shell that stood proud to a moon which, flat sovereign red gold, was already poised full faced to a dying world. (p. 177)

The second quotation is excerpted from a passage of over three hundred words devoted to the roosting of the starlings.

It seems almost inevitable that a writer whose method of composing a novel is to 'carry it in my head. When I say carry I mean the *proportions* . . .',[22] should come to exploit the image of a spiral, because 'a spiral is a figure that *retains its shape* (that is *its proportions*) *as it grows* in one dimension by addition at the open end'.[23] The spiral, then, is prochronistic – it records in its *form* the history of its growth. It is, in other words, the shape of historization; it could almost be an ideogram for the 'idiom of the time'.

The text links its cardinal image to other forms of transordinalism. The day on which the action is set is the Founder's Day of the Institute, and the high point of commemoration is the Dance which everyone looks forward to all day. The specific dance, which is a categorically 'spiralling dance' (p. 187), is naturally the waltz of *Loving*. Working in concert are the other motifs of 'reeling chandeliers' (p. 231) and the faceting of 'eyes, much greater than jewels' and 'more fabulous gems for eyes' (p. 198); but the image of the spiral is the axis about which these other motifs rotate: 'It seemed they danced like a whirling funnel . . . that spiralling orderly . . . revolved about her' (p. 197); 'each child . . . pulled at her partner's waist to speed it, to gyrate quicker' (p. 231). The momentum of the waltz is such as to make the Institute itself appear to rotate, in another example of textual parallax, which takes the sensible world out of man's control: 'While they hurried closer the whole edifice began to turn, even wooden pins which held the panelling noiselessly revolved to the greater, ever greater sound' (p. 200). The Institute is the microcosmic image of a centralized, planned society, but this foreboding of a structural revolution is also afforded by Sebastian's little lecture at the centre of the book. The Economics tutor (whose nickname is 'old "Cause and Effect" ') defines his society in terms of its efficiency – ' "a self compensating mechanism, in, or of, equipoise" ' (p. 118) – but his description of its organizing relations is suggestively archaic: ' "There are, naturally, individual tensions, what one might describe as instances of disintegration or even of centrifugal action, whereby certain appear, now and again, to be flung out into the periphery of outer darkness" ' (p. 117). The threat of a Miltonic expulsion is one of the overtones of a time-honoured cosmology affecting the account of relations of parts to whole:

'But an incautious movement towards the centre,' he went on with an effort, 'towards the shaft upon which our little world revolves, that is to say upon the State which employs us at our main function, that of spinning like tops on our own axis,' and here he gave one of his cracked laughs to point the jest, 'can only fracture the spinning golden bowl, the whole unit, and bring the lot to nought, in other words, reduce us to the lowest, the unemployable.' (p. 118)

Sebastian's argument is a self-compensating mechanism, a tautological nonsense: its meaning is the alienism of logic. His lecture is the mimicry of an almost pre-Copernican, even Dantean, view of a concentric universe, a hierarchy whose apex is the transcendent Logos; but curiously enough (or not so curiously, given Sebastian's ambivalence), the image of the spinning golden bowl at the centre is distinctly transordinal. The associations are strong: first, with the golden bowl in Henry James's novel of that title, where the bowl, already cracked, is broken more or less simultaneously with the discovery of an adultery. This can be thought of as a 'loving' transordinalism, marriage being an adaptative arrangement. A complementary 'dying' transordinalism is provided by the reference to the golden bowl of Ecclesiastes, 12.6:

6 Or ever the silver cord be loosed, or the golden bowl be broken, or the pitcher be broken at the fountain, or the wheel broken at the cistern.

7 Then shall the dust return to the earth as it was: and the spirit shall return unto God who gave it.

The 'loving' and 'dying' tendencies are given a recursive rhythm by the spinning of the bowl. This rhythm is reflected in the diurnal rotation of the planet; the spirals of starlings occur at dawn and dusk, with the dawn passage consisting of a single sentence which synecdochically represents the diurnal scope of the whole book. The daily cycle is also made to symbolize the yearly cycle, so that the Institute and its environs undergo what appears to be an absolute seasonal contrast. During the day, it is almost unbearably hot, 'with the great sun beating stretched earth as a brass hand on a tom tom' (p. 75), while at night the moon gives everything a kind of snow-bound aspect: 'it covered everything with salt, and bewigged distant trees' (p. 189). This pseudo-winter brings the final insensibility of 'no eyes . . . nor ears' (p. 245), turning 'each of these three related people into someone alien, glistening, frozen eyed, alone' (p. 189). When the book finally runs out of time, it does so lingering on the impression of a sub-zero world: 'Lovesick, she walked as someone will who, in a dream, can find herself on frozen wastes where the frost is bright then black, but will still keep warm with the warmth of bed, although that imagined world outside stayed cold, dead cold' (p. 245). The symbolism of the seasons is aided by the fact that Founder's Day makes it the occasion of 'a year's end' (p. 199). The periodicity of 'dying' is extended from the diurnal to the planetary; the text opens with the suggestion of a primeval landscape and closes in the aftermath of its own twilight invocation to 'a dying world' (p. 177).

At the medial point of the dawn passage, sandwiched by two semi-colons in the diurnal sentence, is an image of what the 'dying' tendency leads to: 'a thousand dots revolving on a wave, the shape of a vast black seashell pointed to the morning' (p. 19). The seashell indicates a return to the inanimate, the characteristic regression of the 'death instincts'. *Pack my Bag* had already made the connection anecdotally: 'Some formation of the hills round brought no louder than as seashells echo the

blood pounding in one's ears noise of gunfire through our
windows all the way from France so that we looked out and
thought of death in the sound and this was sweeter to us than
rollers tumbling on a beach' (*Pack my Bag*, p. 40).[24] The sea-
shell is only one of several items of sterile debris scattered
among the metaphors and similes of the text: 'A knee which
. . . burned there like a piece of tusk burnished by shifting
sands' (p. 56); 'the girl who . . . combed out the heavy hair
a colour of rust over a tide-washed stovepipe on a shore' (p. 58).
The debris (which accomplishes the naturalism of man) is
either littoral or very nearly so, and with a shift of attention
from beachcombing to the beach itself this littoral sidelight
becomes even more obvious: 'he cautiously lifted boots one after
the other in an attempt to avoid cold lit veins of quartz in
flagstones underfoot because these appeared to him like sunlight that catches in sharp glass beneath an incoming tide,
where the ocean foams ringing an Atlantic' (p. 245). The
transordinal jump here is from the terrestrial to the marine,
with the spiral actually standing on a coast-line between the
two. The amphibian status of the spiral is behind the recurring
alignment of flocking birds with whispering girls:

This set them off in whispers, as a cloud passes the moon, like birds
at long awaited dusk in trees down by the beach. (p. 59)

that clatter of conversation stilled as, with a rustle of a thousand
birds rising from willows about a warm lagoon, the girls stood in
silence . . . Then . . . with another outburst of talk as of starlings
moving between clumps of reeds to roost, in their turn left . . .
(p. 99)

The adjacency, in the dawn passage, of the seashell to 'a
thousand dots revolving on a wave' is repeated in the dusk
passage, where an 'enormous echo of blood, or of the sea'
recalls the effect of a shell held close to the ear. Another spiral,
that of the waltz, brings with it the same echoes of moving
bodies of water; the music, which is 'in full flood' (p. 213),
builds up to 'a torrent, to spread out, to be lost in the great
space of this mansion, to die when it reached the staff room
to a double beat, the water wheel turned by a rustling rush of
leaf thick water' (p. 199). The water wheel, another of the
many turbines to be found – the evening of the Dance is

crisply summed up as 'the whirlpool' (p. 234) – requires a
context that is generally aqueous, rather than just marine, or
perhaps an accessory context that is recognizably fluvial:
'inevitably as tumbled water, the dance delivered them over,
two leaves that touch beneath a weir, caught in the eddies'
(p. 231). The waltz is identified with 'loving', but the whirlpool, the water wheel, the weir, the river choked with leaves,
all pose a certain danger, the possibility, even, of dying: the
setting would do for a Pre-Raphaelite Ophelia. Certainly, the
possibility inherent in the writing – 'Then Moira whirled
past, hair spread as if by drowning over Marion's round,
boneless shoulder' (p. 196) – is alive in the minds of the characters who suspect that Mary may have drowned: ' "She's
down under water in the lake of course" ' (p. 83). Merode,
Mary's 'partner in crime', takes a bath on her return which
offers the writing a chance to reflect on what can be
thought of as the virtual image of Mary's fate: the girl is
'stretched out under electric light and water, like the roots of a
gross water lily which had flowered to her floating head and
hands'; her own body, which is a cadaverous 'chalk white',
seems to her to 'sway as to light winds, as though she were
bathing by floodlight in the night steaming lake, beech
shadowed, mystically warmed' (p. 63). Sleep, as a simulation
of death, entails a 'heavy tide of dreams' (p. 22), a nocturnal
contingency whose ebb and flow is explained by the ascendancy
of the moon. The music (after nightfall) shares the recurrences
of the waltz with those of the 'spring tide' (p. 215); and the
moon, while covering everything 'with salt', is more noticeably
the cause of a figurative high water: 'Her grandfather . . .
waded much as though the moon had flooded each Terrace six
inches deep' (p. 245); 'he saw the beeches like frozen milk, and
frozen swimming-bath blue water, already motionless in a
cascade, soundless from a height, not sixty yards in front' (p.
249); 'Every twenty yards or so there was a separate marsh of
moonlight' (p. 250); 'they were in the centre of the second pool
of moonlight' (p. 252).

The process of writing which carries the text 'in my head.
When I say carry I mean the *proportions* . . .' becomes truly
vortical, pulling the various transordinal manoeuvres ever
inwards to a greater proximity with one another. A littoral

and moonlit setting, for example, becomes littoral and moonlit only with the final revision:

This set them off in whispers, as a cloud passed over the sun, like birds at dusk in trees. (TS, p. 86)

This set them off in whispers, as a cloud passes the moon, like birds at long awaited dusk in trees down by the beach. (p. 59)

And a sustained comparison of the typescript with the published version of a single episode clearly shows this intention thrown up like a continuous wake on what is an otherwise barely ruffled surface:

A great beech had fallen a night or two before, in full leaf, and lay now with its green leaves turning to pale gold. It had brought other vast limbs down as well . . . blue sky above was opened to Elizabeth and Sebastian and the bare ground between standing beeches was lit at this place by a glare of sunlight . . . and where their way had been clear, past grave trunks, was now this dying mass which lay still . . . The full sunlight . . . was a load, a great cloak to clothe them that turned the man's brown city suit to a scarecrow's habit . . . and, as Elizabeth cried out, "Now do mind, take care, it's your best suit," he had parted a screen of leaves, that hung before him like masses of grapes on a barrow . . . he looked down on a girl stretched out, whom he did not know to be Merode, whose red hair was streaked across her white face and matted by tears, who was in pyjamas that had one leg torn to the knee which, brilliantly polished over

A great beech had fallen a night or two earlier, in full leaf, lay now with its green leaves turned to pale gold, *as though by the sea.* It had brought more vast limbs down along with it . . . colourless sky was suddenly opened to Elizabeth and Sebastian *above a cliff of green. The wreckage beneath* standing beeches was lit at this place by a glare of sunlight . . . and where their way had been *dim, on a sea bed* past grave trunks, was now this dying, brilliant mass which lay exposed . . . The sudden sunlight . . . was a load, a great cloak to clothe them, *like a depth of warm water* that turned the man's brown city outfit to *a drowned man's clothes* . . . and, as Elizabeth cried out, "Now do mind, take care, it's your best suit," he had parted a screen of leaves that hung before him *bent to the tide, like seaweed in the ocean* . . . he looked down on a girl stretched out, whom he did not know to be Merode, whose red hair was streaked across a white face and matted by *salt* tears, the bone beneath, shone in this sort of alcove she had made for herself, in the fallen tree, burned like a piece of tusk burnished on a wheel revolving so fast that it had no edges and was white . . . (TS, pp. 78–80)

who was in pyjamas and had one leg torn to the knee. A knee which, brilliantly polished over bone beneath, shone in this sort of *pool* she had made for herself in the fallen *world of birds*, burned there like a piece of tusk burnished *by shifting sands*, or else a wheel revolving at such speed that it had no edges and was white . . . (pp. 54–6, my emphasis)

The writing undergoes a 'sea-change' in every sense, producing a 'rich and strange' texture in a book with the working title of 'Dying' (the passage just quoted offers the spectacle of a 'dying, brilliant mass'); it might have been composed to the programme that one can derive from Ariel's song in *The Tempest*:

> Full fadom five thy father lies;
>   Of his bones are coral made;
> Those are pearls that were his eyes:
>   Nothing of him that doth fade,
> But doth suffer a sea-change
> Into something rich and strange.[25]

Allowing for a transposition of gender, there is plenty of evidence of the drowned man in *Concluding*, and of the submarine transformation of the body into something rare and precious: the slanting sun turns Moira's 'skin to coral' (p. 138), while another 'redhead' (perhaps Moira herself) 'caught fire with sun like a flare and, out of the sun, eyes, opening to reflected light, like jewels enclosed by flesh coloured anemones beneath green clear water when these yawn after shrimps, disclosed great innocence' (p. 109). Ariel's song, with its submarine, dying brilliance, is the quintessence of transordinalism. But *Concluding*'s relationship with *The Tempest* may be more complex than the allusions to the song would permit.

The play is, of course, the source for the title of Huxley's *Brave New World*, another fable of the totalitarian future. And this detail is suggestive of the kind of ironic parallels to be found between Shakespeare and Green. Rock and Prospero

are comparable figures, since both have a background of
scientific achievement even though Rock's knowledge is
superannuated as opposed to Prospero's expertise in his 'art';
Rock has prematurely 'drowned' his books 'not one of which
he had read in years' (p. 5), and supplants the occult competence of Prospero with an all-round impercipience. However,
persistent alterations to the typescript have made Rock into a
'sage' rather than just an 'old man', thus forcing a context of
uncommon knowledge and abilities. Rock's cottage stands in
the same relation to the Institute as Prospero's island 'cell' does
to Milan; both are political antibodies, with Prospero's actual
expulsion from Milan being mirrored by Rock's potential
eviction from the Institute grounds. The ménage of Ariel and
Caliban becomes that of the three animals which between
them represent aspects of both material grossness and im-
material grace. Something of Caliban also turns up in George
Adams who, like Caliban, is 'the woodman', bereaved of his
wife as Caliban had been of Sycorax. Adams's bitterness
towards Rock at the prospect of losing his cottage to the latter
matches Caliban's resentment at Prospero's invasion of his isle;
but Rock is also his own woodman, and is even indirectly
linked with bestiality, in the anonymous letter received by
Miss Baker and Miss Edge: ' "Who is there furnicates besides
his goose?" ' (p. 164).

Miranda and Ferdinand are not so much ironically paralleled
as travestied in the figures of Elizabeth and Sebastian; Sebastian
is, of course, the name of another character in *The Tempest* –
the one who, with Antonio, is the most Machiavellian, or, if
you will, 'managerialist' (Burnham followed the publication
of his *The Managerial Revolution* with that of *The Machiavellians*).
The qualities of Miranda are more likely to be found in the
girl students, all of whose names begin with the letter M. But
if Rock is an aggregate of Prospero and Caliban, the girls are
a compound of Miranda and Ariel; Merode seems to have
'just come on her own out of thin air', p. 78 (more like Ariel
than was the case in the typescript, where she only seemed to
'appear out of nowhere'), while Mary ' "won't simply disappear into thin air, surely . . ." ' (p. 172). Merode is freed
from the beech tree just as Ariel had been released from the
'cloven pine', but the change of liberating agent is significant:

Prospero, with his stern benevolence, is replaced by Sebastian, the weak-willed bureaucrat. The girl emerges from the tree (brought down by a 'tempest'?), from the naturalism of man, from the forest which surrounds Rock's cottage, only to re-enter the Institute; the treatment she receives there is ironically contradistinctive to the manner of Prospero's and Miranda's reabsorption into the body politic.

Prospero's 'art' is magic; it breaks the laws of nature and opposes by its very secrecy the knowledge of the world that has been ordained – it is transordinal, like Rock's 'Great Theory' which, although forgotten and therefore secret, still works antibiotically as the inverse of 'managerialism', as 'poison to the younger men, who think they've exploded it' (p. 47). 'Managerialism' may have pensioned off the Deity – a simple 'Thank you' being the form adopted for saying Grace – but it is Rock, the dying 'sage', and the girl students with their 'loving' qualities, who are the heretics; Edge and Baker in their 'sanctum' sound like the high priestesses of an official religion: ' "We stand on guard over the Essential Goodness of this great Place . . . we owe it to the Trust, with which you and I have been privileged, Baker, to cast out evil hanging over the heads of our students root and branch, this we must do, or forfeit all selfrespect" ' (pp. 165–7). Their incantatory confidence has to be measured against a substratum of magic, rituals, spells, superstitions, and rumours. Beneath what they regard as the sacred 'Precincts' (p. 167) of the Institute, directly under the 'flower hung cavern' (p. 205) of a Hall where the most important festival in the 'managerialist' Calendar is being kept, are the cellars decorated with 'sprays of azalea filched from above stairs' (p. 226) where cultic ceremonies take place involving Rock and the girls. Rock goes on a kind of journey to the Underworld, through the servants' green baize door that had separated one 'kingdom' from another in *Loving*, there to have revealed to him the mysteries of an underground sect; Edge's joking reference to the Gunpowder Plot invokes a similar context of religious dissidence and of physical undermining. Below stairs, the girls seem to be in receipt of unofficial communications on their radio, so that theirs is a positive version of the apostasy which Rock negatively commits by never bothering to read his mail or his newspapers:

'He employed the daily newspaper, which he never read, only in the outside lavatory' (p. 35). The central ritual of this troglodyte society is the quintessentially 'loving' gesture of kissing, the most appropriate gesture for 'forgetting to be as they taught' (*Pack my Bag*, p. 22), because everything they will have been taught is to make them think of their own bodies as 'unfunctional' (p. 48). The adolescent girls can only begin to discover themselves as sexual beings through a kind of lotus-eating, and in fact Moira is elsewhere described as taking 'a whole azalea right into her mouth' (p. 82). Overhead, all the while, the spiralling waltz performs the function of another 'soft ritual' (p. 195); ritual, as Koestler reminded us, being 'the bridge between freedom and destiny', a form of recurrence which forgets, makes redundant, all that has superseded the lost experience of a homogeneous world.

Founder's Day, the Saint's Day of 'managerialism', occurs *vis à vis* the night of an 'all-powerful' (p. 189) new moon, with its synergism of man and nature. Rock, whose name unifies man with nature, is merged 'as if by magic' (p. 190) into the shadows of the mansion which reminds him of Petra. But the power of the occult has most effect on Edge; although she was there at the disclosure of the doll, she needs reassuring later on that it is not, after all, a voodoo effigy: ' "Were there pins in? Had it a painted Heart?" ' (p. 142). Edge is the figure-head of 'managerialism' and yet she is more prone than any of the other characters to irrational fears; it is an open secret 'known throughout the Institute, that she had a terror of rabbits dead' (p. 141). And at daybreak, she is helpless from fear of the bat (a creature of the night) which Baker lets out of the window. Her fears associated with 'dying' – fear of the doll, fear of rabbits – are complemented by an equivalent recklessness in 'loving': a minimum amount of intoxication, the enjoyment of two cigarettes rather than just one, leads directly to her proposal of marriage to Mr Rock. Edge is the embodiment of the contradiction whereby the entire personnel of a State-owned Institute conducts itself throughout the day on the basis of rumours and superstitions. Mrs Blain's characterization of the place as 'this perplexed establishment' (p. 114) is almost clairvoyant; the girls especially work by hearsay, each one pretending to share the secret, possessed by none, of Mary's disappearance. No interpretation of events is ever shared: everyone to his own version.

The circulation of rumours is the model for reading the text, which has no probable outcomes, no resolution of its mysteries. *Dying* becomes *Concluding* because its writing is always going through the appearance of reaching a conclusion without ever doing so; it plays a game with our horizontal method of storing information for use later on. The most it will allow is the working hypothesis which a horizontal, lineal, reading will later discard as useless. The text cannot be reasoned out; it offers the alternatives of a weak conjecture or a strong conjuration; it opposes the horizontal organizing relations of a novel with the vertical 'spell' of persistent, recurring, transordinal laws. Certain of these spells are cast vertically through one after another of Green's works; so that *Concluding* appears as the *summa* of all his triadic combinations: 'He groaned a third time' (p. 5); 'Then the cry came a third time . . .' (p. 10); 'the mist was rolling back, even below her third Terrace . . .' (p. 15); 'The sinking sun partitioned their room into three, as it came in by three windows' (p. 163); 'Then a third concourse came out of the west . . .' (p. 177); ' "For the third time, Melissa! Shut up, will you?" ' (p. 184); 'When the music began a third time . . .' (p. 195); ' "Come on, just three times round the floor" ' (p. 222); 'The three left music' (p. 231); 'The cry came a third time . . .' (p. 249); the text is even divided into three parts. Just as the official celebration of Founder's Day takes place in the Hall at exactly the same time as its ceremonial traducement in a crypt, so *Concluding* itself works by a simultaneity of levels. It is a *crypto-novel*, in which the patterns of volition coincide unfavourably with the patterns of explanation: to read it is to 'cross the i's and dot the t's' (p. 130). The experience is akin to a psychoanalytical transference, in that learned relations are unlearned with a different map of the same terrain. Faced with the text of *Concluding*, it is in terms of the novel that we seek to *explain*. And yet the language of explanation is always *dying* in *Concluding*: dying, it allows this sort of a novel to synchronize with the temporality of the universal flesh; it produces an idiom of temporality. The coherent deformation of the learned relations between text and world is a kind of anamorphosis: viewed from the perspective of a novel, the text appears distorted or even nonsensical, but from another angle, or by reflection, its internal relations dance a new measure, create a new sense. Rock's insistence on an inconclusive finale – ' "We shall never know the truth," he said' (p. 253) – affects the reader as an after-image of the perspectival view, when this fades before the vision of an entirely re-ordered world; it is, in other words, the precise inversion of expectations in that moment when Miranda, who waits for the chance to fall in line with the rest of a 'brave new world', encounters the same prescription of 'Concluding "Stay: not yet." '

8 *Nothing, Doting:*
something living which isn't

Nothing and *Doting*, Green's last two books, have almost always been connected with each other by his critics. The reason for this is not far to seek, since what divides them from the rest of the oeuvre is precisely what brings these two works together: a primacy of dialogue over every other conceivable mode of fictional presentation. Dialogue had always been a strong point, often celebrated, in Green's writing but in these two books it is practically lifted free of the matrices in which his other work had taken shape. The disengagement of elements results in the 'rich and strange' texture, which had always maintained the audacity of Green's prose, being degraded to something like its line of least resistance. Syntactical resourcefulness and figurative chicanery merely subside in a string of clichés, totally reliant for their effect on a form of textual parasitism. The opening passage of *Nothing* is an elegant rigmarole of motifs borrowed from *Caught, Loving, Back*, and *Concluding*:

outside a single street lamp was yellow, reflected over a thousand rain drops on the glass, the fire was rose, and Penelope came in . . . and she was dressed in pink which the glow blushed to rose then paled then glowed once more . . . all this spelled marriage, heralded a bride without music by firelight, a black mouth trembling mischief and eyes, huge in one so young, which the fire's glow sowed with sparkling points of rose. (pp. 1–2)

Predictably, the text rounds itself off with a formal reciprocation, both of this material, and of what is episodically related to it in the earlier texts:

the fire glowed a powerful rose and it rained outside so that drops on the dark panes, which were a deep blue of ink, by reflection left small snails' tracks across and down the glass in rose . . . he could see into this eye, into the two transparencies which veiled it, down to that last surface which at three separate points glowed with the firc's same rose . . . three great furnaces quiescent in her lovely head just showing through eye-holes to warn a man, if warning were needed, that she could be very much awake, did entirely love him with molten metal within her bones, within the cool back of her skull which under its living weight of hair was deeply, deeply known by his fingers. (p. 244)

The undoubted pleasure which this writing brings is one of nostalgia, of recognition rather than of invention. Green's evasion of what he sees as the false consciousness of the time by means of the deliberate construction of a second nature degenerates into something that is merely secondary: a side-show of luxury items, generally inhering in what can loosely be called description, however fragmentary or indirect this might be. In *Nothing*, when the six-year-old Penelope intrudes on her mother in conference with brother Philip, how much resonance is imparted to her gesture of laying finger to lips which is not to be had without reading *Loving* and *Back*? And how awkwardly insistent would *Nothing*'s interest in physical deterioration seem, without a knowledge of the place this has always held in Green's writing? Apart from the unfortunate Arthur Morris who succumbs, after the initial amputation of a toe, to the loss of an ankle, and finally to that of a whole leg, there is mention of a defunct individual named William Smith whose wife had left him when she ' "couldn't face pouring the whisky down his throat when he lost his arms" ' (p. 172). John Pomfret, one of the book's main characters, develops diabetes, while at the very end, Dick Abbot's choking fit brought on by kissing Liz Jennings combines 'loving' and 'dying' attributes without coming to any point beyond the recension of Raunce's phallic convulsion in the finale of *Loving*: 'his face grew more purple and at last black, as his staring eyes appeared to fight an enemy within . . . until, when his red eyes were almost out of their sockets he began to be able to draw breath once more and what was plainly a glow of ease started to pale him, to suffuse his patient, gentle orbs' (*Nothing*, p. 243). *Doting*'s attempt to have the reader reconciled to these sciolistic manoeuvres by means of a sort of consultative archness is too complacent; almost unbelievably, the text refers on its first page to a scene in a railway station, where 'three weeks later' Peter is to 'carry a white goose under one arm, its dead beak almost trailing the platform' (p. 1).

This devaluation of the 'fabulous apparatus' of earlier work occurred in a period when Green was publishing a series of four essays: theoretical pronouncements on the immediate future of the novel.[1] Between August 1950 and August 1951, he was repeating the claim that 'description' in the novel ought to cede in importance to 'dialogue':

how is the reader's imagination to be fired? For a long time I thought this was best lit by very carefully arranged passages of description. But if I have come to hold, as I do now, that we learn almost everything in life from what is done after a great deal of talk, then it follows that I am beginning to have my doubts about the uses of description. No; communication between the novelist and his reader will tend to be more and more by dialogue, until in a few years' time someone will think up something better.[2]

Green argues the inevitability of this shift in emphasis, bringing the novel in line with the conditions under which it is produced and read; but his incidental assertion that every writer 'must always be changing his own style so as not to be trapped by the clichés which he is continually creating for himself'[3] is a tactical error which betrays what is actually the case: Green's new litigiousness is an attempt to provide an external alibi for what is really an internally generated change. He has promised the novel to dialogue as the result of a stylistic aversion rather than as a timely response to social and cultural constraints. And in the knowledge that his writing now has less than ever to do with an 'idiom of the time' his struggle to prove otherwise appears quite desperate, as it shrinks a whole clause of ratification to the single defiant word 'No'.

Green relies on a method of contagious images, forcibly implicating the novel in the sheer pace of developments generally among the arts and communications. He creates a false exigence by limiting the scope of his prognosis to the 'next ten years'. Complex figurations like those in *Finnegans Wake* requiring 'painful application' are disqualified quite simply because 'most people do not have the leisure'.[4] Books must grow physically smaller, owing to mounting costs of production; the rather loose analogy here is with paintings, which are said to grow smaller in proportion as houses do. Within the work itself, the narrative units are reduced in size under the influence of the cinema, while in 'five years' time' (the novel really will have to be on its toes) 'television will have a profound effect on novelists, and that narrative already split up into small scenes, will be split still further'.[5] The optimum state of contemporary writing has to be in the steady rediffusion of dialogue, because 'We do not write long letters any more, we pick up the telephone instead. Instead of reading, we listen to the wireless or watch television.'[6] This purification of the means of communication is carried out in the name of 'conventional understanding', in a passive rather than an active regard of conditions of knowledge, 'the reason being that we do not have time to define what we mean in conversation'.[7] The logical terminus of these drastic adaptations is assimilation with the lowest common denominator of shared knowledge. Green is adamant that 'if you want to create life the one way not to set about it is by explanation'.[8] But all that this amounts to under the new dispensation is that 'the writer cannot use too much material that has to be explained';[9] 'The argument is that we cannot go outside everyday life to create something between reader and writer in narrative.'[10] What the text projected on this basis cuts out is the dissentient adequacy of Green's more complex writing. The 'idiom of the time' had derived its strength and purpose from the way it had divided its attention between the explicable and the inexplicable – its unreflecting side had demanded the invention of an unrepeatable method of reading which would apprise the reader of the history of his own formation. In *Nothing* and *Doting*, those few passages which Green would term 'descriptive' can only function according to the memory of their antecedents in *Caught*, *Loving*, *Back*, and *Concluding*; their only meaning is in the knowledge of repetition:

Standing prepared, empty, curtained, shuttered, tall mirrors facing across laid tables crowned by napkins, with space rocketing transparence from one glass silvered surface to the other, supporting walls covered in olive coloured silk, chandeliers repeated to a thousand thousand profiles to be lost in olive gray depths as quiet as this room's untenanted attention, but a scene made warm with

mass upon mass of daffodils banked up against mirrors, or mounded
once on each of the round white tables and laid in a flat frieze about
their edges, – here then time stood still for Jane, even in wine bottles
over to one side holding the single movement, and that unseen of
bubbles rising just as the air, similarly trapped even if conditioned,
watched unseen across itself in a superb but not indifferent pause of
mirrors. (*Nothing*, p. 82)

This is less a description of vacancy than a congestion of
familiar images whose opportunism can be judged by comparing
this usage of the participial adjective 'untenanted' with that
in 'Before the Great Fire', where 'untenanted' takes the strain
of a political reading of *Loving*. Even more insouciant is *Doting*'s
aggravation of a St Peter theme: an unrewarding obduracy,
expertly compassed by Bruce Bassoff:

During the book Peter is a fisherman, and Diana refers several times
to the number of fish he has caught (he ends up with twelve). The
night club where they gather is called Rome, where they are to
watch some wrestlers as part of the stage show. At one point 'a near
miracle occurred', and they are served their meals. Peter keeps
returning to his 'goblet' throughout the meal. He at first wets himself with ice water from the wine bottle but later avoids this baptis-
mal act by being more careful. Peter keeps saying 'Oh God' through
the scene and says it for the last time when a conjuror comes on
stage. This evocation of Roman decadence and of a priggish and
ineffectual Simon Peter is rather a heavy joke which undermines the
delicate farce of the book.[11]

What the failure of the St Peter theme does achieve is a surreptitious endorsement of the reasonableness of writing as mere
reflection; Green is cooking his own book to advance the claim
of dialogue. The adequacy of reflection and dialogue is as
confused as I have made it sound. Green stubbornly insists that
any 'literary' work 'has to be argued by the viewer, and if and
when it is successful it therefore grows into a work of conscious
imagination on the part of the viewer'.[12] And he clings to the
heretical idea that the only means of achieving this is by the
assurance of writing opaquely: 'the future function of narrative
prose is not to be clear'.[13] Where he diverges from the line he
had set out to follow in 'Apologia' is in holding to the view that
this unclearness does not correspond to a necessary reduction
but to an increase in the degree of reflectiveness: all that one

has to do is to be scrupulously faithful to the half-truths of real dialogue in real 'life', because 'In life the intimations of reality are nearly always oblique.'[14] Unclearness is what one has to represent, not the means of dissolving a fixed representation; Green is actually saying that an accomplished obliquity would incur the triumph of pure representation: 'the future of novels must surely be to leave characters alive enough to go on living the life they have led in the book'.[15] Both in *Nothing*, and in *Doting*, the almost complete abolition of a regulating author ensures that indefiniteness cannot be assigned to any strategic insecurity of authorial knowledge. Green stipulates, in 'The English Novel of the Future', that 'the writer will keep any direct statement from himself out of his narrative' and indeed, authorial responsibility ceases to be an issue in the fiction itself. In *Doting* particularly, the author appears in possession of only subsidiary intelligence, and his is the only replaceable lack of precision in a regularly indefinite text: 'Nothing else of consequence passed that night between them' (p. 102); 'They laughed, finished their drinks, and went separate ways' (p. 138); 'Shortly afterwards they left, went their separate ways, without anything else of significance having passed' (p. 226).

Where Green's practice, in *Nothing* at least, outgrows the theoretical design is in the choice of what all the indirect answers of the dialogue palpably avoid. Every tangential response of one character to another is an attempt to redress a balance of power, in accordance with which knowledge is equal to a gain, and ignorance to a loss. What none of the characters, except possibly Jane, knows – what is the 'unknown' knowledge, the 'nothing' which prompts everything each one of them says – is whether or not the proposed marriage between Mary and Philip would involve these two in a relationship of incest. Philip may be the illegitimate son of Jane Weatherby and John Pomfret; and Jane floats this possibility to prevent the marriage of Philip to Pomfret's daughter Mary, while engineering the alternative marriage of Pomfret and herself. The text draws to a close with its own version of *Concluding*'s ' "We shall never know the truth" ' : ' ". . . Oh but we shall never get at the whole truth . . ." ' (p. 228). There is no way of knowing the truth, but the pretence of knowledge is what regulates the balance of power, and the balance is adjusted by none as effectively as by the reader who is the only impartial recipient of all the clues. These, although they amount to 'nothing', are constant and various. Philip's obsession with wanting to get to know his relatives lends colour to the importance of a genealogical research. When he eventually meets up with his uncle Ned, the latter is found to harbour an inexplicably violent antipathy to Jane: ' "It simply seems he detests Mamma and won't have her mentioned in his presence hardly" ' (p. 142). This is only partly accounted for by the mention of a past possibility of 'cross divorces' involving Jane and her husband and John and his wife. Jane herself is unusually vulnerable in being unable to pronounce the word 'incestuous':

'But oh John I have warned Philip if not once then quite a thousand times. No but the whole picture has grown so enormous in his poor head I really believe he feels deep down inside him that he must, simply must find a wife so close that the marriage could almost turn out to be incestious John.'

'Incestuous. So you're afraid he'll never start a family is that it?' Mr. Pomfret did not appear to take the conversation seriously. (p. 76)

Jane also makes constant references to her daughter Penelope as a 'saint' with 'sacred little ears'; a 'desperate brave little martyr'; a 'sad longsuffering angel': as if to compensate for the 'unholiness' of Philip's putative illegitimacy. The other characters suspect that she uses Penelope as a 'shield', attributing neuroses to the child which encode her own concerns; and Penelope's name is abbreviated to 'Pen', because she is effectively the pen Jane writes with. In this context of manipulations and submissions, it is noteworthy that *Party Going*'s burden, 'fellow feeling', is specifically defined as being tantamount to 'real politeness' (p. 103), a simple matter of the correct and tasteful observance of rules. It is this correctness and tastefulness which Jane falls back on in her only moment of real powerlessness, when Philip announces the engagement she is ignorant of, during his twenty-first birthday party. Jane's knowledge of deportment and etiquette turns what is initially a defeat on her side into a spectacularly triumphal performance:

And when Jane came to their table she folded Mary Pomfret into so wonderful an embrace while the child half rose from her chair to greet it that not only was the girl's hair not touched or disarranged

in this envelopment, but as Mrs. Weatherby took the young lady
to her heart it must have seemed to most the finest thing they had
ever seen, the epitome of how such moments should be, perfection
in other words, the acme of manners, and memorable as being the
flower, the blossoming of grace and their generation's ultimate
instinct of how one should ideally behave. (p. 109)

Jane regains her control precisely because Mary and Philip
have no knowledge of 'how one should ideally behave': 'It
was noticeable how frightened the girl looked, as was perhaps
only natural' (p. 110). And much of the action in the book
consists of attempts on the part of these members of the younger
generation to alleviate their condition of powerlessness and
ignorance; Mary journeys to Brighton to interview Jane, and
visits Arthur Morris in hospital; Philip visits Arthur Morris, and
journeys to his uncle Ned. This scheme gives the absence of an
author its most extreme justification, since if the author knew
everything, or even a great deal, there would effectively be
nothing to read *for*.

   In a sense, there is almost nothing to read for in *Doting*, or
rather there is nothing worth the argument of a reader who is to
'make an act of conscious imagination to fuse the narrative,
if this is capable of it, into a work of art with a life of its own'.[16]
The knowledge withheld in *Doting* is not of the certainty of an
incestuous relationship, but of ordinary heterosexual relationships, and far less is at stake. Diana Middleton, proceeding on the
false assumption that her husband Arthur has committed
adultery with the young Annabel Paynton, keeps him guessing
as to whether she has done the same with his oldest friend,
Charles Addinsell. The married couple are exercised by
doubts over the exact nature of the relationship between
Charles and Annabel, even though the only extramarital love-
making in the book involves Charles and Annabel's friend,
Claire Belaine. All that holds the reader's interest is the comedy.
The text recovers and dissipates the writing process adopted for
Nothing, just as *Nothing* had rendered inanimate the 'idiom of
the time'. Green is quite precisely writing to a programme in
which humour is the only dividend of 'something living which
isn't': 'to create life between writer and reader, humour should
in future be the bridge. After humour the ingredients can be
expressed in a family tree:

HUMOUR

SATIRE   REALISM   FANTASY   PORNOGRAPHY

There may be many who at this point will turn away in disgust . . .'[17]

It would be rash to speculate, in the absence of sufficient biographical data, on the reasons for Green's lengthy silence between the publication of *Doting* in 1952 and his death in 1974. But one can at least discover a trend in his latest work, away from a form of writing which exceeds the ordinary capacity of a novel to reflect its time, and which clarifies a margin below which reading does not question its method. This attempted transection of conditions of knowledge, which I have been identifying as the 'idiom of the time', is progressively withdrawn from the texts of *Nothing* and *Doting*. The dogmatic timeliness of the theoretical pronouncements during the same period is a means of compensating for the anxiety which must have increased as *Doting* proved incapable of a sufficiently dynamic regulation of the indefinite. For whatever reason, the writing was once again engrossed as an evasive amenity, so that the same libidinal imperative which inaugurated Green's career appeared to be uppermost at its close. It was as if, once it had become impossible any longer to hide behind the formalization of untrustworthiness in an 'idiom of the time', once 'Henry Green' had become recognizable by his own clichés, the project of evasion found resort, by a perverse logic, in the extreme trustworthiness of dialogue as reflection. Whatever else was in play, once it became obvious that *Doting* was an alarmingly premature reprise of *Nothing* in most respects, Green ceased to write.

Notes

1. *Blindness, Living:* the living idiom

1 British Library Loan 67/1 consists of a typescript with the pencil addition, 'Early typescript of Blindness'.
2 Nikolai Gogol, *Dead Souls*, translated by David Magarshack (Harmondsworth: Penguin, 1961), p. 276, my emphasis. The Everyman edition of 1915, which is mentioned elsewhere in the typescript of *Young and Old*, is less succinct: 'the neighbourhood would seem to have become converted into one great concert of melody' (London: Dent, 1915), p. 272.
3 See Yvon Taillandier, *Corot* (Lugano: Uffici Press, n.d.).
4 Shakespeare, *King Lear*, edited by Kenneth Muir, The Arden Shakespeare (London: Methuen, 1964), IV. vi. 151ff.
5 Robert Browning, *Poetical Works 1833–1864*, edited by Ian Jack, (Oxford University Press, 1970), p. 399.
6 'πλεκταῖς ἐώραις': Οἰδίπους τύραννος, l. 1264, *Sophoclis Fabulae*, edited by A. C. Pearson (Oxford University Press, 1928).
7 Hippocrates, 'The Sacred Disease', in the edition of W. H. S. Jones (London and Cambridge, Mass., 1931), vol. 2, pp. 129ff.
8 See Jeffrey Mehlman, '*Cataract*: Diderot's Discursive Politics, 1749–1751', in *Glyph Two*, edited by Sussman and Weber (Baltimore and London: Johns Hopkins University Press, 1977), p. 37.
9 As does the fictional name Haye, and the name of the central character of *Caught*, Roe.
10 Sigmund Freud, 'Dostoevsky and Parricide', *Standard Edition of the Complete Psychological Works*, edited by J. B. Strachey (London: Hogarth Press, 1953–74), vol. 21, p. 180.
11 Harvey Breit, 'Talk with Henry Green – and a P.S.', *New York Times Book Review*, 19 February, 1950, p. 29.
12 Freud, 'Dostoevsky and Parricide', p. 187, n. 2.
13 'Composition as Explanation', collected in *Look at me now and here I am: Writings and Lectures 1911–1945* (London: Peter Owen, 1967), p. 29.
14 Sir Colin Anderson, in *Brian Howard: Portrait of a Failure*, edited by Marie-Jacqueline Lancaster, p. 121.

15 See Goronwy Rees, *A Chapter of Accidents* (London: Chatto and Windus, 1977).

16 See Auden, Preface to *Collected Shorter Poems 1927–1957* (London: Faber, 1966).

17 Terry Southern, 'The Art of Fiction xxii, Henry Green', in *Paris Review*, 5 (Summer 1958), 61–77.

18 See Ian A. Gordon, *The Movement of English Prose* (London: Longman, 1966), for the Anglo-Saxon element in modern English.

19 See Green's 'interim autobiography', *Pack my Bag*: 'I had taken English as my school and that meant learning Anglo-Saxon' (p. 213).

20 T. S. Eliot, *Collected Poems 1909–1962* (London: Faber and Faber, 1963), p. 69.

21 Giorgio Melchiori, *The Tightrope Walkers: Studies of Mannerism in Modern English Literature* (London: Routledge and Kegan Paul, 1956), p. 194.

22 John Russell, 'There It Is', *Kenyon Review* 26 (Summer 1964), p. 442.

23 Shakespeare, *Henry V*, edited by John H. Walter, The Arden Shakespeare (London: Methuen, 1954), ii, iii. 14–15.

24 See Mikhail Bakhtin, *Rabelais and his World*, translated by H. Iswolsky (New York, 1968).

25 See 'An Unfinished Novel', *The London Magazine*, vol. 6, no. 4 (April 1959), 11–17, for Green's acknowledgement of Lawrence.

26 *Psychoanalysis and the Unconscious* (London: Heinemann, 1961), p. 227.

27 Richard Ellmann, *James Joyce* (Oxford University Press, 1965), p. 536.

28 Ibid., p. 725. The change of mind is pointed out by Frank Kermode in *The Genesis of Secrecy: On the Interpretation of Narrative* (Cambridge, Mass.: Harvard University Press, 1979), pp. 66–7.

29 Milton, *Paradise Lost*, edited by Alastair Fowler (London: Longman, 1971), p. 112, ll. 488–95.

30 *A History of the English Church and People*, translated by Leo Sherley-Price (Harmondsworth: Penguin, 1968), p. 127.

31 Melchiori, *The Tightrope Walkers*, p. 193.

32 'Preface to the American Edition of *New Poems*', collected in *Phoenix: The Posthumous Papers of D. H. Lawrence* (London: Heinemann, 1936), p. 222.

2. *Party Going*: a border-line case

1 John Russell, 'There It Is', *Kenyon Review* 26 (Summer 1964), 443.

2 Coleridge, 'The Rime of the Ancyent Marinere', in W. Wordsworth and S. T. Coleridge, *Lyrical Ballads*, edited by R. L. Brett and A. R. Jones (Edinburgh: Constable, 1965), p. 12.

3 The formulation is an apt one in the context of a highly artificial portrait of the 'idle party'. A parallel with the ship on the ocean is enforced by the crowd which converges on the station: 'Now they came out in ones and threes and now a flood was coming out and spreading into streets round' (p. 14). Julia leans over 'stagnant water', which is like the 'slimy sea' of the poem, and sees three seagulls: 'She thought those gulls were for the sea they were to cross that evening' (p. 19). It seems appropriate that the wedding guest is 'party going' when he is stopped, and the act of narration is given prominence: 'The wedding guest he beat his breast, / Yet he cannot chuse but hear.'

4 Kenneth Burke, *The Philosophy of Literary Form. Studies in Symbolic Action* (Baton Rouge: Louisiana State University Press, 1941), pp. 10–11.

5 Georg Groddeck, 'The Meaning of Illness', reprinted in *The Meaning of Illness: Selected Psychoanalytic Writings*, translated by Gertrud Mander (London: Hogarth Press, 1977), p. 199.

6 On p. 72 of *Party Going* there is a catalogue of illnesses with a general effect on the *constitution*.

7 Groddeck, 'The Meaning of Illness', p. 200.

8 W. H. Auden, *The Orators*, in *The English Auden: Poems, Essays, and Dramatic Writings, 1927–1939*, edited by Edward Mendelson (London: Faber, 1977), p. 62.

9 An elaborate joke is constructed on the number three. Whenever an 'arbitrary' number is called for, it is always determined as three: 'in ones and threes', 'three seagulls', 'under the clock . . . there were three', 'every third person', 'at that three things happened', 'three sitting rooms', 'three men', 'if I whistle three times', 'three people', 'three deep', 'these three bits', and although there are two hotel porters, Max *believes* there are three.

See Bruno Bettelheim on the significance of this choice, in *The Uses of Enchantment: The Meaning and Importance of Fairy Tales* (Harmondsworth: Penguin, 1978):

> Three is a mystical and often a holy number, and was so long before the Christian doctrine of the Holy Trinity. It is the threesome of snake, Eve, and Adam which, according to the Bible, makes for

carnal knowledge. In the unconscious, the number three stands for sex, because each sex has three visible sex characteristics: penis and the two testes in the male; vagina and the two breasts in the female.

The number three stands in the unconscious for sex also in a quite different way, as it symbolizes the oedipal situation with its deep involvement of three persons with one another – relations which, as the story of 'Snow White' among many others shows, are more than tinged with sexuality . . . Thus, three symbolizes a search for who one is biologically (sexually), and who one is in relation to the most important persons in one's life. Broadly put, three symbolizes the search for one's personal and one's social identity. From his visible sex characteristics and through his relations to his parents and siblings, the child must learn with whom he ought to identify as he grows up, and who is suitable to become his life's companion, and with it also his sexual partner. (pp. 219–20)

10 Groddeck, 'The Meaning of Illness', pp. 200–1.
11 Repressed vision had been associated with Ocdipal guilt in Green's first novel, *Blindness*.
12 William Empson, 'Marvell's Garden', in *Some Versions of Pastoral* (London: Chatto and Windus, 1935), p. 120.
13 Ibid., p. 128. See the relevant stanza of 'The Garden':

> Meanwhile the mind, from pleasures less,
> Withdraws into its happiness:
> The mind, that ocean where each kind
> Does straight its own resemblance find,
> Yet it creates, transcending these,
> Far other worlds, and other seas,
> Annihilating all that's made
> To a green thought in a green shade.

Andrew Marvell, *The Complete Poems*, edited by Elizabeth Story Donno (Harmondsworth: Penguin, 1972), p. 101.

14 Cf. John Haye's epileptic fit in *Blindness*: 'it was as if there were something straining behind his eyeballs to get out' (p. 252).
15 British Library Loan 67/2 consists of: (A), one complete typescript with manuscript corrections and additions; (B), pp. 1–62 of an earlier typescript with manuscript corrections entitled *Going In A Party*; and a few assorted manuscript pages relating to a very early plan of the novel – according to which the group of friends actually arrives in the South of France by the start of Chapter two. The sentence I have quoted is from TS(A), p. 90.
16 Empson, *Some Versions of Pastoral*, p. 127.
17 In an earlier version of the quoted passage, the doves 'do that through an arch' (TS(B), p. 11).
18 It is feasible that the essay provides even the names of the two

most neurotic characters – Julia and Alex – in the following citation:

> Only for him no cure is found,
> Whom Juliana's Eyes do wound . . .

> every Mower's wholesome heat
> Smelled like an Alexander's sweat.

19 Empson, *Some Versions of Pastoral*, p. 125.
20 Ibid., p. 119.
21 Groddeck, 'The Meaning of Illness', p. 200.
22 In Freudian analysis the house is a symbol of the woman's body: an association which surfaces in the popular notion of the windows as the eyes of a house; the hotel has 'lidded windows' (p. 145) and there may be a reference to the infantile theory of sexuality in the fact that Miss Fellowes is carried up 'the back way' (p. 59).
23 See Green's autobiography, *Pack my Bag*: 'We could not often go to this place and when we did it was as if to an assignation, a lost world stretching back to the time we were children and had a corner in the shrubbery which we had made ours, behind where Poole used to burn dead leaves' (p. 141).
24 See *Pack my Bag*: 'I had gone for this odd hat which I had painted in alternate rings of red and yellow' (p. 111). In an earlier version, the collection of charms had included 'two glass eyes' (MS).
25 It also bears comparison with the lowering winter weather of *The Castle*, its callous officials and narrative contradictions.
26 See *Pack my Bag*: 'But we, a year or two past puberty . . . imagined women as one dreams at one's desk of a far country unvisited with all its mystery of latitude and place' (p. 116).
27 Roland Barthes, *Mythologies*, translated by Annette Lavers (Frogmore: Paladin, 1973), p. 151.
28 Sigmund Freud, 'The Taboo of Virginity', translated by Joan Rivière, *Collected Papers IV* (London: Hogarth Press, 1925), p. 224, my emphasis.
29 While at Eton, Green was a member of the Society of Arts, a club of aesthetes dominated by Harold Acton and Brian Howard. According to one writer, 'imagery of fishes, aquariums, and baths is dominant in all Harold Acton's imaginative work. It is clearly enough appropriate to his highly relaxed and contemplative kind of narcissism; the central experience it returns to is the sensual pleasure of lying in a bath.' Martin Green, *Children of the Sun* (London: Constable, 1977), p. 193.

30 See Frank Kermode, *The Classic* (London: Faber and Faber, 1975), p. 111.
31 Sigmund Freud, 'Fetishism', *International Journal of Psycho-Analysis*, vol. 9, part 2 (April 1928), 163.
32 They establish a context of fixed relations which depends on strict contiguity: 'They had all, except for Angela Crevy, been in that same party twelve months ago *to the same place*' (p. 71, my italics). The spatial investment is part of the attempt to give memory a hard surface.
33 See *Pack my Bag*: 'Every lane so it now seems was sunken, tufts of grass and wild flowers overhung our walks' (p. 42).
34 Although the hotel is completely sealed off (and this fact is continually mentioned) Amabel somehow manages to get in; the only available access is by way of fiction.

3. *Pack my Bag*: the poetics of menace

1 Hugh Sykes Davies, 'An Epilaugh for Surrealism', *The Times Literary Supplement*, 13 January 1978.
2 *The Spectator*, 15 September, 1939; cited by Robert Hewison in *Under Siege: Literary Life in London 1939–1945* (London: Weidenfeld and Nicolson, 1977), p. 9.
3 Cited by Virginia Woolf in *Three Guineas* (Harmondsworth: Penguin, 1977), p. 62.
4 Ibid., p. 197, n. 18.
5 *Lions and Shadows* (London: Hogarth Press, 1938), p. 74.
6 'To the Young Writers and Artists Killed in the War; 1914–18', *The Eton Candle*, vol. 1, 1922.
7 *Collected Poems*, edited by C. Day Lewis (London: Chatto and Windus, 1963), p. 42.
8 *Infants of the Spring* (London: Heinemann, 1976), p. 68.
9 *F.S.P.* (London: Chatto, 1942), pp. 32–5.
10 Collected in *Look at me now and here I am*, pp. 21–30.
11 Felix Guattari, 'Everybody Wants to Be a Fascist', *Semiotext(e)*, vol. 2, no. 3 (New York, 1977), 96.
12 Cited in Mass-Observation's report, *War Begins at Home*, edited and arranged by Tom Harrisson and Charles Madge (London: Chatto, 1940).
13 Jacques Lacan, 'The function and field of speech and language in psychoanalysis', in *Ecrits. A Selection*, translated by Alan Sheridan (London: Tavistock, 1977).
14 Guattari, 'Everybody Wants to Be a Fascist', 96.
15 Kenneth Burke, *Philosophy of Literary Form*, p. 41.

16 'Women's Exile', *Ideology and Consciousness*, no. 1 (May 1977), 65.
17 Sigmund Freud, 'Hysterical Phantasies and their Relation to Bisexuality', in *On Psychopathology*, the Pelican Freud Library, vol. 10 (Harmondsworth: Penguin, 1979), p. 94.

4. *Caught:* the idiom of the time

1 Hewison, *Under Siege*, p. 83.
2 Ibid., p. 80.
3 Mass-Observation, *War Begins at Home*, p. 187.
4 Elizabeth Bowen, 'Contemporary', review of *In My Good Books* by V. S. Pritchett, *New Statesman*, 23 May 1942.
5 Hewison, *Under Siege*, p. 89.
6 William Sansom, *Fireman Flower and other stories* (London: Hogarth Press, 1944), p. 111.
7 Edwin Muir, Review of *Four Quartets*, *New Statesman*, 20 February 1943.
8 T. S. Eliot, 'The Genesis of *Four Quartets*', *New York Times Book Review*, 29 November 1953.
9 Bowen, 'Contemporary'.
10 Henry Green, letter to Rosamond Lehmann, quoted in Lehmann, 'An Absolute Gift', *The Times Literary Supplement*, 6 August 1954.
11 At one point in the manuscript of *Caught*, (MS, p. 22) the name Sebastian is written in the place of Christopher. Sebastian is the name of the writer's own son, to whom the novel is dedicated.

In this analysis, several references are made to the manuscripts and typescripts of *Caught* in the British Library. These papers are not yet in order. Among them are one incomplete typescript pp. 1–349, with manuscript corrections and additions, which I refer to as the typescript. There are also pp. 1–90 of a manuscript representing an earlier stage of composition, which I refer to as the manuscript. Apart from these two series of papers there remain miscellaneous fragments of manuscripts and typescripts representing different stages of composition again. When a reference is made to any of these, an attempt is made to specify it by one means or another.

12 Henry Green, 'A Rescue', in *Penguin New Writing*, 4 (March 1941), 93.
13 Henry Green, 'Mr Jonas', in *Penguin New Writing*, 14 (July–September 1942), 20.
14 Edwin Muir, 'The Natural Man and the Political Man', in *New Writing and Daylight* (London: Hogarth Press, 1942).

15 See *The Neuroses in War*, edited by Emanuel Miller (London: Macmillan, 1940) and *International Journal of Psycho-Analysis* and *Journal of Abnormal and Social Psychology* for this period.

16 R. D. Gillespie, *Psychological Effects of War on Citizen and Soldier* (London: Chapman and Hall, 1942), p. 33.

17 Mass-Observation, *War Begins at Home*, p. 70.

18 Ibid.

19 Constantine Fitzgibbon, *The Blitz* (London: Allen Wingate, 1957), pp. 6–7.

20 Henry Reed, *The Novel Since 1939* (London: British Council, 1949).

21 W. R. Bion, 'The "War of Nerves": Civilian Reaction, Morale and Prophylaxis', in *The Neuroses in War*, edited by Emanuel Miller, p. 185.

22 Sansom, *Fireman Flower*, p. 150.

23 Stephen Spender, 'September Journal', in *The Thirties and After* (London: Fontana, 1978), p. 122.

24 See lines 33–40 of 'The Garden':

> What wondrous life is this I lead!
> Ripe apples drop about my head;
> The luscious clusters of the vine
> Upon my mouth do crush their wine;
> The nectarene, and curious peach,
> Into my hands themselves do reach;
> Stumbling on melons, as I pass,
> Ensnared with flowers, I fall on grass.

Andrew Marvell, *The Complete Poems*, p. 101.

25 Eliot, 'Burnt Norton', in *Collected Poems*, pp. 189–90.

26 T. S. Eliot, *The Family Reunion*, in *Collected Plays* (London: Faber and Faber, 1962), pp. 106–7.

27 Eliot, 'Little Gidding', in *Collected Poems*, p. 222.

28 *The Tightrope Walkers*. The Lawrence text is, of course, the one featured in my analysis of *Living*.

29 Lawrence, 'Preface to the American Edition of *New Poems*', in *Phoenix*, p. 219.

30 And the water-lily, in the company of rose-coloured steam, bobs up to the surface of the text in 'Mr Jonas': 'It was as though three high fountains which, through sunlight, would furl their flags in rainbows as they fell dispersed, had now played these up into a howling wind to be driven, to be shattered, dispersed, no longer to fall to sweet rainbows, but into a cloud of steam rose-coloured beneath, above no wide water-lilies in a pool, but into the welter of yellow banner-streaming flames.'

31 Marcel Proust, *Swann's Way*, translated by C. K. Scott Moncrieff (London: Chatto and Windus, 1966), p. 62.

32 On one occasion, Hilly's body is a winter landscape suddenly brought to life: 'The relief he experienced when their bodies met was like the crack, on a snow silent day, of a branch that breaks to fall under a weight of snow, as his hands went like two owls in daylight over the hills, moors, and wooded valleys, over the fat white winter of her body' (p. 117). Roe is taking possession of her body, just as Max does of Amabel in a comparable image in *Party Going*: 'Looking at her head and body, richer far than her rare fur coat, holding as he did to these skins which enfolded what ruled him, her arms and shoulders, everything, looking down on her face which ever since he had first seen it had been his library, his gallery, his palace, and his wooded fields he began at last to feel content and almost that he owned her' (p. 226).

33 In the published version of the novel, several emendations to the typescript have removed a compulsive extension of this marine imagery in the character of Richard Roe:

Published version: 'and, as he clutched at her arm, which was not there, above the elbow, he shook at leaving this, the place he got back to her nearest, his ever precious loss' (p. 34)

Typescript: 'and he clutched at her arm, above the elbow, he would be leaving this, who was now, by all she was to him, the stretch, the lake under the mountain, the ship that bore him' (TS, p. 56)

Published version: 'the scene was his wife's eyes, wet with tears he thought, her long lashes those black railings, everywhere wet, but, in the air . . .' (p. 37)

Typescript: 'the scene was the colour of his wife's eyes, the wet about might have been machined steel and over all was that stretch, the trough of lake-water grey light joining earth and sky, but, in the air . . .' (TS, p. 61)

34 Sigmund Freud, 'The Transformations of Puberty' (1905), *On Sexuality*, the Pelican Freud Library, vol. 7 (Harmondsworth: Penguin, 1977), p. 148.

35 Lacan, *Ecrits*, p. 142.

36 Karl Mannheim, *Man and Society*, translated by E. Shils (London: Routledge and Kegan Paul, 1940).

37 Virginia Woolf, 'Thoughts of Peace in an Air Raid', in *Collected Essays, IV*, (London: Hogarth Press, 1967), p. 174.

38 George Stonier, *Shaving through the Blitz* (London: Jonathan Cape, 1943), p. 46.
39 Erich Fromm, *The Fear of Freedom* (London: Kegan Paul, 1942), p. 91.
40 Bion, 'The "War of Nerves" ', p. 184.
41 Fitzgibbon, *The Blitz*, p. 133.
42 P. 112. In *Who's Who*, Green defines his recreation as 'Romancing over the bottle, to a good band'.
43 Mass-Observation, *War Begins at Home*, p. 251.
44 Fromm, *The Fear of Freedom*, pp. 143–4.
45 Elizabeth Bowen, *The House in Paris* (London: Jonathan Cape, 1935) p. 154.
46 Elsewhere, the marriage vow is satirically twisted into a seal of promiscuity: 'he saw them hungrily seeking another man, oh they were sorry for men and they pitied themselves, for yet another man with whom they could spend last hours, to whom they could murmur darling, darling, darling it will be you always; the phrase till death do us part being, for them, the short ride next morning to a railway station' (p. 63).
47 Green, 'Mr Jonas', pp. 15–16.
48 Graham Greene, *The Ministry of Fear* (London: Heinemann, 1943), p. 193.
49 Ibid., p. 114.
50 Spender, in *The Thirties and After*, p. 102.
51 Patrick Hamilton, *Hangover Square* (London: Constable, 1941), p. 193.
52 By contrast, the roses in the rose garden 'stared' in order to fall in with Roe's designs.
53 Willy Goldman, 'The Way We Live Now', *Penguin New Writing*, 3 (1941).
54 Tom Harrisson, *Living Through the Blitz* (Harmondsworth: Penguin, 1978), p. 321.
55 Fromm, *The Fear of Freedom*, p. 136.
56 Ibid, p. 168.
57 Bowen, 'Contemporary'.
58 P. 13. One can see the germs of this sentence in *Blindness* – 'the sea with violet patches over grey where the seaweed stained it, silver where the sun rays met it' (p. 83) – and in the adolescent prose poem, 'Barque', which Green reproduces in *Pack my Bag* (p. 164).
59 Breit, 'Talk with Henry Green – and a P.S.'.
60 Southern, 'The Art of Fiction, xxii – Henry Green'.

61 'Very umprincipiant through the trancitive spaces!', James Joyce, *Finnegans Wake* (London: Faber and Faber, 1939), p. 594.
62 Henry Green, 'Apologia', *Folios of New Writing* (Autumn 1941), London: at the Hogarth Press, p. 51.

In his own practice, Green can be seen re-writing to increase the degree of unclearness: in the manuscript, the phrase 'the silence once broken, by a warplane flying low over the tops of trees' is rearranged to be more discomforting: 'the silence once broken, flying low over the tops of trees, by a warplane.' (MS, p. 6).
63 Green, 'Apologia', pp. 50–1.
64 Elizabeth Bowen, 'Summer Night', in *Look at All Those Roses* (London: Jonathan Cape, 1941), p. 194.
65 Stephen Spender, *World Within World* (London: Readers Union, 1953), p. 236.
66 Mass-Observation, *War Begins at Home*, p. 148.
67 It is winter – 'the ground was under snow' (p. 172) – as it was on Roe's previous visit when the memory of his wife was distorted into a spring setting. The seasonal balance resembles that of *Four Quartets*, where the autumnal episode of 'Burnt Norton' is revised in the winter landscape of 'Little Gidding'.
68 Mass-Observation, *War Begins at Home*, p. 424.

5. *Loving:* a fabulous apparatus

1 Howard Erskine-Hill, *The Social Milieu of Alexander Pope* (New Haven and London: Yale University Press, 1975), p. 283.
2 Elizabeth Bowen, *Bowen's Court* (London: Longman, 1942), p. 20.
3 Ibid., p. 21.
4 See, for example, Columella, *De Re Rustica*, edited and translated by H. B. Ash (3 vols., London and Cambridge, Mass., 1960–8), VIII. xi. 3, and Varro, *Rerum Rusticarum*, edited and translated by W. D. Hooper, revised by H. B. Ash (London and Cambridge, Mass., 1934), III. vi.
5 Evelyn Waugh, *Brideshead Revisited* (London: Chapman and Hall, 1945).
6 Bowen, *Bowen's Court*, p. 451.
7 H. A. Mason, *Humanism and Poetry in the Early Tudor Period* (London: Routledge and Kegan Paul, 1959), p. 274.
8 Ibid., p. 278.
9 The decor is comparable to that of the Vidame de Poitier's house, as described by Madame de Créquy in a passage that Green was later to incorporate in the text of *Back* (p. 95).

10 Erskine-Hill, *The Social Milieu of Alexander Pope*, p. 282.
11 See *O.E.D.*: 'Welsh, v. *Racing*. Also welch (Of obscure origin.) *trans*. To swindle (a person out of money laid as a bet.)'.
12 Cf. the analysis of Mark Girouard in *Life in the English Country House: A Social and Architectural History* (New Haven and London: Yale University Press, 1978): 'The peculiar character of Victorian servants' wings was the result of early-nineteenth-century arrangements being revised to make them more moral and more efficient. Efficiency involved analyzing the different functions performed by different servants, giving each function its own area and often its own room, and grouping the related functions into territories accessible to the gentry part of the house which they serviced. Morality meant – in addition to compulsory attendance at daily prayers and Sunday church – separation of the sexes *except when they were under suspicion . . .*' (p. 276, my emphasis).
13 'She will drown me with her eyes and hair, lank coils of seaweed hair around me, my heart, my soul. Salt green death.' James Joyce, *Ulysses* (London: Bodley Head, 1960), p. 313.
14 'Lancelot' is a legendary name, associated with the 'old kings', and connoting betrayal. Little Lancelot is reminiscent of the man in *Living* 'that had lengths cut out of his belly . . . Black it was' (p. 5).
15 Eliot, *Collected Poems*, p. 65.
16 'Marina', ibid., p. 115.
17 'Before the Great Fire', *The London Magazine*, vol. 7, no. 12 (December 1960).
18 W. B. Yeats, *Collected Poems*, second edition (London: Macmillan, 1950), p. 132.
19 Stéphane Mallarmé, 'Quant au Livre', in *Oeuvres Complètes*, edited by Mondor and Jean-Aubry (Paris: Gallimard, 1945), p. 386.
20 Maurice Merleau-Ponty, *The Prose of the World*, translated by John O'Neill (London: Heinemann, 1974), p. 132.
21 Bettelheim, *The Uses of Enchantment*, p. 25.
22 Bettelheim, *The Uses of Enchantment*, p. 11.
23 Both of Green's stories, 'A Rescue' and 'Mr Jonas', are concerned with the danger of engulfment, and the title of the second of these refers to a specifically oral incorporation: that of Jonah and the Whale.
24 Southern, 'The Art of Fiction, xxii – Henry Green'.
25 Shakespeare, *Antony and Cleopatra*, edited by M. R. Ridley, The Arden Shakespeare (London: Methuen, 1965), ii. ii. 190ff.

26 Shakespeare, *Cymbeline*, edited by J. M. Nosworthy, The Arden Shakespeare (London: Methuen, 1955), II. iv. 87ff.

27 Ibid., II. iv. 70–1.

28 Eliot, *The Waste Land*, in *Collected Poems*, p. 66, ll. 94–6.

29 *Antony and Cleopatra*, v. ii. 88–90.

30 See, for example, Columella, *De Re Rustica*, VIII. xi. 5.

31 Gustave Flaubert, *Bouvard and Pécuchet*, translated by A. J. Krailsheimer (Harmondsworth: Penguin, 1976), p. 262.

32 Pliny, *Historia Naturalis*, x. xxii. 43: 'On being praised it spreads out its jewelled colours directly facing the sun, because in that way they shine more brightly; at the same time, it makes its tail as curved as a shell, so as to find a corresponding amount of shade for its other colours, which actually gleam more brightly in the shade, and it draws into one cluster all the eyes of its feathers which it is proud to have on view' (author's translation).

33 Cicero, *De Finibus Bonorum et Malorum*, III. v. 18: 'Other things, however, have no use but seem to be intended for some kind of ornament, like the tail of a peacock or the multicoloured feathers of doves' (author's translation).

34 Lucretius, *De Rerum Natura*, II, 798–809: 'For what colour could there be in the pitch dark? Indeed, colour is changed by the light itself, because it reflects back the impact of direct or slanting light; this is apparent in the sunlit plumage around the neck and nape of a dove, for sometimes this is as ruddy as bright bronze, while at other times from a certain angle it seems to mingle emerald greens with coral. The same is true of a peacock's tail which, when it is filled with a strong light, changes colour as it is turned. Since these colours occur through the incidence of light, you must not imagine that they could occur without it' (author's translation).

35 Lewis and Short, *A Latin Dictionary* (Oxford University Press, 1879).

36 See my chapter on *Caught*, 'The idiom of the time'.

37 Southern, 'The Art of Fiction XXII – Henry Green'.

38 Alan Ross, 'Green, with Envy', *The London Magazine*, vol. 6, no. 4 (April 1959).

39 Southern, 'The Art of Fiction XXII – Henry Green'.

40 Henry Green, 'An Unfinished Novel', *The London Magazine*, vol. 6, no. 4 (April 1959).

6. *Back:* the prosthetic art

1 My account is derived from Mass-Observation's report on demobilization, edited by Tom Harrisson and H. D. Willcock, *The Journey Home* (London: Advertising Service Guild, 1944).
2 Ibid., p. 111.
3 Ibid., p. 86.
4 'Towards a Theory of Schizophrenia', by Gregory Bateson, Don D. Jackson, Jay Haley, and John H. Weakland. The essay is reproduced in Bateson's *Steps to an Ecology of Mind* (London: Paladin/Granada, 1973), p. 180.
5 Mark, 14.30. Green's earliest published writing (it is cited by him in *Pack my Bag*, pp. 27–8) is a childhood sermon on the meaning of Peter's Denial.
6 Bateson, *Steps to an Ecology of Mind*, p. 182.
7 'A case of paranoia running counter to the psychoanalytic theory of the disease', in *On Psychopathology*, the Pelican Freud Library, vol. 10 (Harmondsworth: Penguin, 1979), p. 153.
8 Eugen Bleuler, *Dementia Praecox or the Group of Schizophrenias* (New York: International Universities Press, 1950), cited in J. Laplanche and J.-B. Pontalis, *The Language of Psycho-analysis* (London: Hogarth Press and the Institute of Psycho-analysis, 1973), p. 409.
9 British Library Loan 67/6, TS, p. 15.
10 'ART. IV. – *Souvenirs de la Marquise de Créqui, 1710 à 1800* – Tomes premier et second. Paris 1834', *The Quarterly Review*, vol. 51, no. 102 (London, 1834), 391–9.
11 Ibid.
12 Palinurus, *The Unquiet Grave* (London: Curwen Press for Horizon, 1944).
13 *Poetical Works*, edited by H. W. Garrod (Oxford University Press, 1956), p. 219, l. 15.
14 Edward Stokes, *The Novels of Henry Green* (London: Hogarth Press, 1959), p. 232.
15 Southern, 'The Art of Fiction XXII – Henry Green'.
16 Malcolm Cowley (ed.), *The Faulkner—Cowley File: Letters and Memoirs: 1944–62* (New York, 1966), p. 38f.
17 It is worth recalling at this point Green's youthful preoccupation with 'the story of Judas, I believe it haunts all little boys' (*Pack my Bag*, p. 85).
18 See for example, Giovanni Bellini's 'The Agony in the Garden' in the National Gallery, London.
19 Russell, 'There It Is'.

7. *Concluding:* the sea-change

1 See Orwell's estimate of Burnham, 'James Burnham and the Managerial Revolution', in *The Collected Essays, Journalism and Letters of George Orwell, Volume Four: In Front of Your Nose 1945–1950* (Harmondsworth: Penguin, 1970), pp. 192–215.

2 *War Begins at Home.*

3 Arthur Koestler, *The Yogi and the Commissar* (London: Jonathan Cape, 1945), p. 239.

4 Ibid., p. 228.

5 Ibid., p. 233.

6 Ibid., p. 231.

7 Ibid., p. 241.

8 Ibid., p. 236.

9 Ibid., p. 242.

10 Ibid., p. 244.

11 Cited by Stephen Heath in *The Nouveau Roman: A Study in the Practice of Writing* (London: Elek, 1972), pp. 95 and 182.

12 Maurice Merleau-Ponty, *The Visible and the Invisible*, translated by Alphonso Lingis (Evanston: Northwestern University Press, 1968), p. 135.

13 Koestler, *The Yogi and the Commissar*, p. 245.

14 Fromm, *The Fear of Freedom*, p. 18.

15 Collected in *Steps to an Ecology of Mind*, pp. 423–40.

16 Ibid., pp. 439–40.

17 British Library Loan 67/7 consists of one complete typescript without manuscript corrections which differs textually from the published version.

18 Koestler, *The Yogi and the Commissar*, p. 245.

19 Merleau-Ponty, *The Visible and the Invisible*, p. 141.

20 Ibid., p. 143.

21 Ibid., p. 133.

22 Southern, 'The Art of Fiction XXII – Henry Green'.

23 Gregory Bateson, *Mind and Nature: A Necessary Unity* (Glasgow: Fontana/Collins, 1980), p. 21.

24 *Pack my Bag* would be an equal candidate with *Concluding* for a working title of 'Dying'. Both books qualify as 'swan songs'; and *Pack my Bag*'s figuration of 'loving' as a 'marriage with sympathetic swans' would appear to insist on the fusion of 'Eros' and 'Thanatos': 'I found two swans floating past locked in a fight or love I did not know, their necks entwined one head fastened on the other, both half drowned with barely beating wings' (p. 137).

25 Shakespeare, *The Tempest*, edited by Frank Kermode, The Arden Shakespeare (London: Methuen, 1964), I. ii. 399–404.

8. *Nothing, Doting*: something living which isn't

1 These were, in chronological order, 'The English Novel of the Future', *Contact*, no. 1 (August 1950), 21–4, 'A Novelist to his Readers: Communication without Speech', *The Listener*, 44, (9 November 1950), 505–6, 'A Novelist to his Readers – II', *The Listener*, 45 (15 March 1951), 425–7, and 'A Fire, a Flood, and the Price of Meat', *The Listener*, 46 (23 August 1951), 293–4.
2 'A Novelist to his Readers: Communication without Speech', p. 506.
3 'The English Novel of the Future', p. 23.
4 Ibid., p. 22.
5 Ibid.
6 Ibid.
7 Ibid.
8 'A Novelist to his Readers: Communication without Speech', p. 505.
9 'A Fire, a Flood, and the Price of Meat', p. 293.
10 'The English Novel of the Future', p. 24.
11 *Toward 'Loving': The Poetics of the Novel and the Practice of Henry Green* (Columbia, S.C.: University of South Carolina Press, 1975), p. 116.
12 'The English Novel of the Future', p. 21.
13 Ibid., p. 22.
14 Ibid., p. 23.
15 Ibid.
16 Ibid.
17 Ibid., p. 24.

Bibliography

Primary sources

Green, Henry. 'Apologia'. *Folios of New Writing* (Autumn 1941), 44–51
Back. London: Hogarth Press, 1946
'Before the Great Fire'. *The London Magazine*, vol. 7, no. 12 (December 1960), 12–27
Blindness. London: Hogarth Press, 1977
Caught. London: Hogarth Press, 1943
Concluding. London: Hogarth Press, 1948
Doting. London: Hogarth Press, 1952
'The English Novel of the Future'. *Contact*, no. 1 (August 1950), 21–4
'A Fire, a Flood, and the Price of Meat'. *The Listener*, (23 August 1951), 293–4.
'Firefighting'. *Texas Quarterly*, vol. 3, no. 4 (1960), 105–20
Living. London: Hogarth Press, 1929
Loving. London: Hogarth Press, 1945
'The Lull'. *New Writing and Daylight* (Summer 1943), 11–21
'Mr Jonas'. *Penguin New Writing*, 14 (July–September 1942), 15–20
Nothing. London: Hogarth Press, 1950
'A Novelist to his Readers: Communication without Speech'. *The Listener*, 44 (9 November 1950) 505–6
'A Novelist to his Readers – II'. *The Listener*, 45 (15 March 1951), 425–7
Pack my Bag. London: Hogarth Press, 1940
Party Going. London: Hogarth Press, 1939
'A Rescue'. *Penguin New Writing*, 4 (March 1941), 88–93
'The Spoken Word as Written'. Review of *The Oxford Book of English Talk*, edited by James Sutherland. *The Spectator*, 4 September 1953, p. 248
'An Unfinished Novel'. *The London Magazine*, vol. 6, no. 4 (April 1959), 11–17

Secondary sources

Addison, Paul. *The Road to 1945; British politics and the Second World War*. London, 1975
Allen, Walter. 'An Artist of the Thirties'. *Folios of New Writing*, (Spring 1941), 149–58
'Henry Green'. *Penguin New Writing*, 25 (1945), 144–55
Anonymous. 'A Poet of Fear'. Review of *Concluding*. *The Times Literary Supplement*, 25 December 1948, p. 726
Arts Council of Great Britain. *Thirties; British Art and Design before the War*. Catalogue of the Hayward Gallery Exhibition, edited by Jennifer Hawkins and Marrianne Hollis. London, 1979
Auden, W. H. *Collected Shorter Poems 1927–1975*. London: Faber, 1966
  The English Auden: Poems, Essays, and Dramatic Writings 1927–1939. Edited by Edward Mendelson. London: Faber, 1977
Auden, W. H., and Isherwood, Christopher. *On the Frontier*. London: Faber, 1938
Bakhtin, Mikhail. *Rabelais and his World*. Translated by H. Iswolsky. New York, 1968
Barthes, Roland. *Image—Music—Text*. Essays, selected and translated by Stephen Heath. London: Fontana/Collins, 1977
  Mythologies. Translated by Annette Lavers. Frogmore: Paladin, 1973
  Le plaisir du texte. Paris: Seuil, 1973
  Sade / Fourier / Loyola. Translated by Richard Miller. New York: Hill and Wang, 1976
Bassoff, Bruce. *Toward 'Loving'; The Poetics of the Novel and the Practice of Henry Green*. Columbia, S.C.: University of South Carolina Press, 1975
Bateson, Gregory. *Mind and Nature; A Necessary Unity*. Glasgow: Fontana/Collins, 1980
  Steps to an Ecology of Mind. London: Paladin/Granada, 1973
Bede. *A History of the English Church and People*. Translated by Leo Sherley-Price. Harmondsworth: Penguin, 1968
Bersani, Leo. 'The Subject of Power'. *Diacritics*, vol. 7, no. 3 (Fall 1977), 2–21
Bettelheim, Bruno. *The Uses of Enchantment: The Meaning and Importance of Fairy Tales*. Harmondsworth: Penguin, 1978
Bion, W. R. 'The "War of Nerves": Civilian Reaction, Morale, and Prophylaxis'. *The Neuroses in War*. Edited by Emanuel Miller. London: Macmillan, 1940
Bleuler, Eugen. *Dementia Praecox or the Group of Schizophrenias*. New York: International Universities Press, 1950

Bowen, Elizabeth. *Bowen's Court*. London: Longman, 1942
  'Contemporary'. Review of *In My Good Books* by V. S. Pritchett.
    New Statesman, 23 May 1942
  The House in Paris. London: Jonathan Cape, 1935
  Look at All Those Roses. London: Jonathan Cape, 1941
  Seven Winters. Dublin: Cuala Press, 1942
Breit, Harvey. 'Talk with Henry Green – and a P.S.'. *New York
    Times Book Review*, 19 February 1950, p. 29
Browning, Robert. *Poetical Works 1833–1864*. Edited by Ian Jack.
    Oxford University Press, 1970
Burke, Kenneth. *A Grammar of Motives*. New York, 1945
  The Philosophy of Literary Form. Studies in Symbolic Action. Baton
    Rouge: Louisiana State University Press, 1941
Calder, Angus. *The People's War; Britain 1939–1945*. London:
    Jonathan Cape, 1969
'Cato'. *Guilty Men*. London: Gollancz, 1940
Churchill, Thomas. '*Loving*: A Comic Novel'. *Critique*, vol. 4 (1961),
    29–38
Cicero. *De Finibus Bonorum et Malorum*. Edited and translated by
    H. Rackham. London and Cambridge, Mass.: Loeb Classical
    Library, 1967
Cole, G. D. M. and M. *The Condition of Britain*. London, 1937
Columella. *De Re Rustica*. Edited and Translated by H. B. Ash
    (E. S. Forster and E. H. Heffner). 3 vols., London and
    Cambridge, Mass.: Loeb Classical Library, 1960–8
Connolly, Cyril. *Enemies of Promise*. London: Routledge, 1938
  The Unquiet Grave. London: Curwen Press for Horizon, 1944
Cowley, Malcolm (ed.). *The Faulkner—Cowley File: Letters and
    Memoirs: 1944–62*. New York, 1966
Créquy, La Marquise de. *The French Noblesse of the XVIII Century*.
    Translated by Mrs Colquhon Grant. London: John Murray,
    1904
Deleuze, Gilles. *Proust and Signs*. Translated by Richard Howard.
    London: Allen Lane, 1973
Dickens, Charles. *Bleak House*. Harmondsworth: Penguin, 1971
Dostoevsky, Feodor. *Crime and Punishment*. Translated by Constance
    Garnett. London: Dent, 1911
Doughty, C. M. *Travels in Arabia Deserta*. With an Introduction by
    T. E. Lawrence. London, 1908
Eliot, T. S. *Collected Plays*. London: Faber and Faber, 1962
  Collected Poems, 1909–1962. London: Faber and Faber, 1963
  'The Genesis of *Four Quartets*'. *New York Times Book Review*,
    29 November 1953

Ellmann, Richard. *James Joyce*. Oxford University Press, 1965
Empson, William. *Seven Types of Ambiguity*. Harmondsworth: Penguin, 1973
Some Versions of Pastoral. London: Chatto and Windus, 1935
Erskine-Hill, Howard. *The Social Milieu of Alexander Pope*. New Haven and London: Yale University Press, 1975
The Eton Candle. vol. 1 (1922)
Faulkner, William. *Soldiers' Pay*. Harmondsworth: Penguin, 1976
The Sound and the Fury. Harmondsworth: Penguin, 1964
Fitzgibbon, Constantine. *The Blitz*. London: Allen Wingate, 1957
Flaubert, Gustave. *Bouvard and Pécuchet*. Translated by A. J. Krailsheimer. Harmondsworth: Penguin, 1976
Three Tales. Translated by Robert Baldick. Harmondsworth: Penguin, 1961
Forster, E. M. *Howards End*. Harmondsworth: Penguin, 1941
Foucault, Michel. *Discipline and Punish; The Birth of the Prison*. Translated by Alan Sheridan. London: Allen Lane, 1977
The History of Sexuality. Volume 1: An Introduction. Translated by Robert Hurley. London: Allen Lane, 1979
Freud, Sigmund. 'A case of paranoia running counter to the psychoanalytic theory of the disease'. *On Psychopathology*. The Pelican Freud Library, vol. 10. Harmondsworth: Penguin, 1979
'Dostoevsky and Parricide'. *Standard Edition of the Complete Psychological Works*. 24 vols. Edited by J. B. Strachey. vol. 21, London: Hogarth Press, 1953–74.
'Fetishism'. *International Journal of Psycho-Analysis*, vol. 9, part 2 (April 1928)
'Hysterical Phantasies and their Relation to Bisexuality'. *On Psychopathology*. The Pelican Freud Library, vol. 10. Harmondsworth: Penguin, 1979
'The Taboo of Virginity'. Translated by Joan Rivière. *Collected Papers IV*. London: Hogarth Press, 1925
'The Transformations of Puberty' (1905). *On Sexuality*. The Pelican Freud Library, vol. 7. Harmondsworth: Penguin, 1977
Fromm, Erich. *The Fear of Freedom*. London: Kegan Paul, 1942
Fussell, Paul. *The Great War and Modern Memory*. Oxford University Press, 1975
Genette, Gérard. *Figures III*. Paris: Seuil, 1972
Gillespie, R. D. *Psychological Effects of War on Citizen and Soldier*. London: Chapman and Hall, 1942
Girouard, Mark. *Life in the English Country House: A Social and Architectural History*. New Haven and London: Yale University Press, 1978

Glover, Edward. 'Notes on the Psychological Effects of War Conditions on the Civilian Population'. *International Journal of Psycho-Analysis* (1941)

Gogol, Nikolai. *Dead Souls*. Translated by David Magarshack. Harmondsworth: Penguin, 1961

Goldman, Willy. 'The Way We Live Now'. *Penguin New Writing*, 3 (1941)

Gordon, Ian A. *The Movement of English Prose*. London: Longman, 1966

Gordon, James, Sansom, William, and Spender, Stephen. *Jim Braidy: The Story of Britain's Firemen*. London: Lindsay Drummond, 1943

Green, Martin. *Children of the Sun*. London: Constable, 1977

Greene, Graham. *The Ministry of Fear*. London: Heinemann, 1943
A Sort of Life. London: Bodley Head, 1971

Groddeck, Georg. *The Book of the It*. Translated by V.M.E. Collins. New York: Vintage Books, 1949
The Meaning of Illness: Selected Psychoanalytic Writings. Translated by Gertrud Mander. London: Hogarth Press, 1977

Guattari, Felix. 'Everybody Wants to Be a Fascist'. *Semiotext(e)*, vol. 2, no. 3 (1977), 87–98

Gwynn-Browne, Arthur. *F.S.P.* London: Chatto, 1942

Hall, James. 'The Fiction of Henry Green: Paradoxes of Pleasure-Pain'. *Kenyon Review*, 19 (Winter 1957), 76–88

Hamilton, Patrick. *Hangover Square*. London: Constable, 1941

Hampson, John. *Saturday Night at the Greyhound*. London: Hogarth Press, 1931

Harrisson, Tom. *Living Through the Blitz*. Harmondsworth: Penguin, 1978

Hawthorne, Nathaniel. *The Scarlet Letter and Selected Tales*. Harmondsworth: Penguin, 1970

Heath, Stephen. *The Nouveau Roman: A Study in the Practice of Writing*. London: Elek, 1972

Hewison, Robert. *Under Siege: Literary Life in London 1939–1945*. London: Weidenfeld and Nicolson, 1977

Hippocrates. Edited by W. H. S. Jones. London and Cambridge, Mass.: Loeb Classical Library, 1931

Holden, Inez. *Night Shift*. London: John Lane, 1941

Howe, Irving. 'Fiction Chronicle'. *Partisan Review*, no. 16, 10 October 1949

Hynes, Samuel. *The Auden Generation: Literature and Politics in England in the 1930's*. London: Bodley Head, 1976

Ingham, H. S. (ed.). *Fire and Water: An NFS Anthology*. London: Lindsay Drummond, 1942

Irigaray, Luce. 'Women's Exile'. *Ideology and Consciousness*, no. 1 (May 1977), 62–76

Isherwood, Christopher. *Lions and Shadows*. London: Hogarth Press, 1938

James, Henry. *The Golden Bowl*. London: Bodley Head, 1971
The Spoils of Poynton. Harmondsworth: Penguin, 1963

Jones, Ernest. 'The Psychology of Quislingism'. *International Journal of Psycho-Analysis* (1941)

Jonson, Ben. *The Poems. The Prose Works*. The Oxford Jonson, vol. 8. Edited by C. H. Herford, Percy and Evelyn Simpson. Oxford University Press, 1970

Joyce, James. *Finnegans Wake*. London: Faber and Faber, 1939
Selected Letters. Edited by Richard Ellmann, London: Faber and Faber, 1975
Ulysses. London: Bodley Head, 1960

Kafka, Franz. *The Castle*. Translated by Willa and Edwin Muir. London: Secker and Warburg, 1930
Metamorphosis (under the title *The Transformation*). Translated by Willa and Edwin Muir. London: Secker and Warburg, 1933
The Trial. Translated by Willa and Edwin Muir. London: Gollancz, 1935

Keats, John. *Poetical Works*. Edited by H. W. Garrod. Oxford University Press, 1956

Kermode, Frank. *The Classic*. London: Faber and Faber, 1975
The Genesis of Secrecy: On the Interpretation of Narrative. Cambridge, Mass.: Harvard University Press, 1979

Koestler, Arthur. *The Yogi and the Commissar*. London: Jonathan Cape, 1945

Kuleshov, Lev. *Kuleshov on Film*. Edited and Translated by Ronald Levaco. Berkeley, Los Angeles, London: University of California Press, 1974

Labor, Earle. 'Green's Web of Loving'. *Critique*, vol. 4 (1961), 29–40

Lacan, Jacques. *Ecrits. A Selection*. Translated by Alan Sheridan. London: Tavistock, 1977

Lancaster, Marie-Jacqueline (ed.). *Brian Howard: Portrait of a Failure*

Laplanche, J., and Pontalis, J.-B. *The Language of Psycho-analysis*. London: Hogarth Press and the Institute of Psycho-analysis, 1973

Lawrence, D. H. *Fantasia of the Unconscious* and *Psychoanalysis and the Unconscious*. London: Heinemann, 1961

Phoenix: The Posthumous Papers of D. H. Lawrence. London: Heinemann, 1936

Lehmann, Rosamond. 'An Absolute Gift', *The Times Literary Supplement*, 6 August 1954

Loos, Anita. *Gentlemen Prefer Blondes*. London: Brentano's, 1926

Lucretius. *De Rerum Natura*. Edited by Cyril Bailey. Oxford University Press, 1922

Macciocchi, Maria-Antonietta. 'Female Sexuality in Fascist Ideology'. *Feminist Review*, 1 (1979), 67–82

Mallarmé, Stéphane. *Oeuvres Complètes*. Edited by Mondor and Jean-Aubry. Paris: Gallimard, 1945

Mannheim, Karl. *Man and Society in an Age of Reconstruction: Studies in Modern Social Structure*. Translated by E. Shils. London, 1940

Marvell, Andrew. *The Complete Poems*. Edited by Elizabeth Story Donno. Harmondsworth: Penguin, 1972

Mason, H. A. *Humanism and Poetry in the Early Tudor Period*. London: Routledge and Kegan Paul, 1959

Mass-Observation. *The Journey Home*. Edited by Tom Harrisson and H. D. Willcock. London: Advertising Service Guild, 1944
    War Begins at Home. Edited and arranged by Tom Harrisson and Charles Madge. London: Chatto, 1940

Mehlman, Jeffrey. '*Cataract*: Diderot's Discursive Politics, 1749–1751'. *Glyph Two*. Edited by Sussman and Weber. Baltimore and London: Johns Hopkins University Press, 1977

Melchiori, Giorgio. *The Tightrope Walkers: Studies of Mannerism in Modern English Literature*. London: Routledge and Kegan Paul, 1956

Merleau-Ponty, Maurice. *The Prose of the World*. Translated by John O'Neill. London: Heinemann, 1974
    The Visible and the Invisible. Translated by Alphonso Lingis. Evanston: Northwestern University Press, 1968

Miller, Emanuel (ed.). *The Neuroses in War*. London: Macmillan, 1940

Milton, John. *Paradise Lost*. Edited by Alastair Fowler. London: Longman, 1971

Mitford, Nancy. *Pigeon Pie*. London: Hamish Hamilton, 1940

Muir, Edwin. 'The Natural Man and the Political Man'. *New Writing and Daylight*. London: Hogarth Press, 1942
    Review of *Four Quartets* by T. S. Eliot. *New Statesman*, 20 February 1943

Orwell, George. *Animal Farm*. London: Secker and Warburg, 1945
    'James Burnham and the Managerial Revolution'. *The Collected Essays, Journalism and Letters of George Orwell, Volume Four: In*

Front of Your Nose 1945–1950. Harmondsworth: Penguin, 1970, pp. 192–215

Owen, Wilfred. *Collected Poems*. Edited by C. Day Lewis. London: Chatto and Windus, 1963

Palinurus. *See* Connolly, Cyril

Pliny. *Historia Naturalis*. Edited and translated by H. Rackham and W. H. S. Jones. London and Cambridge, Mass.: Loeb Classical Library, 1961

Powell, Anthony. *To Keep the Ball Rolling, Volume One: Infants of the Spring*. London: Heinemann, 1976

Pritchett, V. S. 'The Future of Fiction'. *New Writing and Daylight*, 7 (1946), 97f

Propp, Vladimir. 'Fairy Tale Transformations' (1928). *Readings in Russian Poetics*. Edited by Matejka and Pomorska. Cambridge, Mass., 1971

Proust, Marcel. *Swann's Way*. Translated by C. K. Scott Moncrieff. London: Chatto and Windus, 1966

The Quarterly Review, vol. 51, no. 102 (London, 1834), 391–9

Quinton, Anthony. 'A French View of *Loving*'. *The London Magazine*, vol. 6, no. 4 (April 1959), 25–35

Reed, Henry. *The Novel Since 1939*. London: British Council, 1949

Rees, Goronwy. *A Chapter of Accidents*. London: Chatto and Windus, 1977

Reich, Wilhelm. *The Invasion of Compulsory Sex-Morality*. Harmondsworth: Penguin, 1975

  Listen, Little Man! Harmondsworth: Penguin, 1975

  The Mass Psychology of Fascism. Harmondsworth: Penguin, 1975

Richardson, M. L. *London's Burning*. London: Robert Hale, 1941

Ross, Alan. 'Green, with Envy'. *The London Magazine*, vol. 6, no. 4 (April 1959), 18–24

Russell, John. *Henry Green: Nine Novels and an Unpacked Bag*. New Brunswick, N.J.: Rutgers University Press, 1960

  'There It Is'. *Kenyon Review*, 26 (Summer 1964), 433–65

Said, Edward. *Beginnings: Intention and Method*. Baltimore and London: Johns Hopkins University Press, 1978

Sansom, William. *Fireman Flower and other stories*. London: Hogarth Press, 1944

  Westminster in War. London: Faber and Faber, 1947

Shakespeare, William. *Antony and Cleopatra*. Edited by M. R. Ridley. The Arden Shakespeare. London: Methuen, 1965

  Cymbeline. Edited by J. M. Nosworthy. The Arden Shakespeare. London: Methuen, 1955

Henry V. Edited by John H. Walter. The Arden Shakespeare. London: Methuen, 1954

King Lear. Edited by Kenneth Muir. The Arden Shakespeare. London: Methuen, 1964

The Tempest. Edited by Frank Kermode. The Arden Shakespeare. London: Methuen, 1964

Sophocles. *Sophoclis Fabulae.* Edited by A. C. Pearson. Oxford University Press, 1928

Southern, Terry. 'The Art of Fiction xxii – Henry Green'. *Paris Review,* 5 (Summer 1958), 61–77

Spender, Stephen. *The Thirties and After.* London: Fontana, 1978

World Within World. London: Readers Union, 1953

Stedman, H. W. *Battle of the Flames.* London: Jarrolds, 1942

Stein, Gertrude. *Look at me now and here I am: Writings and Lectures 1911–1945.* London: Peter Owen, 1967

Stokes, Edward. *The Novels of Henry Green.* London: Hogarth Press, 1959

Stonier, George. *Shaving through the Blitz.* London: Jonathan Cape, 1943

Sweet, Henry. *An Anglo-Saxon Reader.* Oxford University Press, 1876

Swift, Jonathan. *A Tale of a Tub, The Battle of the Books, and other satires.* London: Dent, 1909

Sykes Davies, Hugh. 'An Epilaugh for Surrealism'. *The Times Literary Supplement,* 13 January 1978

Taillandier, Yvon. *Corot.* Lugano: Uffici Press, n.d.

Toynbee, Philip. 'The Novels of Henry Green'. *Partisan Review,* 16 (May 1949), 487f

Upward, Edward. *The Railway Accident and Other Stories.* Harmondsworth: Penguin, 1972

Varro. *Rerum Rusticarum.* Edited and Translated by W. D. Hooper, revised by H. B. Ash. London and Cambridge, Mass.: Loeb Classical Library, 1934

Vernon, P. E. 'Psychological Effects of Air-Raids'. *Journal of Abnormal and Social Psychology,* vol. 36, no. 4 (1941), 457–76

Wassey, Michael. *Ordeal by Fire.* London: Secker and Warburg, 1941

Waugh, Evelyn. *Brideshead Revisited.* London: Chapman and Hall, 1945

Put Out More Flags. London: Chapman and Hall, 1942

Weatherhead, A. Kingsley. *A Reading of Henry Green.* Seattle: University of Washington Press, 1961

Woolf, Virginia. 'Thoughts of Peace in an Air Raid'. *Collected Essays, IV.* London: Hogarth Press, 1967

Three Guineas. Harmondsworth: Penguin, 1977

Woon, Basil. *Hell Came to London*. London: Peter Davies, 1941

Wordsworth, William, and Coleridge, Samuel Taylor. *Lyrical Ballads*. Edited by R. L. Brett and A. R. Jones. Edinburgh: Constable, 1965

Yeats, William Butler. *Collected Poems*. Second Edition. London: Macmillan, 1950

Index

Acton, Harold, 48 n. 29
Anglo-Saxon Chronicle, 17
Auden, W. H., 16, 34–5, 46, 51, 63

Bassoff, Bruce, 211
Bateson, Gregory, 160, 166, 187
Bede, 28–9
Benoîst-Méchin, Jacques, 25
Bettelheim, Bruno, 36 n. 9, 136
Bowen, Elizabeth, 69, 84, 104, 110, 112
Browning, Robert, 6
Burgess, Guy, 63
Burke, Kenneth, 34
Burnham, James, 181, 182, 202

Chamberlain, Neville, 92–3
Cicero, 147
Clutton-Brock, Alan, 15
Coleridge, Samuel Taylor: 'The Rime of the Ancyent Marinere', 32–3, 39, 40, 41
Connolly, Cyril, 173
Corot, J.-B., 5
Créquy, La Marquise de, 171–3

Dickens, Charles: *Bleak House*, 45
Diderot, Denis, 9
Dostoevsky, Fyodor, 9, 11–12; *Crime and Punishment*, 1, 7, 11
Doughty, Charles, 101

Ecclesiastes, 196–7
Eliot, T. S., 79, 129; 'Burnt Norton', 77–8; *The Family Reunion*, 78; *Four Quartets*, 70, 78; *The Waste Land*, 18–19, 128, 143–4
Empson, William, 38–42 *passim*, 132

Faber, Geoffrey, 53–4
Faulkner, William: *Soldiers' Pay*, 175; *The Sound and the Fury*, 90, 170, 176–7
Flaubert, Gustave, 110, 146

Freud, Sigmund, and Freudian theory, 10–11, 39, 41, 43 n. 22, 47, 84, 95, 168, 188, 189
Fromm, Erich, 97, 98, 187

Gibbon, Edward, 18
Gillet, Louis, 25
Girouard, Mark, 120 n. 12
Gogol, Nikolai, 2–3
Green, Henry (pseudonym of Henry Vincent Yorke): attitude towards brothers, 56–7; attitude towards parents, 57; family home used as war hospital, 57–8; member of Eton Society of Arts, 15–16, 48 n. 29, 56; 'femininity' at school, 63; resignation from school cadet corps, 62–3; attitude towards public schools, 60; youthful rejection of Fascism, 59–60; Oxford undergraduate, 12, 62, 66–7; cinemagoer, 16; attitude towards General Strike, 61–2; engineering apprentice, 12; industrialist, vii; visit to Eire in 1938, 129; auxiliary fireman, 71, 140; *Who's Who* entry, 88 n. 42; eventual silence, 215; characteristics of Henry Green: 'deafness', 154–5; dislike of being photographed vii, 62, 155; use of pseudonym, vii, 10, 41, 62, 172
works of Henry Green: 'Apologia', 101, 211; *Back*, 113 n. 9, **157–80**, 181, 207, 208, 210; 'Before the Great Fire', 129–30, 211; *Blindness*, **1–12**, 38 n. 11, 40 n. 14, 56, 65, 98 n. 58, 175, 190; *Caught*, **68–108**, 109, 122, 128, 131, 132, 135, 142, 157, 165, 175–176, 185–6, 207, 210; *Concluding*, ix, 61, 118, 126, 127, 148, **181–206**, 207, 208, 210, 212; *Doting*, **207–15** *passim*; 'The English Novel

Henry Green—*cont.*
of the Future', 209–10, 211–12,
214–15; 'A Fire, a Flood, and the
Price of Meat', 210; *Living*, **12–
30**, 176; *Loving*, **109–56**, 157, 176,
181–2, 188, 190, 195, 203, 207,
210, 211; 'Mr Jonas', 71, 79 n.
30, 91–2, 139 n. 23; *Nothing*, **207–
215** *passim*; 'A Novelist to his
Readers: Communication
without Speech', 209, 210; *Pack
my Bag*, ix, 16, 17 n. 19, 44 n. 23,
44 n. 24, 49 n. 33, **53–67**, 98 n.
58, 118, 126, 178 n. 17, 197–8,
204; *Party Going*, 30, **31–52**, 58,
76, 78, 81 n. 32, 99, 122, 127,
130, 132, 141, 213; 'A Rescue',
71, 139 n. 23
Greene, Graham, 46; *The Ministry of
Fear*, 69, 73, 92
Groddeck, Georg, 34, 39, 137
Gwynn-Browne, Arthur, 57–8

Hamilton, Patrick; *Hangover Square*, 69,
73, 90, 93
Hampson, John, 14
Hansel and Gretel, 15, 140
Harrisson, Tom, 96–7
Hawthorne, Nathaniel, 48
Hitler, Adolf, 55, 85, 93, 130
Holden, Inez, 73
Howard, Brian, 56
Huxley, Aldous, 201

Irigaray, Luce, 64
Isherwood, Christopher, 46, 56, 57

James, Henry, 196
Jesus Christ, 162–3, 178–9
Jonson, Ben, 111–12
Joyce, James, 135; *Finnegans Wake*,
101, 209; *Ulysses*, 25
Judas Iscariot, 61, 178

Kafka, Franz, 35, 37
Keats, John, 173–4
Koestler, Arthur, 181, 183–4, 186,
189, 204

Lacan, Jacques, 84
Lawrence, D. H., 24–5, 29, 78–9, 89
Lévi-Strauss, Claude, 84
Loos, Anita, 13

Lucretius, 147

Maclean, Donald, 63
Mallarmé, Stéphane, 134–5
Marvell, Andrew, 39–41, 48, 75, 127,
132
Marx, Karl, 185
Mass-Observation, 68, 72, 87, 88, 96,
107, 158, 181
Melchiori, Giorgio, 19, 28–9, 78, 79
Merleau-Ponty, Maurice, 134–5, 186,
187, 192, 194
Milton, John, 26–7, 196
Mitford, Nancy, 84
Muir, Edwin, 70, 71

Needham, Joseph, 186, 188–9
New Writing, 69

Oedipus, 7–8, 91, 175
Ogilvie-Grant, Mark, 15
Orwell, George, 181–4 *passim*
Owen, Wilfred, 56–7

Palinurus, *see* Connolly, Cyril
Pascal, Blaise, 179
Peter the Apostle, 162–3, 177–9, 185,
211
Pliny, 147
Powell, Anthony, 57
Propp, Vladimir, 141
Proust, Marcel, 80, 89

Quarterly Review, The, 171–2

Rabelais, François, 21
Reed, Henry, 73
Reich, Wilhelm, 84
Ross, Alan, 1, 154
Russell, John, 180

Sansom, William, 69–70, 73–4
Shakespeare, William: *Antony and
Cleopatra*, 143–5, *Cymbeline*, 143;
Henry V, 21; *King Lear*, 6; *The
Tempest*, 181, 201–3, 206
Sophocles, 7
Spender, Stephen, 74, 92, 104–5
Stein, Gertrude, 13–14, 29, 49, 58, 177
Stonier, George, 86
Sweet, Henry, 17
Swift, Jonathan, 127–8, 144
Sykes Davies, Hugh, 58

Tchaikovsky, Peter, 15
Times Literary Supplement, The, 14
Tolstoy, Leo; *War and Peace,* 70
Trollope, Anthony, 70–1

Upward, Edward, 46

Wassey, Michael, 95
Waugh, Evelyn, 84, 111–12
Woolf, Virginia, 56, 85

Yeats, W. B., 131, 136
Yorke, Henry Vincent, *see* Green, Henry